YELLOW

52 WEEKS • 52 ARTISTS • ONE ILLUSTRATED YEAR

A Studio OL project by Daniel Humphry and Steve Leard
www.StudioOL.uk

— YELLOW JOURNALISM —

REPORTING THAT EXPLOITS, DISTORTS OR EXAGGERATES THE NEWS TO CREATE SENSATION AND ATTRACT READERS

Welcome to *Yellow*, a celebration of illustration and the artists who continue to make it their own. This book is the culmination of a year-long series that was designed to show how illustration is more than a medium of pretty pictures – that, at its best, it can be as powerful as any photograph, piece of writing or fine art. For the past three years, we've been publishing *OFF LIFE*, a quarterly-ish comic and illustration magazine that's distributed free in shops, galleries and bars. We started that magazine to spread the word about independent comics and illustration, to show there's more to it than people might expect. We love making the magazine, it's picked up some amazing support and a loyal readership bigger than we could've ever hoped, but after a few years we started getting an itchy feeling: is there more we could be saying?

One of the best things about running *OFF LIFE* is visiting illustration shows and scouting all the amazing talent that's currently (always) out there. In summer 2014, we visited a ton of shows and while the work was always beautiful, we couldn't help but ask where the bite was? Where was the artwork addressing issues that are directly affecting artists, young people and society at large: austerity, the cost of living, divide and rule politics, mass surveillance and the increasing attacks on freedom of speech? We knew that the artists on display at these shows were creating such work – you'd see it on their social media feeds and in their magazine commissions – but no galleries seemed to be reflecting it. Not that we could see anyway.

So in November 2014 we unveiled *Yellow*, a project that gave artists a space to illustrate their say on the biggest issues of today. But how to do that? The power of illustration is often in its simplicity and directness, and we wanted *Yellow* to mirror those values. So we came up with the idea of one illustrated year: 52 of the world's most exciting artists illustrating 52 weeks of news, week-by-week as they happen.

The result is this book: 365 days of reaction, opinion, outrage and social comment, drawn from 52 unique perspectives and laid bare in print. Putting *Yellow* together has made us question how we digest news, how we remember the stories and what, 12 months down the line, remains important to us. Now it's time for you to read on and ask those questions of yourself. Enjoy!

DANIEL HUMPHRY & STEVE LEARD

Editor & Art Director of *Yellow*

STANLEY CHOW

THE MANSON WEDDING / 17–23 NOVEMBER

"Charles Manson (80) being allowed to marry Afton Elaine Burton (26) struck me as one of those 'only in America' stories. I've had a fascination with Manson since hearing U2's version of *Helter Skelter*, where Bono shouts 'This is a song Charles Manson stole from The Beatles. We're stealing it back!' I based my artwork on Grant Wood's *American Gothic* painting."

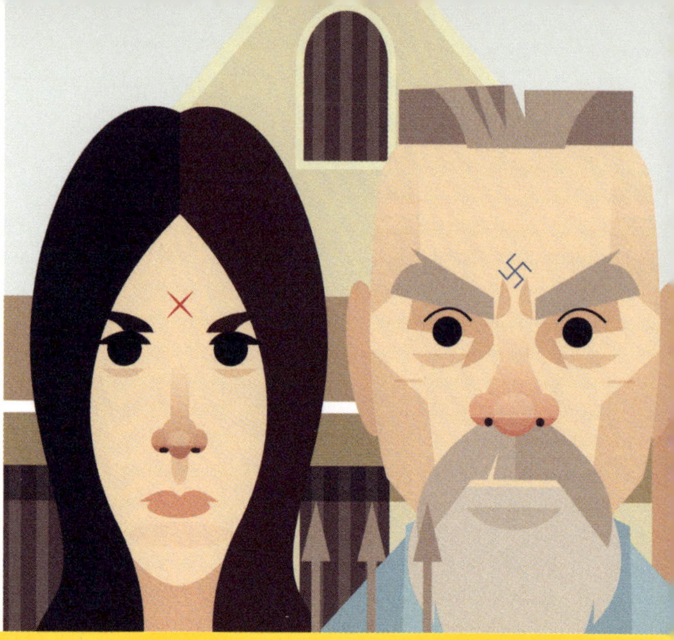

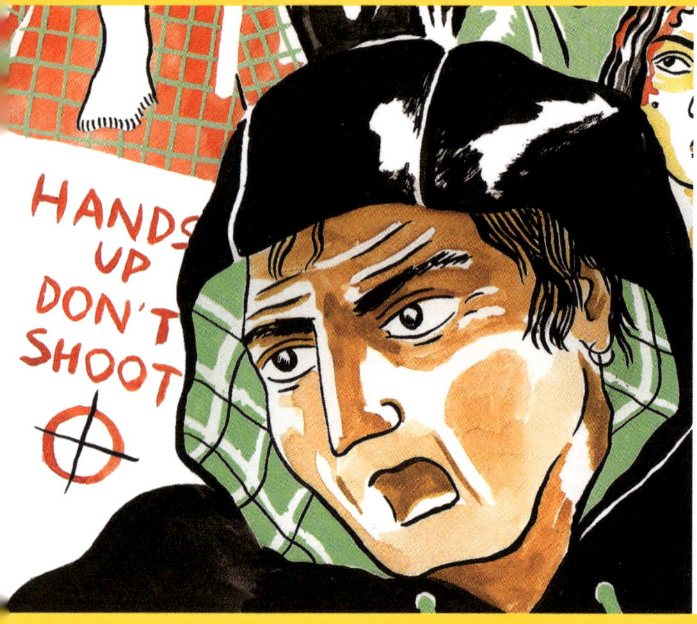

GRACE WILSON

LONDON TO FERGUSON / 24–30 NOVEMBER

"News broke that Darren Wilson – the officer who shot a teenager in Ferguson – would not face charges. The London To Ferguson vigil outside the US Embassy gave it perspective, especially as the events in Ferguson so closely echo those of Mark Duggan in Tottenham in 2011."

TAKAYO AKIYAMA

I AM NOT SORRY / 1–7 DECEMBER

"During my week on *Yellow*, the winner of the Turner Prize was announced and news broke about Shia LaBeouf being raped during part of art performance #IAMSORRY. I wondered what Turner himself would have thought about it? What is 'good art' and 'bad art'?"

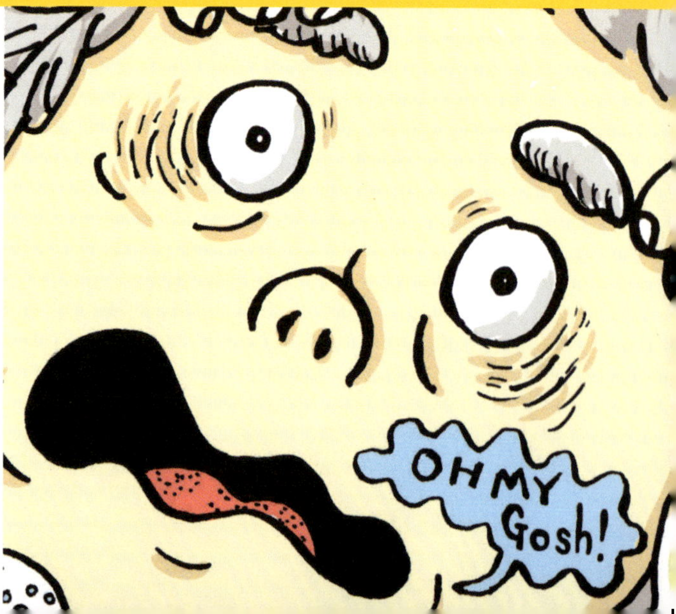

THE PROJECT TWINS

CIA TORTURE REPORTS / 8–14 DECEMBER

"In December, leaked CIA torture reports laid bare the full horror of the agency's activities around the world. We wanted to subvert the CIA logo and so used it along with a chained up figure in a gritty and textured style, which is also confined within the shape of a folder."

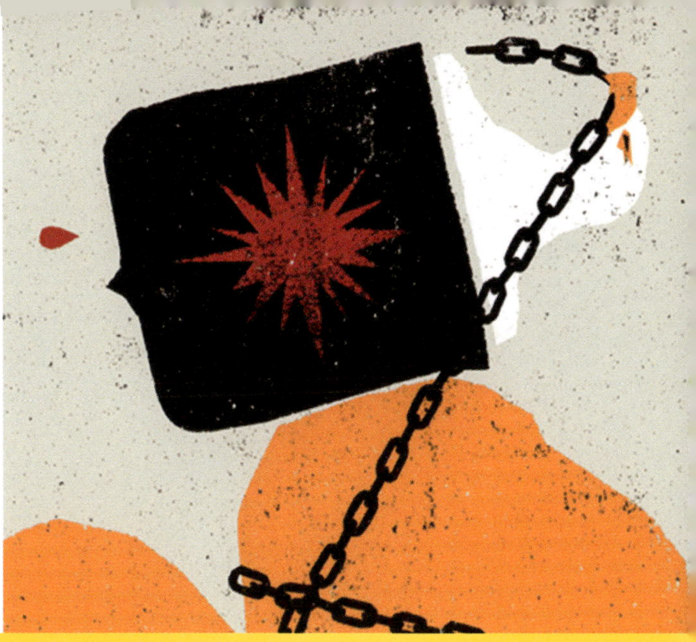

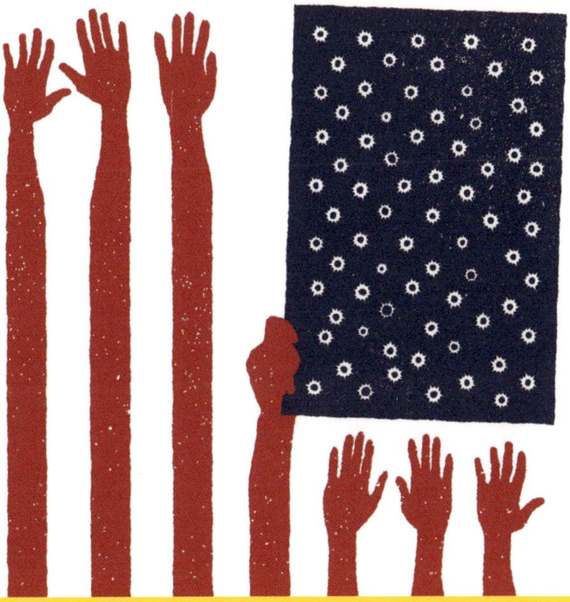

GAVIN STRANGE

DON'T SHOOT / 15–21 DECEMBER

"I read a story from the US about a woman who was aggressively questioned after her boyfriend was shot dead in a Walmart. It struck me how regular fatal shootings with the police are now. There are too many cases to focus on just one, so I wanted to represent the movement protesting against these injustices."

DAN BERRY

LET IT SNOW! / 22–28 DECEMBER

"Scrutinising the news over the Christmas period is difficult. Every sad news report gets magnified through its proximity to tinsel and loved ones, and seems far sadder in comparison. For that reason, thank goodness for the gift of Boxing Day snow!"

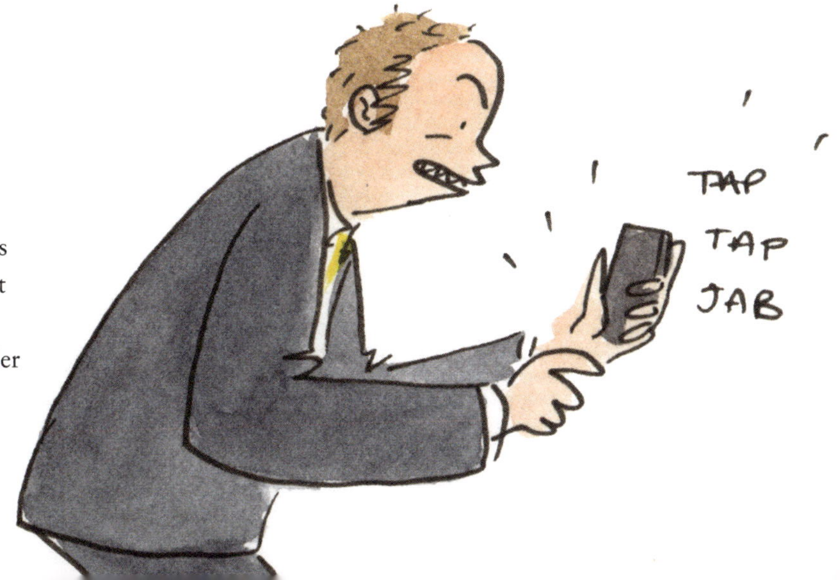

"YOU KNOW,
A LONG TIME AGO
BEING CRAZY
MEANT SOMETHING.
NOWADAYS
EVERYBODY'S CRAZY."

CHARLES MANSON

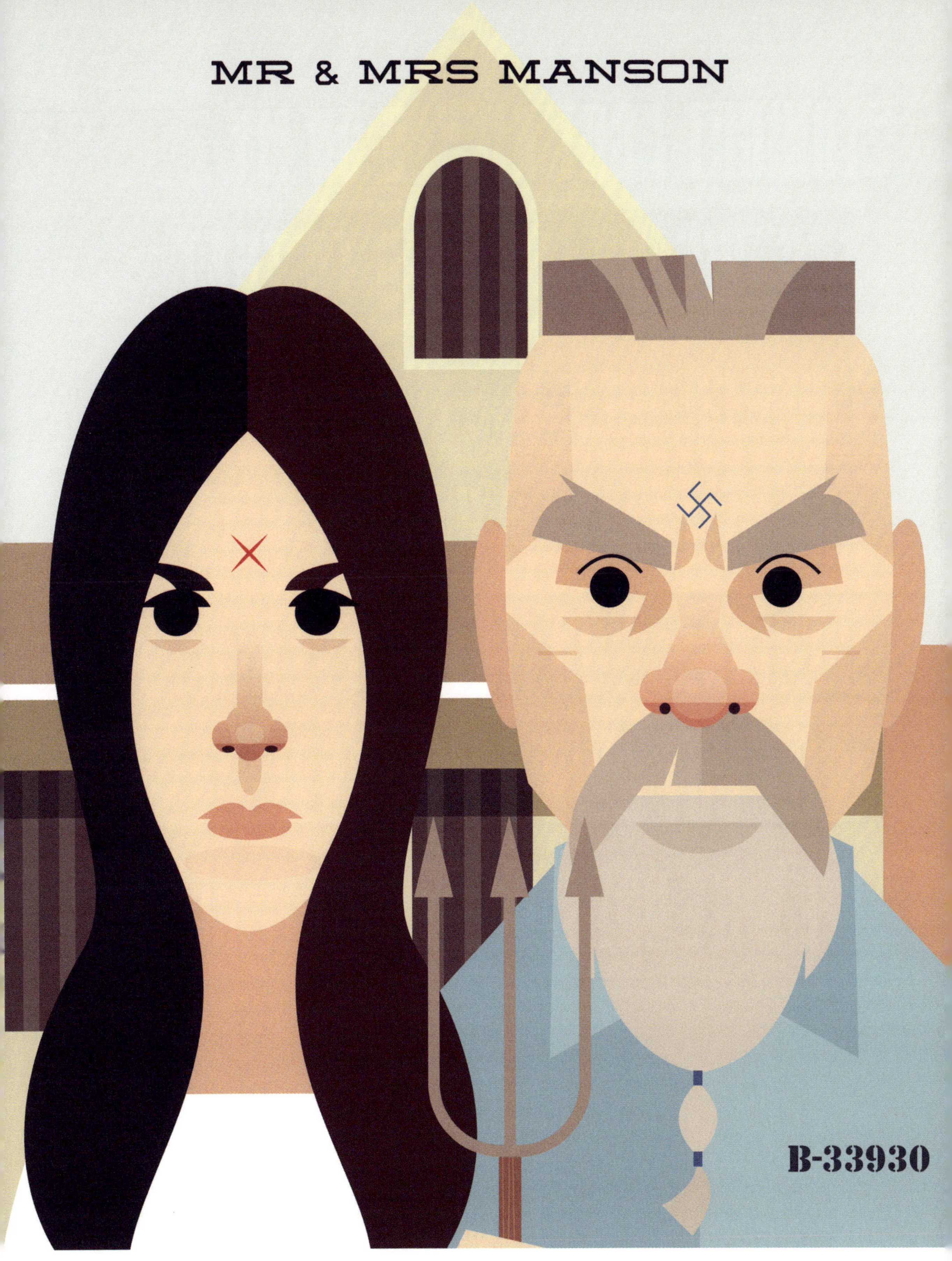
MR & MRS MANSON
B-33930

"TONIGHT I GOT KICKED ON MY ASS, WHEN I LISTENED TO THAT PROSECUTOR... YOU MOTHERFUCKERS GOT ME TODAY... I KNEW IT WAS COMING... YOU MOTHERFUCKERS WILL NOT OWN TOMORROW. WE WILL NOT LIVE IN YOUR FEAR."

KILLER MIKE

ONSTAGE — NIGHT OF THE DARREN WILSON VERDICT

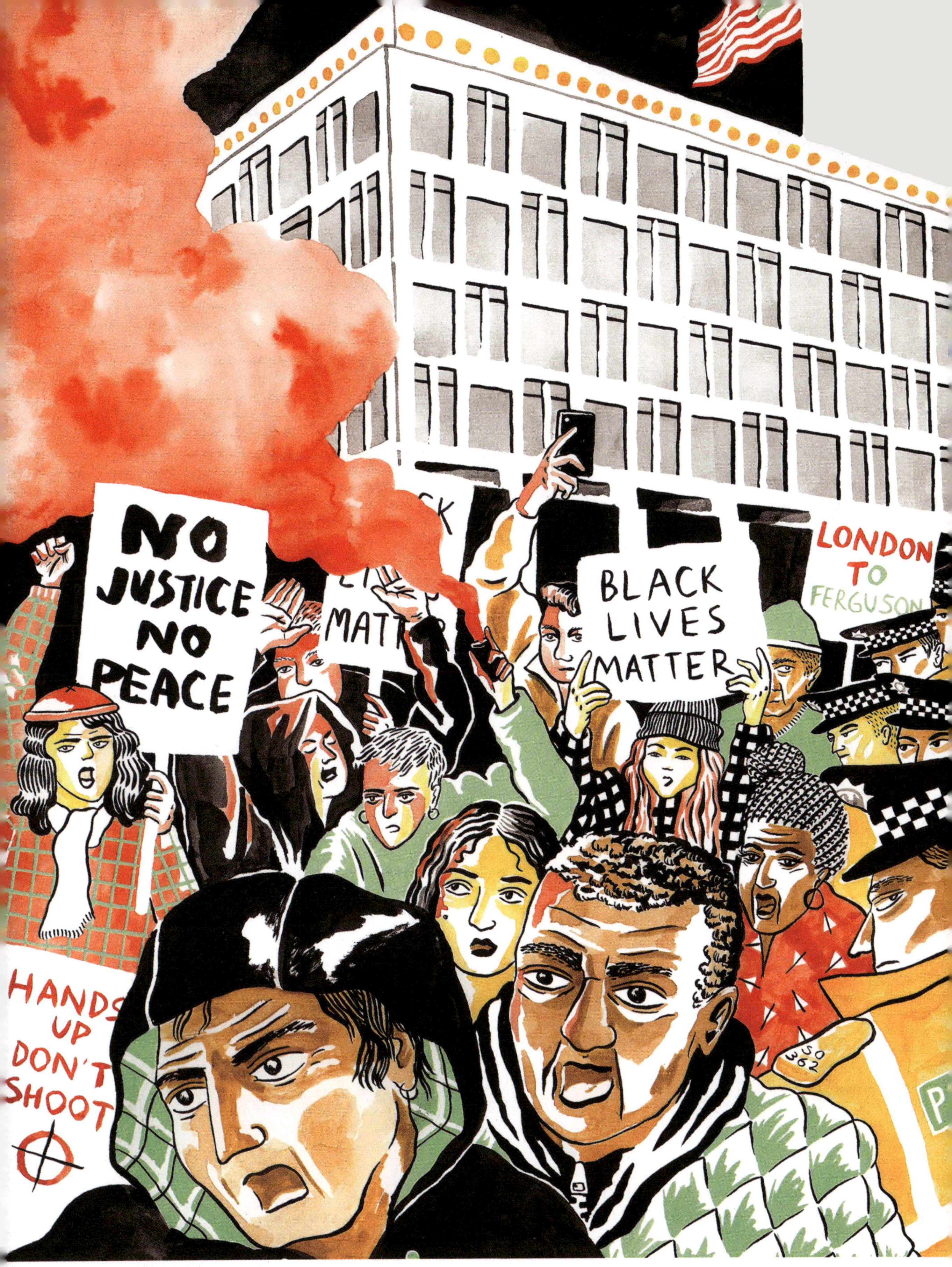
NO JUSTICE NO PEACE
BLACK LIVES MATTER
LONDON TO FERGUSON
HANDS UP DON'T SHOOT
SO 362

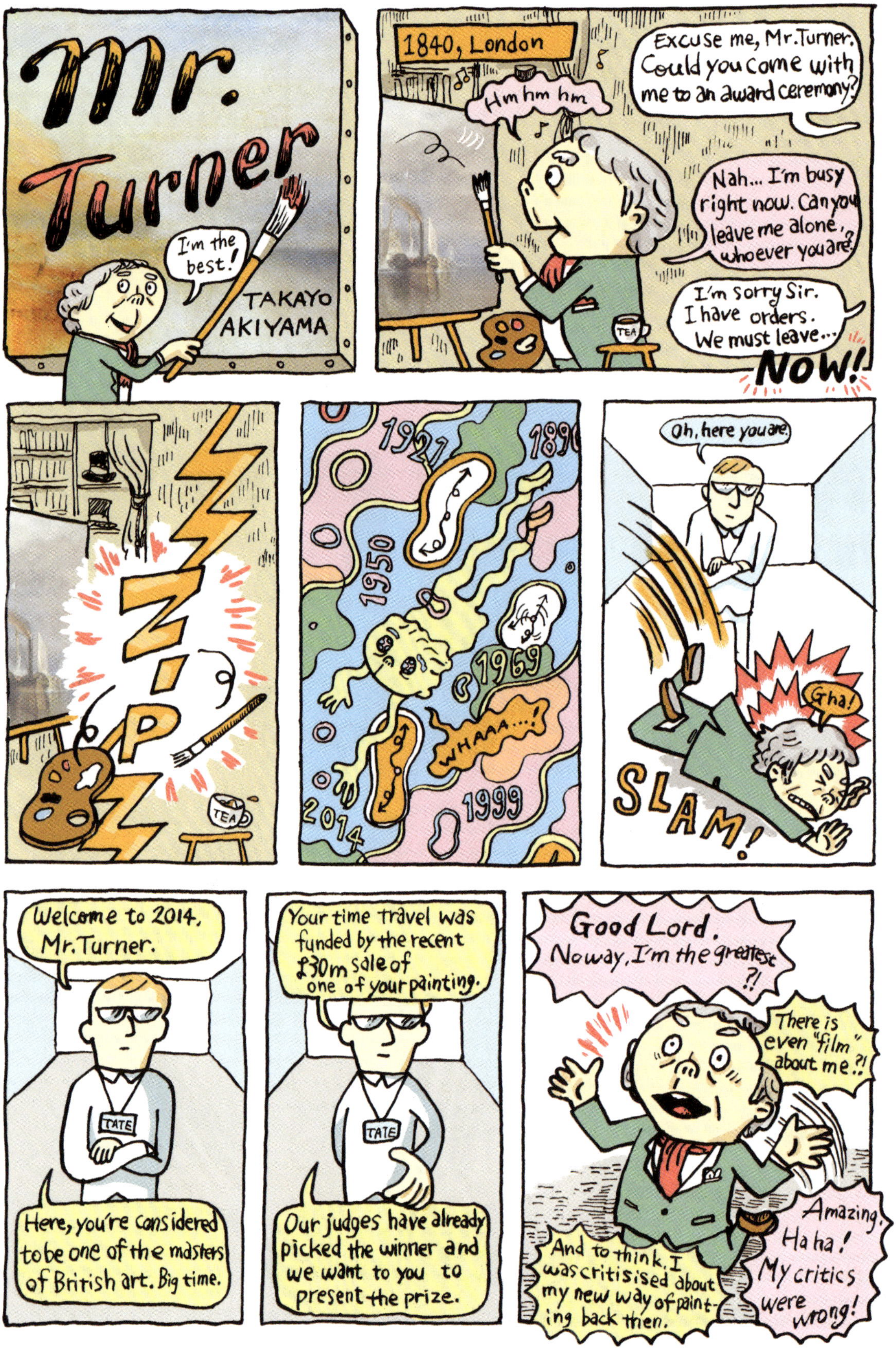
Mr. Turner
TAKAYO AKIYAMA
I'm the best!
1840, London
Hm hm hm
Excuse me, Mr. Turner. Could you come with me to an award ceremony?
Nah... I'm busy right now. Can you leave me alone, whoever you are?
I'm sorry Sir. I have orders. We must leave...
NOW!
ZIP
TEA
1927
1890
1950
1969
WHAAA...!
2014
1999
Oh, here you are.
Gha!
SLAM!
Welcome to 2014, Mr. Turner.
Here, you're considered to be one of the masters of British art. Big time.
TATE
Your time travel was funded by the recent £30m sale of one of your painting.
Our judges have already picked the winner and we want to you to present the prize.
Good Lord. No way. I'm the greatest?!
There is even "film" about me?!
And to think, I was critisised about my new way of painting back then.
Amazing. Ha ha! My critics were wrong!

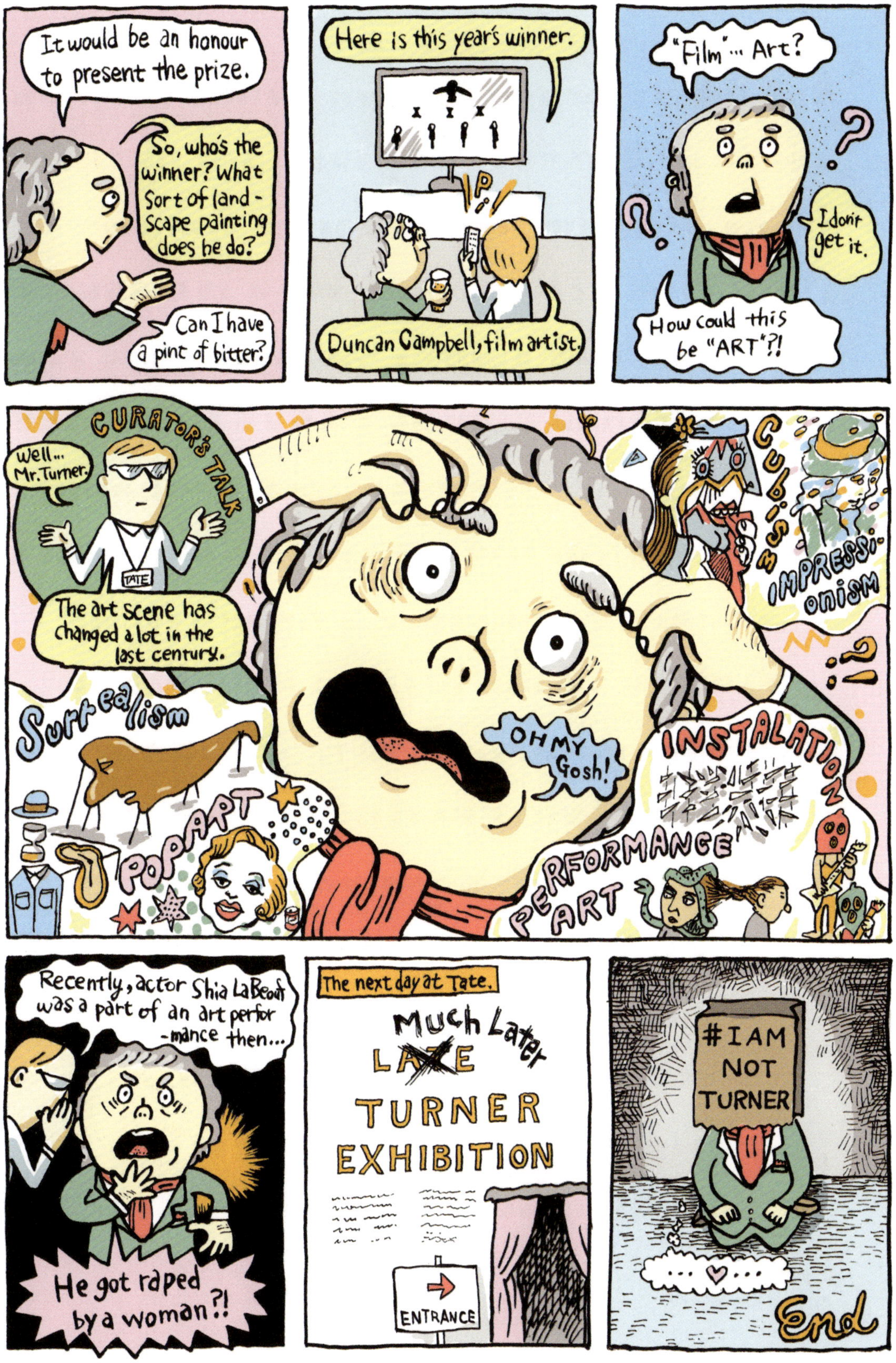
It would be an honour to present the prize.
So, who's the winner? What sort of landscape painting does he do?
Can I have a pint of bitter?
Here is this year's winner.
Duncan Campbell, film artist.
"Film"... Art?
I don't get it.
How could this be "ART"?!
CURATOR'S TALK
Well... Mr. Turner.
TATE
The art scene has changed a lot in the last century.
CUBISM
IMPRESSIONISM
Surrealism
POP ART
OH MY Gosh!
INSTALATION
PERFORMANCE ART
Recently, actor Shia LaBeouf was a part of an art performance then...
He got raped by a woman?!
The next day at Tate.
LATE Much Later
TURNER EXHIBITION
ENTRANCE
#I AM NOT TURNER
... ♥ ...
End

THE INTELLIGENCE COMMUNITY'S ACTIONS MUST ALWAYS REFLECT WHO WE ARE AS A NATION, AND ADHERE TO OUR LAWS AND STANDARDS... INSTEAD, CIA PERSONNEL DECIDED TO INITIATE A PROGRAM OF INDEFINITE SECRET DETENTION AND THE USE OF BRUTAL INTERROGATION TECHNIQUES IN VIOLATION OF US LAW, TREATY OBLIGATIONS, AND OUR VALUES.

Dianne Feinstein, Vice Chairman of the US Senate Select Committee on Intelligence.
(Reference: *The Official Senate Report on CIA Torture*)

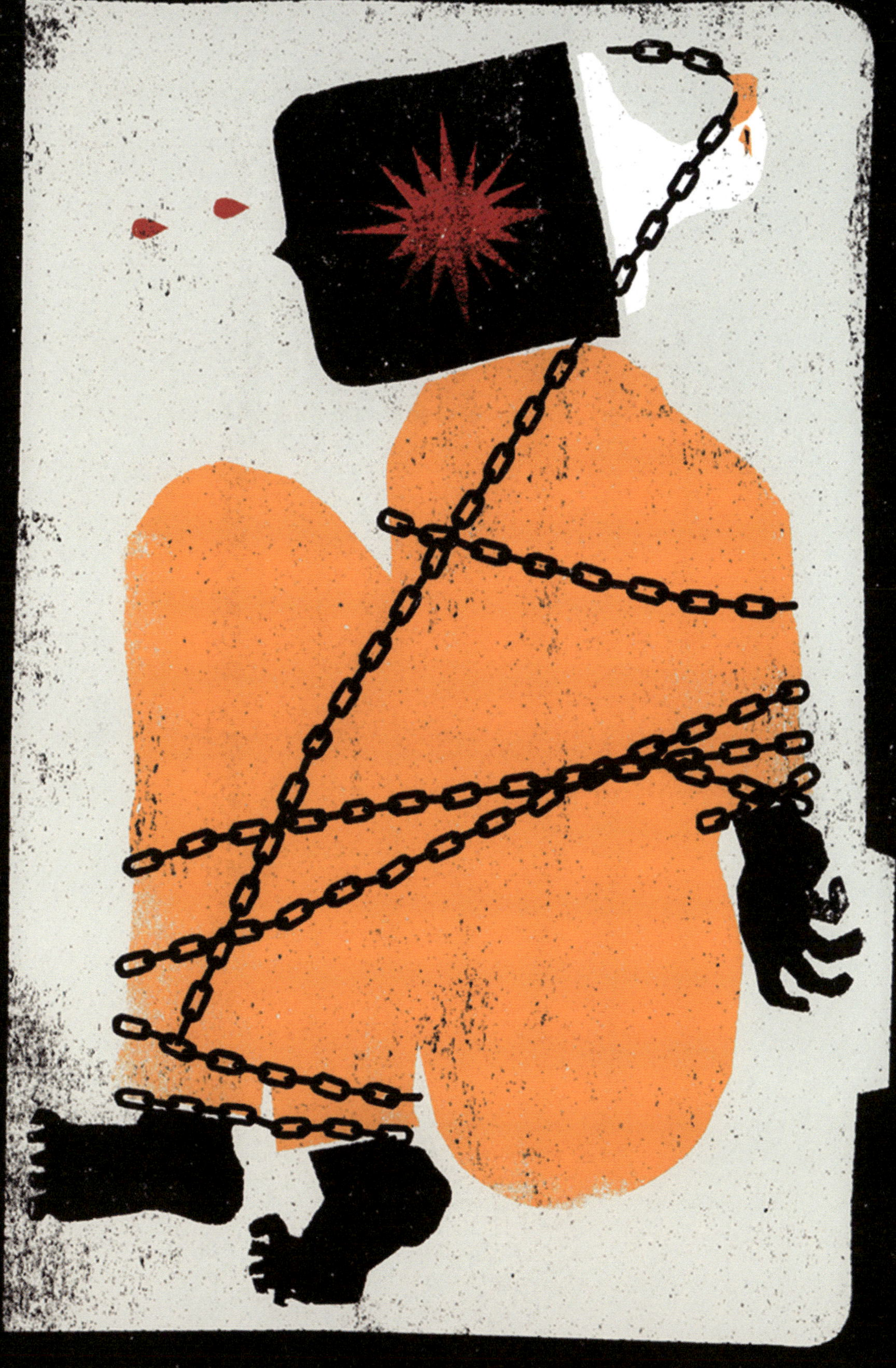

CIA TORTURE REPORTS

THE PROJECT TWINS

DON'T SHOOT

There are a hundred different topics I could have covered for my contribution to *Yellow*. I get on my high horse and rant about things on a daily basis. I'm that annoying dude sharing those posts and viewpoints all the time, so I was stuck for which route to go down until I read this story from the US about a woman aggressively questioned after her boyfriend was shot dead in a Walmart.

It struck me how regular an occurrence this is seeming to be. Violent and fatal confrontations with the police with the victims being shot dead. There are too many sad cases to pick just one to focus on: Trayvon Martin, Michael Brown, Tamir Rice, Eric Garner and many more. I wanted to represent the huge movement of people protesting against these massive injustices – the 'Hands up, don't shoot' gesture is such a powerful one, so turning it into the American flag felt like a way to make something that is commenting on the situation without using words. I hope things start to change in the US, the attitudes to race and firearms, but I fear progress is a long way off. Please police, just stop killing people.

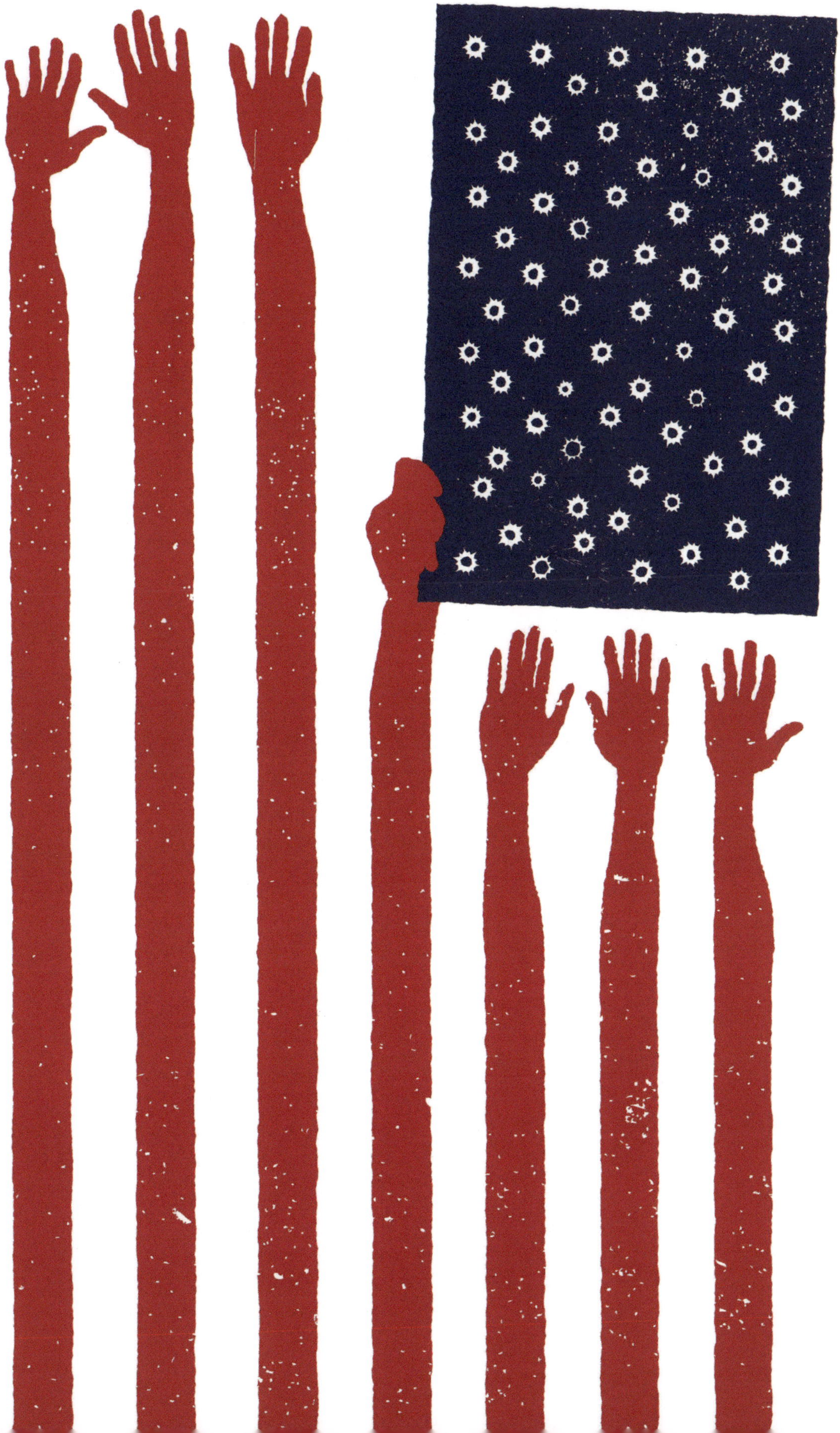

LET IT SNOW!

DAN BERRY

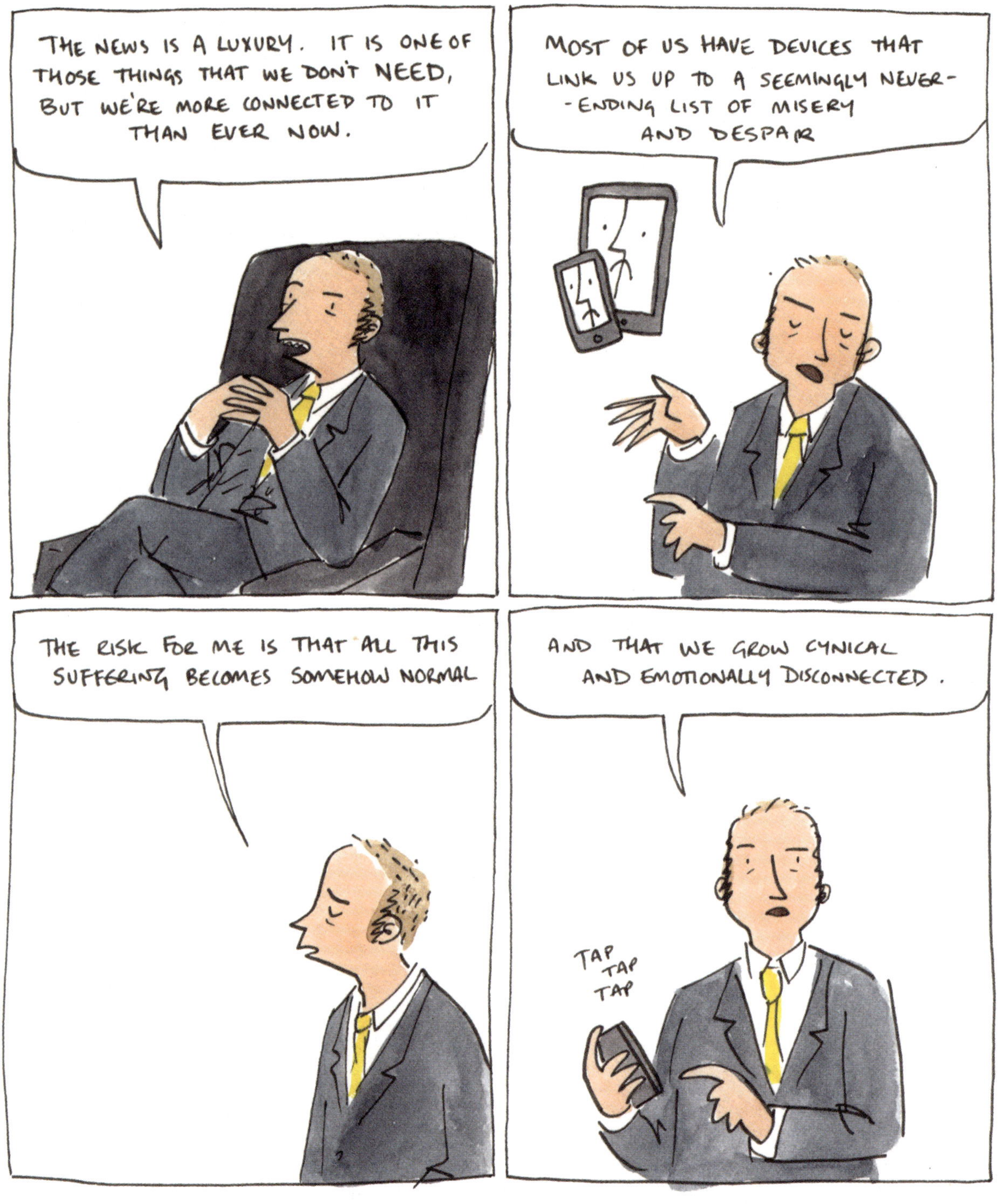

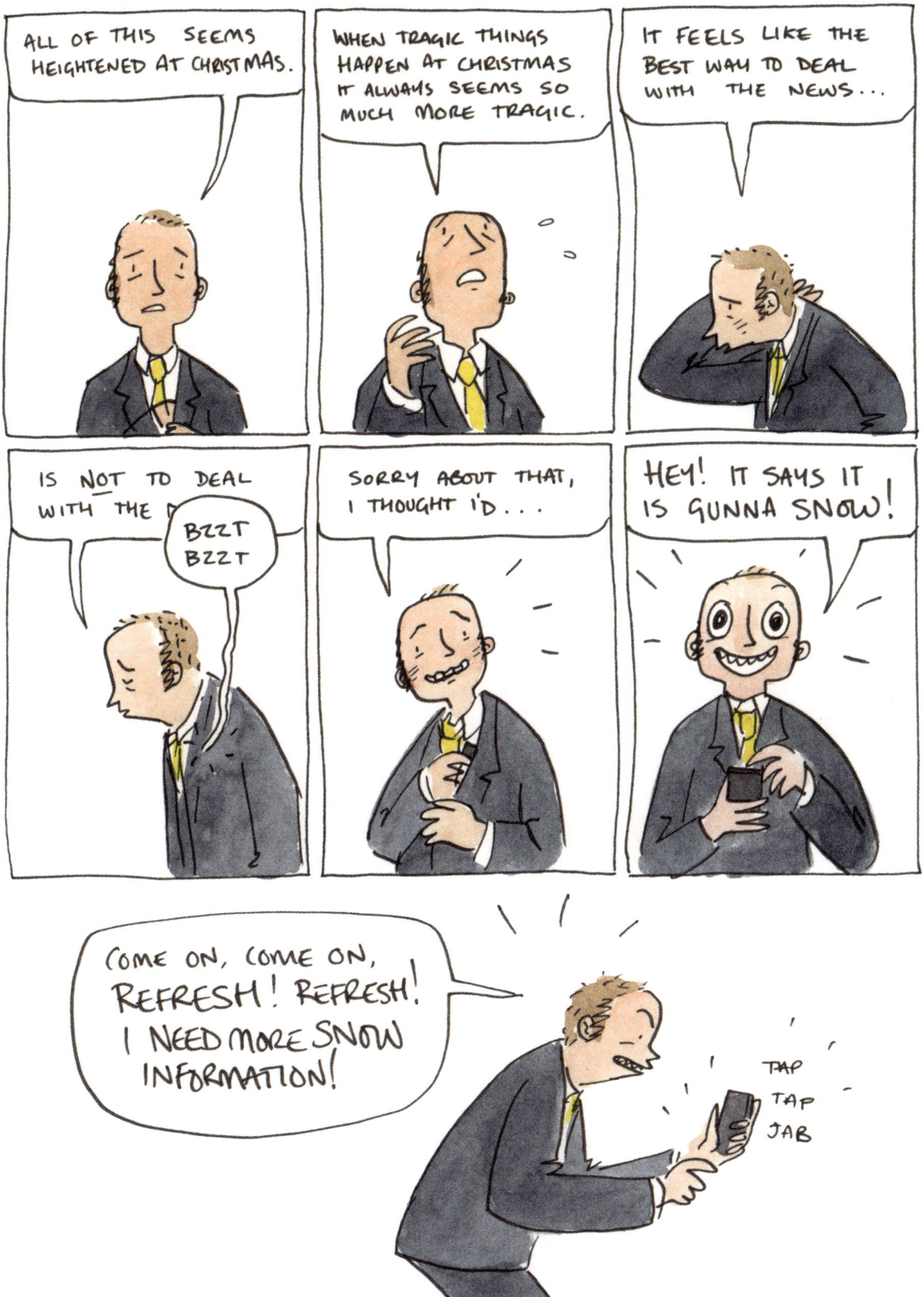
ALL OF THIS SEEMS HEIGHTENED AT CHRISTMAS.
WHEN TRAGIC THINGS HAPPEN AT CHRISTMAS IT ALWAYS SEEMS SO MUCH MORE TRAGIC.
IT FEELS LIKE THE BEST WAY TO DEAL WITH THE NEWS...
IS NOT TO DEAL WITH THE
BZZT BZZT
SORRY ABOUT THAT, I THOUGHT I'D...
HEY! IT SAYS IT IS GUNNA SNOW!
COME ON, COME ON, REFRESH! REFRESH! I NEED MORE SNOW INFORMATION!
TAP
TAP
JAB

JAMIE MILLS

CLIMATE AWARENESS / 29 DECEMBER–4 JANUARY

"I'd been reading articles about action on climate change and powerful people beginning to take a step back, look at the bigger picture and support climate action. My intention for the illustration was to try and capture something about the precariousness and scale of the climate issues that we all face."

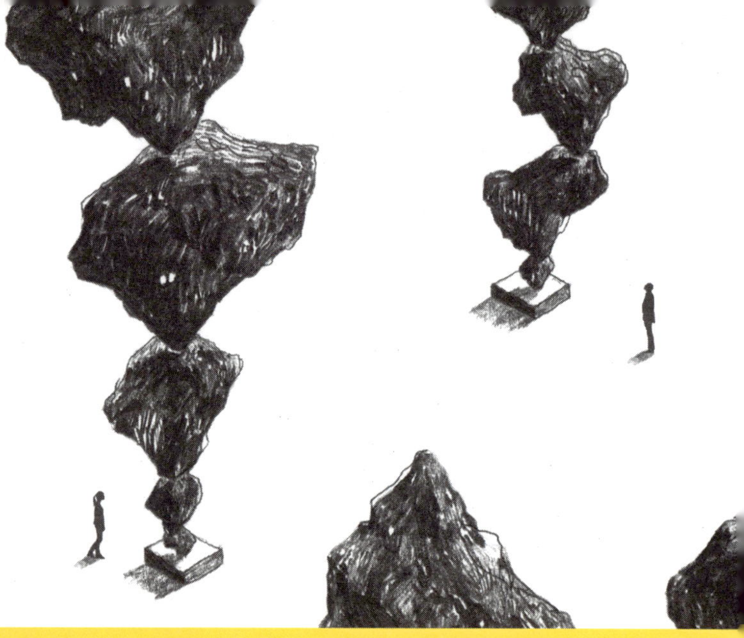

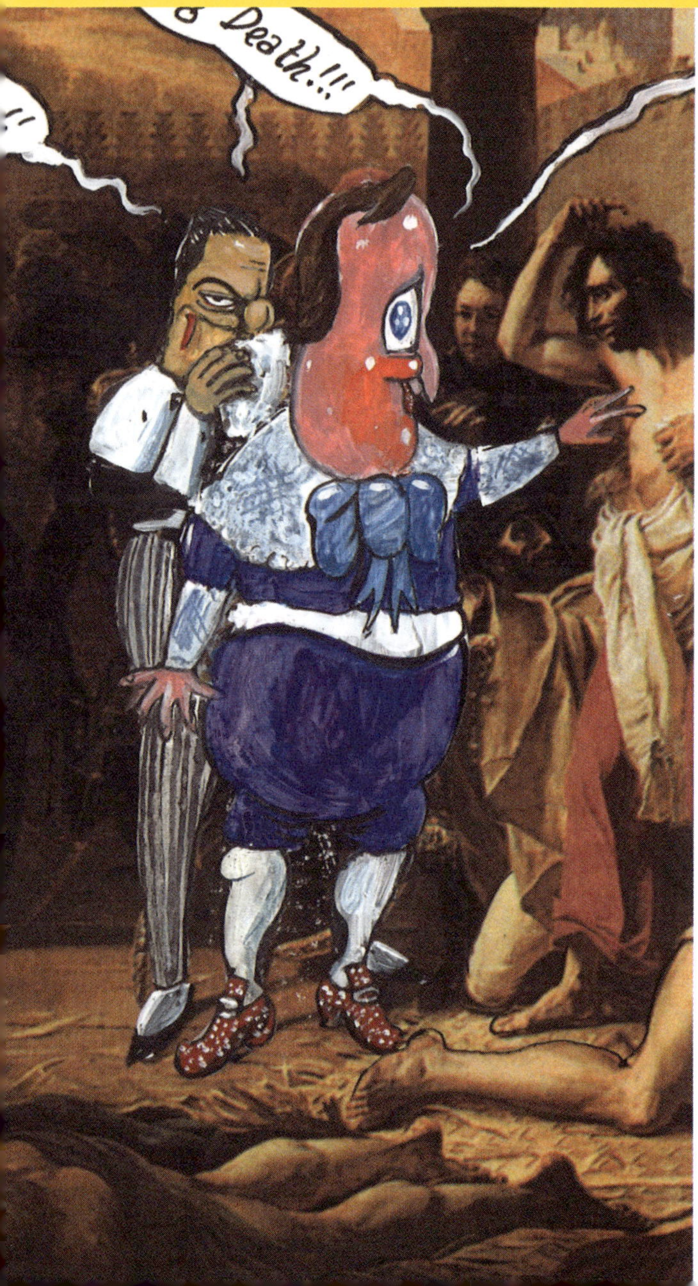

MARTIN ROWSON

CHARLIE HEBDO / 5–11 JANUARY

We started *Yellow* to see what artists could bring to the way we digest news. But never did we imagine that events involving cartoonists would become a story of such deep sadness. In November 2014 we booked *Guardian* cartoonist Martin Rowson to illustrate the week starting Monday 5 January. On Tuesday, Martin submitted his piece, a typically blistering attack on the gutter-antics of UK political parties ahead of election season. But by Wednesday it became clear that another story would need to be addressed. We asked Martin how he'd like to proceed:

"As it's my day job to produce artwork informed by the news, I originally filed before the weekly rush of deadlines overwhelmed me. Back then the big story was the beginning of the interminable 2015 election campaign; as lies, smears and promises began to be hurled across the no-man's land of 'news' while the nation slept on. Then came Wednesday and the murders at *Charlie Hebdo*, including four cartoonists. Hence the second cartoon..."

EVE LLOYD KNIGHT

OSCAR SNUB / 12–18 JANUARY

"I felt frustrated by the lack of diversity in the Oscar nominations, especially Ava DuVernay not being nominated for *Selma*. I hope my piece inspires a sense of quiet confidence, that women like Ava maintain against the monumental odds before them. I'd like to award this Oscar to all the artists who suffer from the fate of inequality."

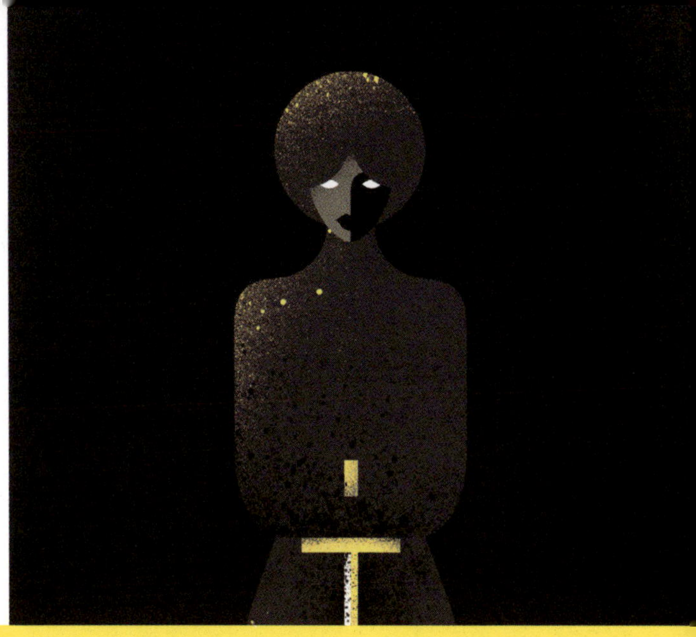

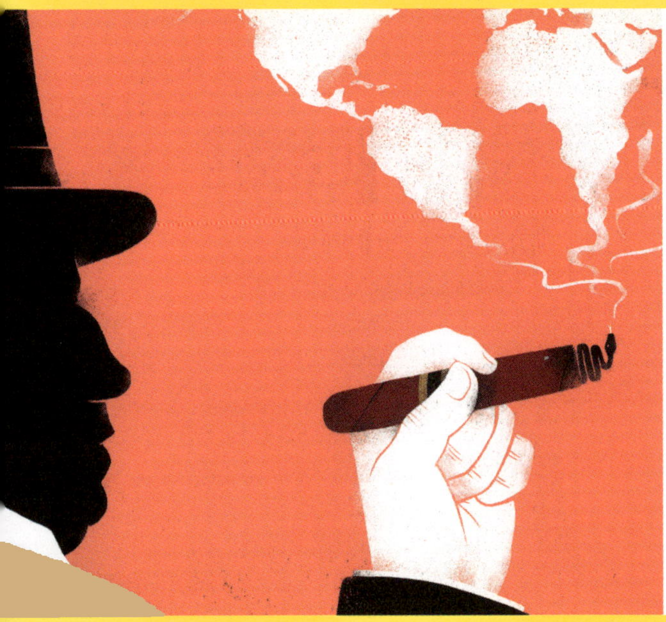

SÉBASTIEN THIBAULT

WEALTH GAP / 19–25 JANUARY

"The subject that inspired me was the extreme wealth of the 1%; where soon 50% of all wealth in the world will be controlled by just 1% of the population. Getting so much money and this kind of pursuit of power is a venom that corrodes the planet – hence the snake reference."

ELLIOT KRUSZYNSKI

LIZARD SQUAD / 26 JANUARY–1 FEBRUARY

"I depicted the shitstorm caused by the 'Lizard Squad' hacker group, who managed to hack into Facebook and shut down its affiliated systems, including Tinder and Instagram. My heart goes out to all the commuter-bros sending dick picks to women on Tinder and stalking their ex-girlfriends on Facebook."

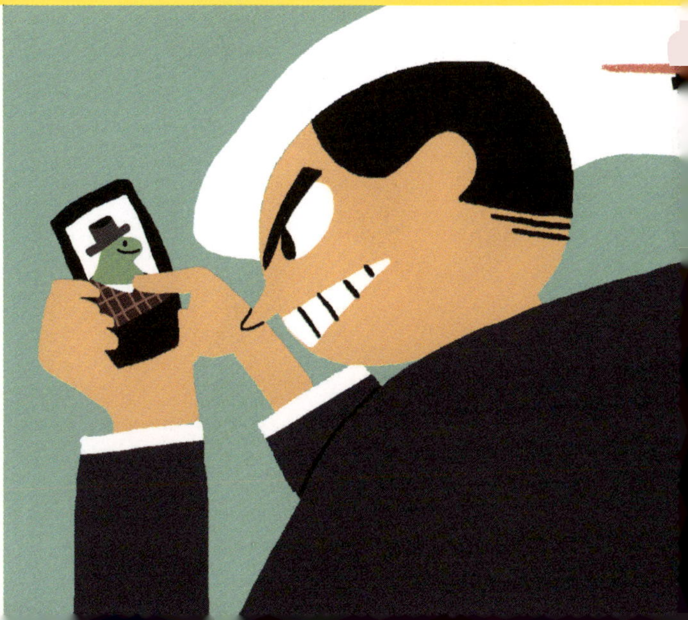

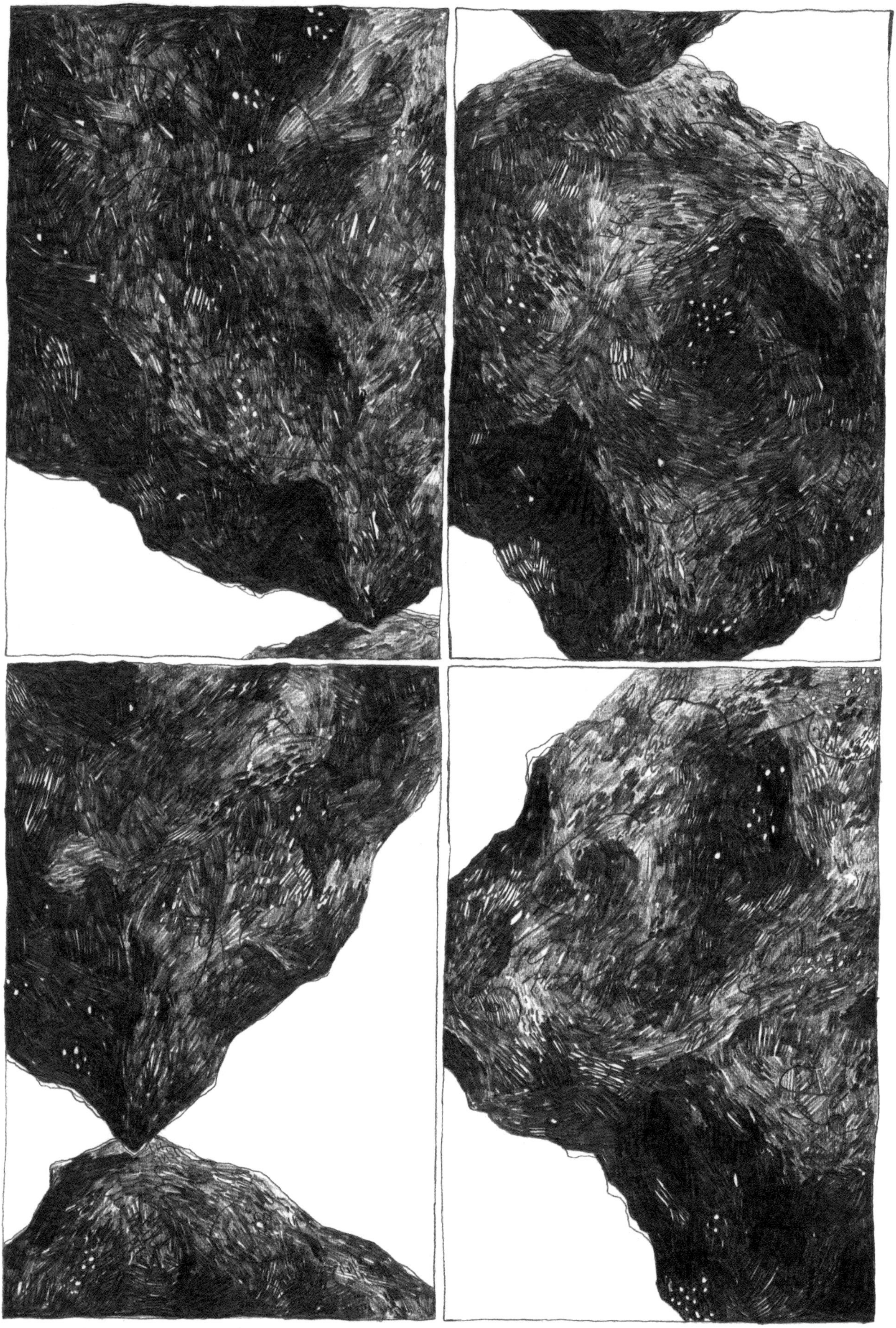

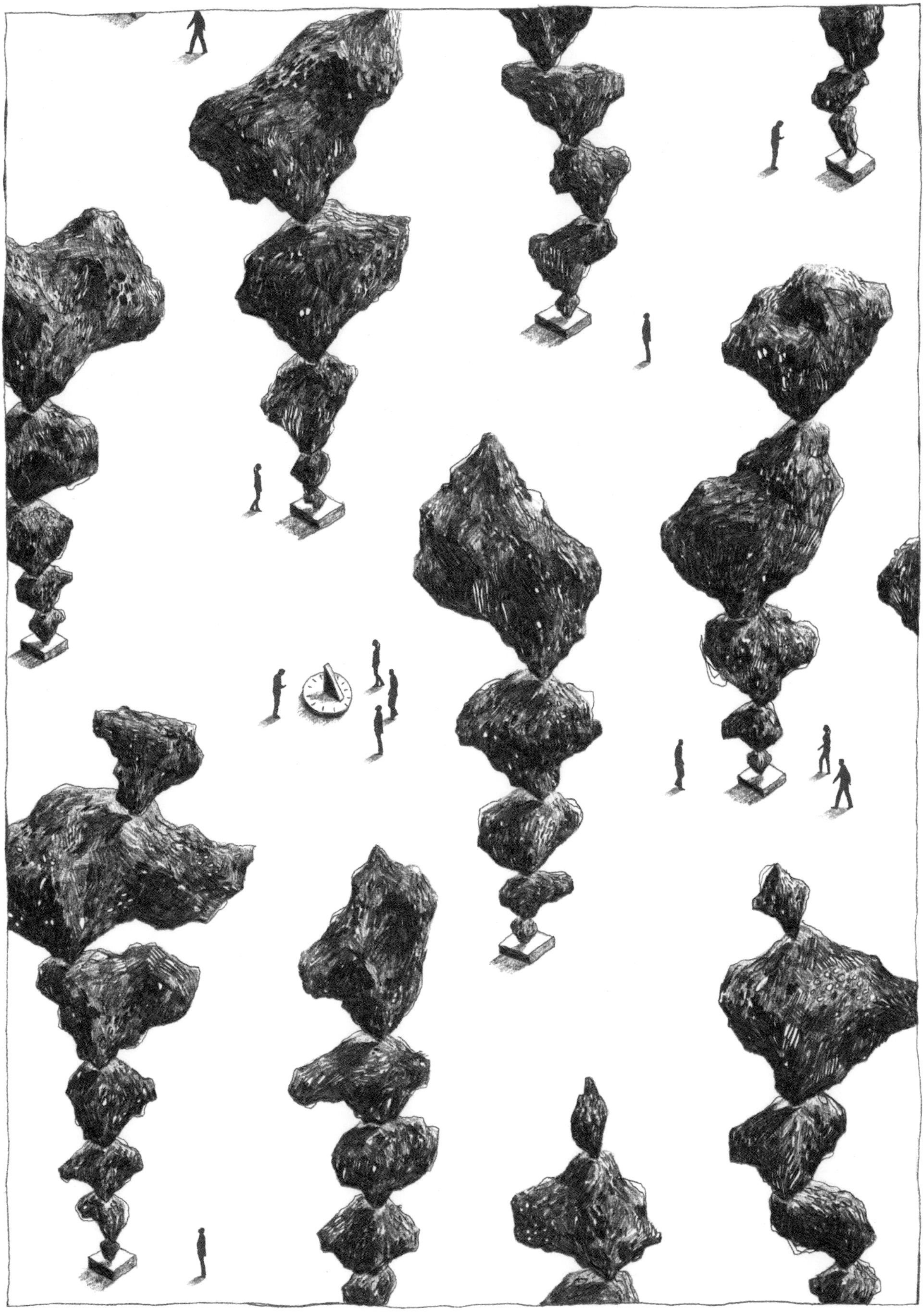

CARTOONS & DESPOTS

Death threats come with the territory. Since the advent of the internet, people around the world who are enraged by my cartoons have been able to threaten to kill me via email.

Over the years these have included Muslims, Zionists, Republican Americans, a few angry Chomskyians, Catholics, Russians, some Serbs, and, I imagine, a large number of teenage boys locked in their bedrooms 'having a laugh'. I've tended to laugh them off, joking that a death threat by email doesn't count. It needs a letter sent to my home address containing one of my loved ones' ears to be taken seriously. However, after the murders of the *Charlie Hebdo* cartoonists Cabu, Wolinski, Tignous and the paper's editor-in-chief Stéphane Charbonnier, there's a terrible temptation to stop laughing. Although that, I believe, would be a fundamental error.

Laughter is one of the things humans do best. Mostly because it makes us feel better. I've been convinced for years that laughter is a hardwired evolutionary survival mechanism that helps humans navigate our way through life without going mad with existentialist terror. That's why we laugh at all those terrifying things like death, sex, other people and the disgusting stuff that pours out of our bodies on a daily basis.

Moreover, we're very good at laughing at those who place themselves above us. That's the basis of the craft I shared with my murdered colleagues in Paris. This universal capacity to use mockery as a form of social control is one of the main things that make us human.

But there appears to be something exquisitely intolerable to the 'serious mind' about mockery when it's in illustrated form. Largely this is due to the way the visual is consumed. Rather than nibbling your way through text, however incendiary, a cartoon floods the eyes, gets swallowed whole and often makes the recipient choke.

Cartoons should be seen more as a kind of sympathetic magic more than anything else. We steal our subjects' souls by recreating them through caricature and then mock them in narratives of our own devising. Worst of all, we then pretend that it's all just a good-natured laugh – it is a laugh, but often a cruel and mocking one. It is, in short, assassination without the blood.

This time it's cartoonists' blood that's been shed; another tragedy among countless others throughout history that shows how hateful laughter is to despots. Which is why, now more than ever, we mustn't stop laughing at them.

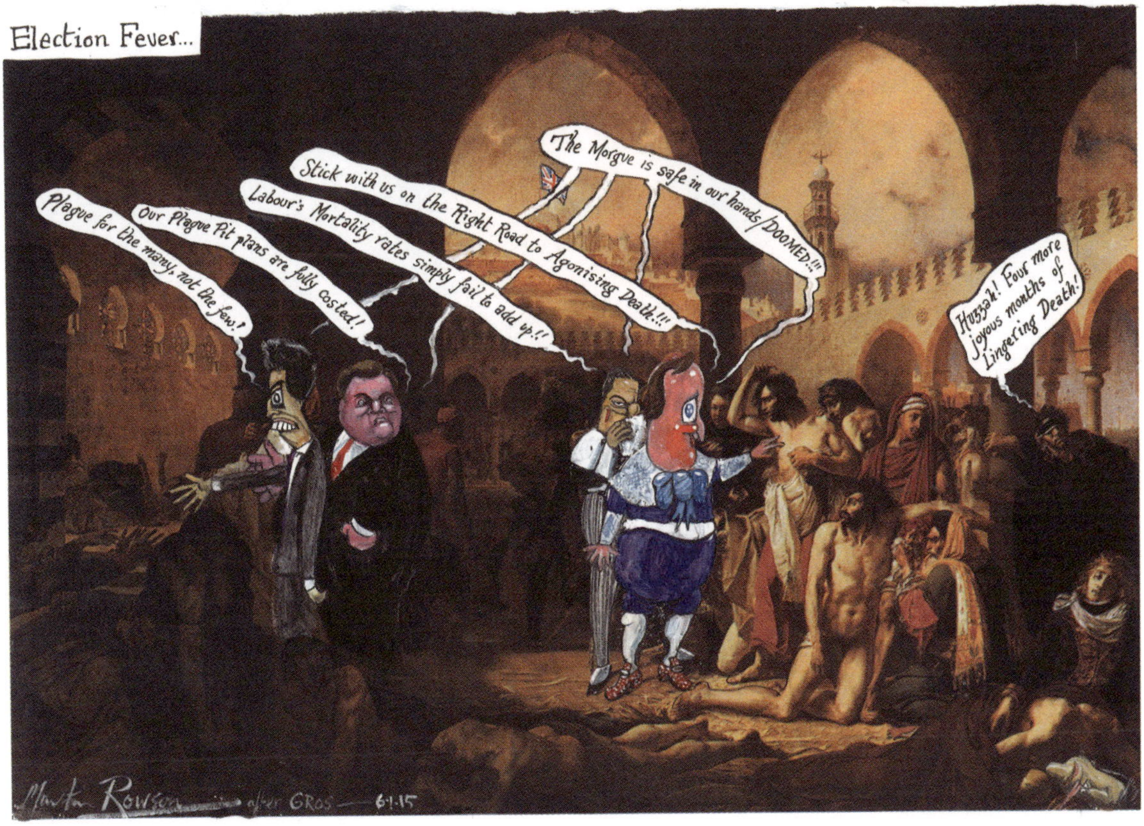
Election Fever...
Plague for the many, not the few!
Our Plague Pit plans are fully costed!
Labour's Mortality rates simply fail to add up!!
Stick with us on the Right Road to Agonising Death!!!
The Morgue is safe in our hands/DOOMED!!!
Huzzah! Four more joyous months of Lingering Death!
Martin Rowson after GROS 6.1.15

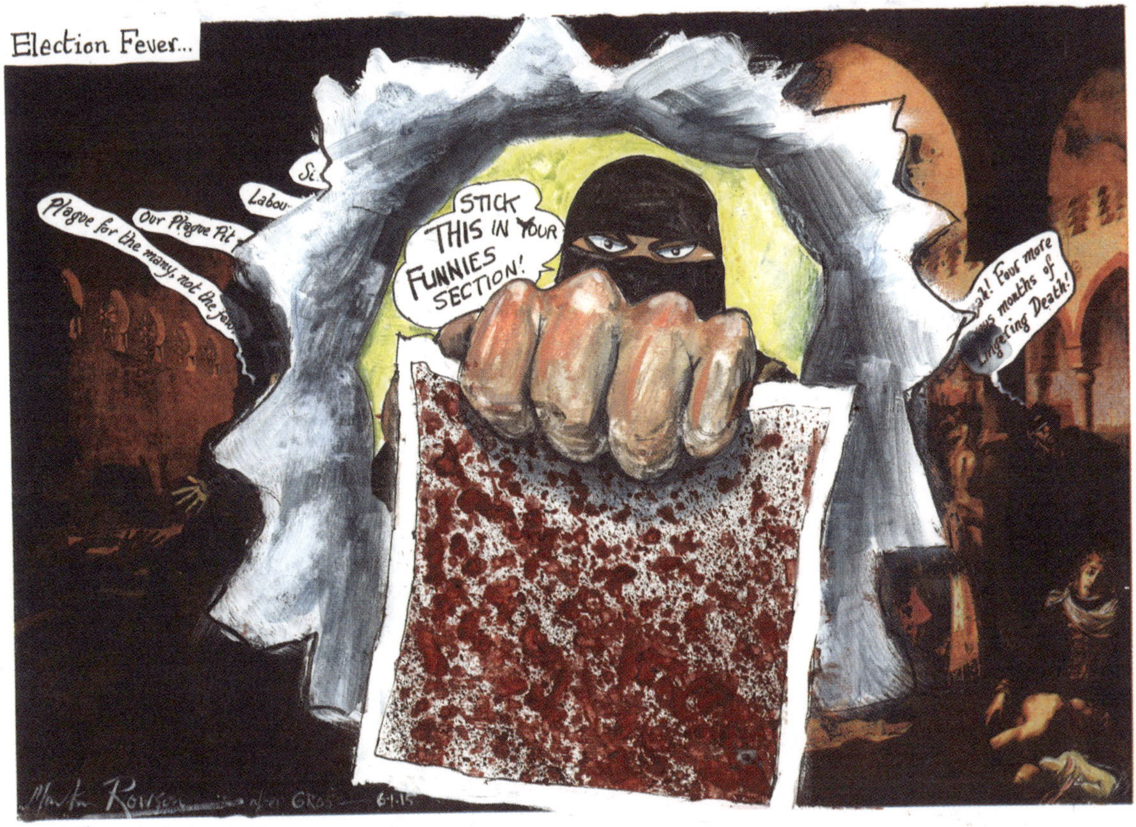
Election Fever...
Plague for the many, not the
Our Plague Pit
Labou
STICK THIS IN YOUR FUNNIES SECTION!
Four more
months of
Lingering Death!
Martin Rowson after GROS 6.1.15

"THE TRADITIONAL MODELS FOR DOING THINGS ARE COLLAPSING, FROM MUSIC TO PUBLISHING TO FILM, AND IT'S A WIDE

OPEN DOOR FOR PEOPLE WHO ARE CREATIVE TO DO WHAT THEY NEED TO DO WITHOUT HAVING INSTITUTIONS BLOCK THEIR ART."

Ava DuVernay, Director, *Selma*

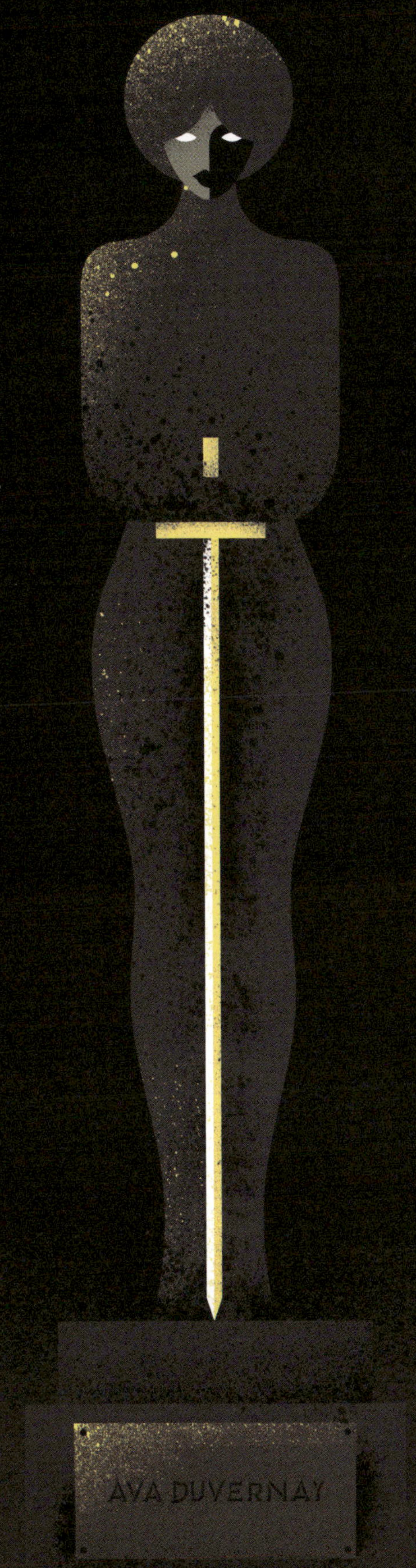
AVA DUVERNAY

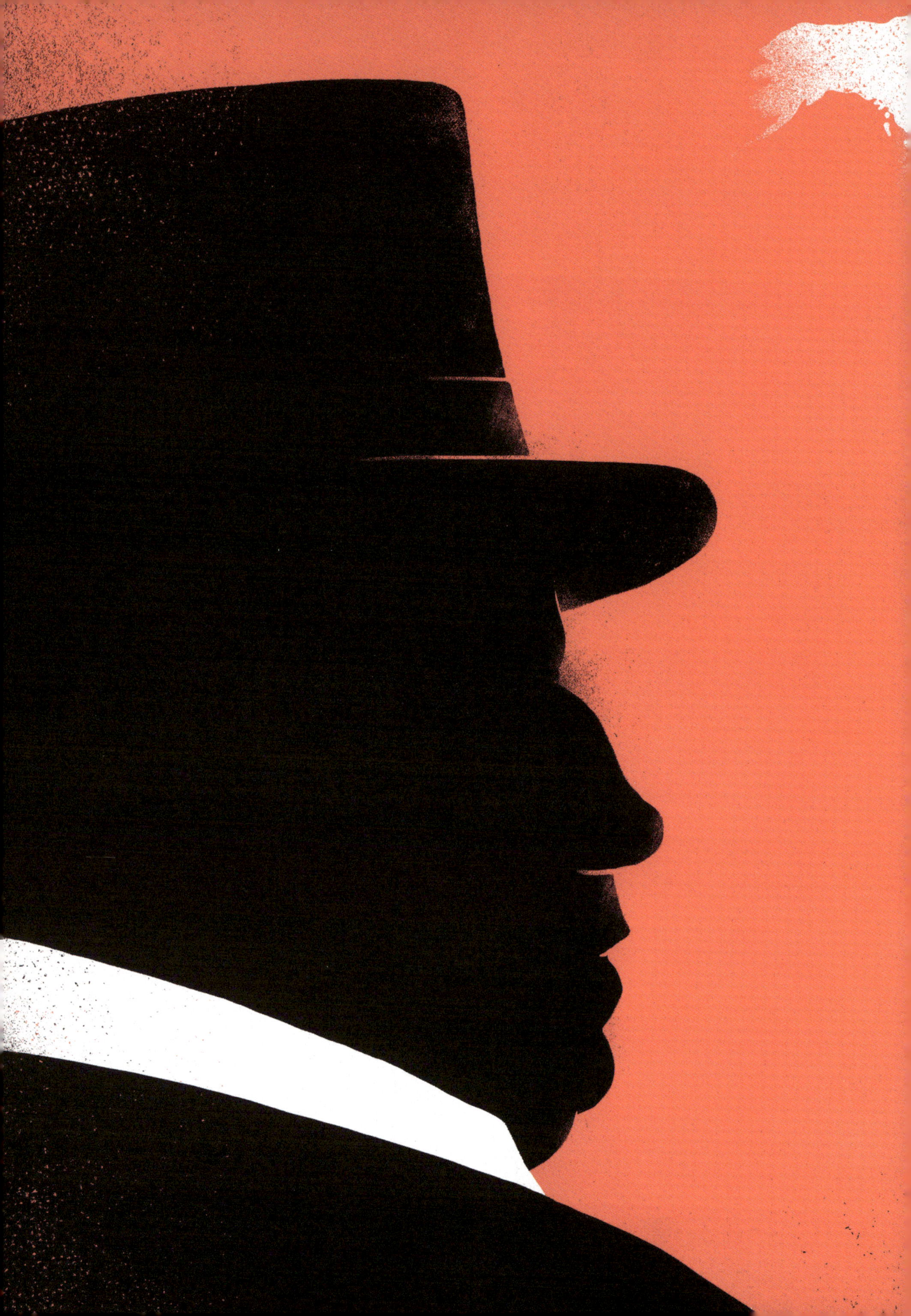

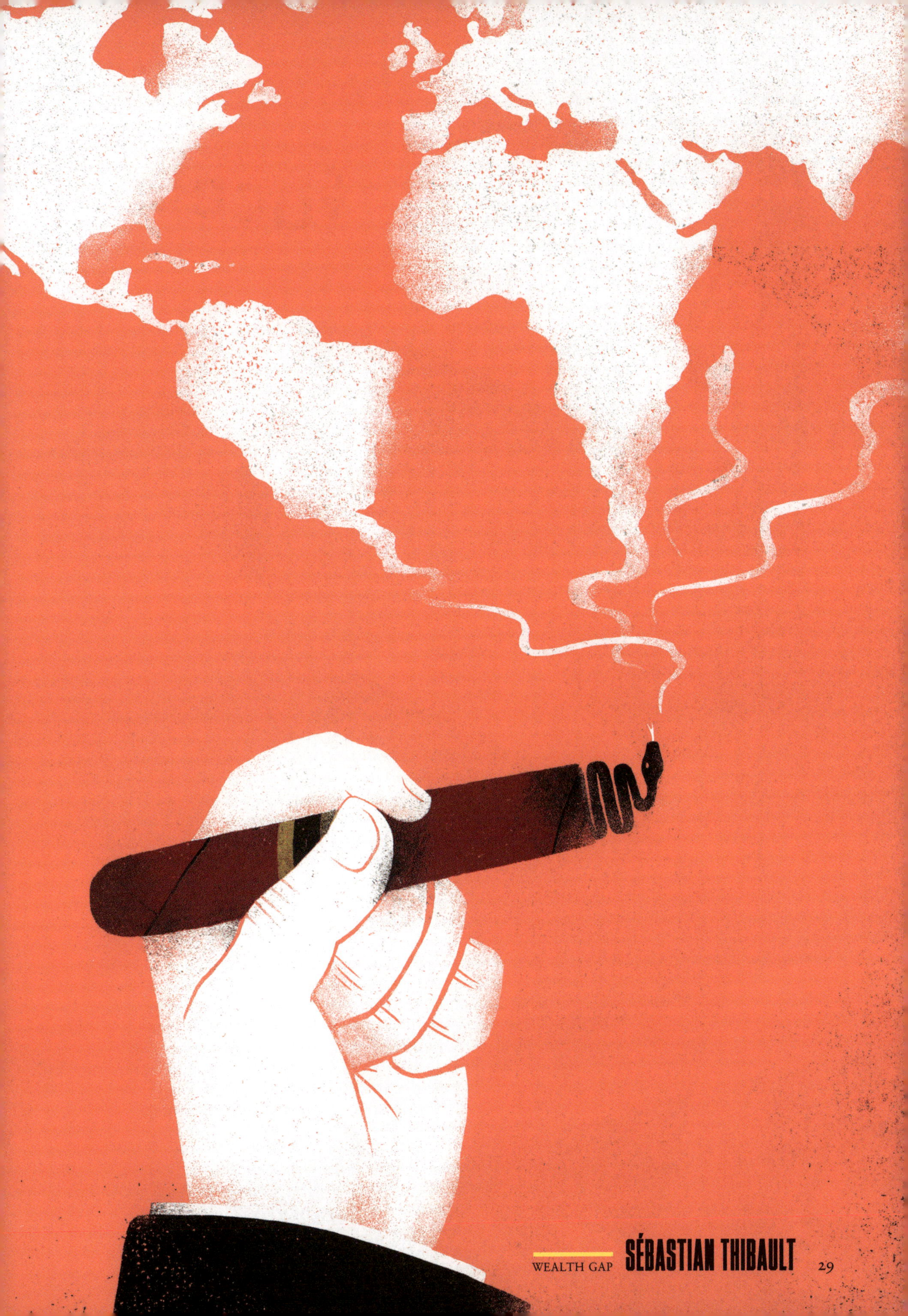

WEALTH GAP **SÉBASTIAN THIBAULT**

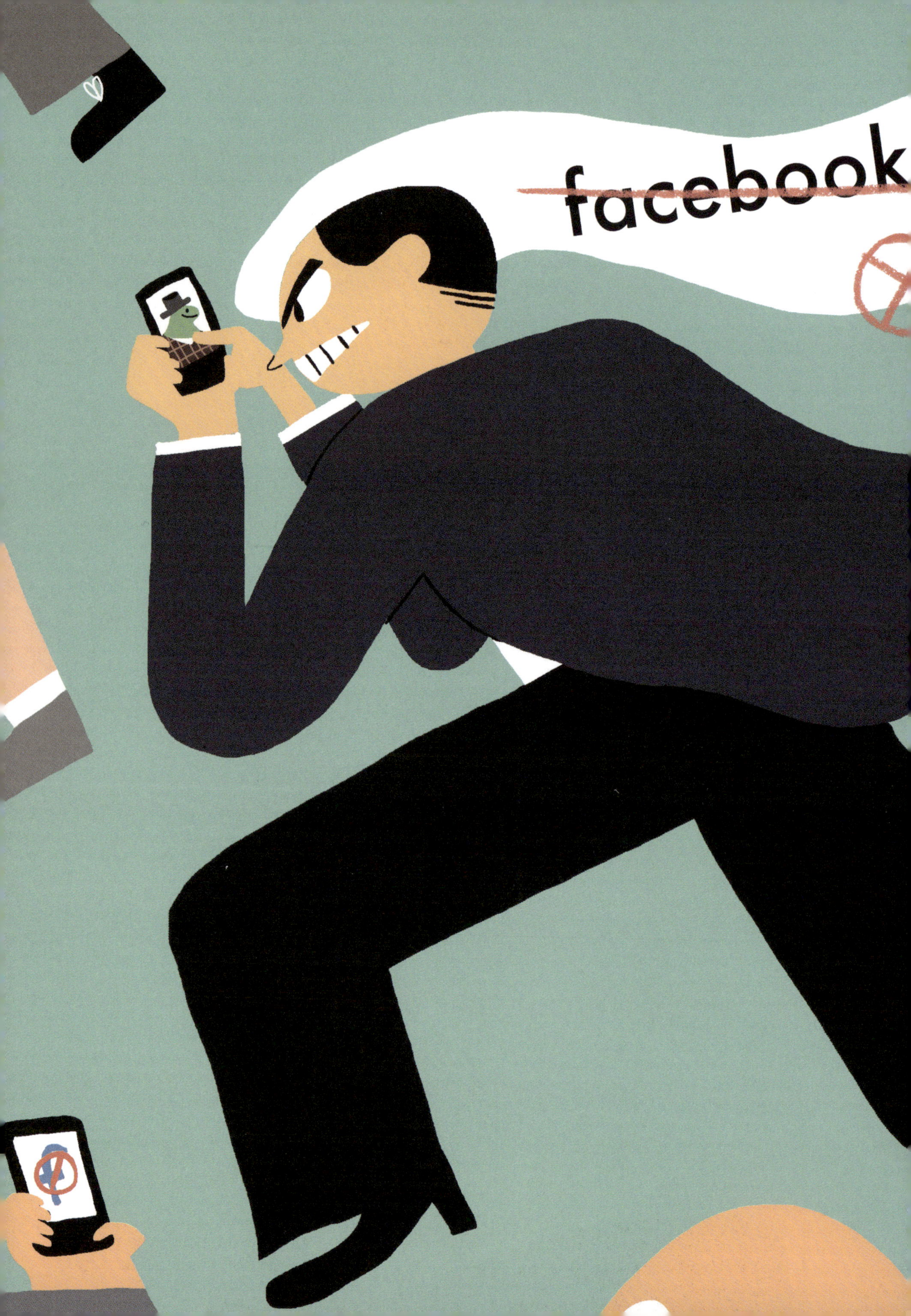
facebook

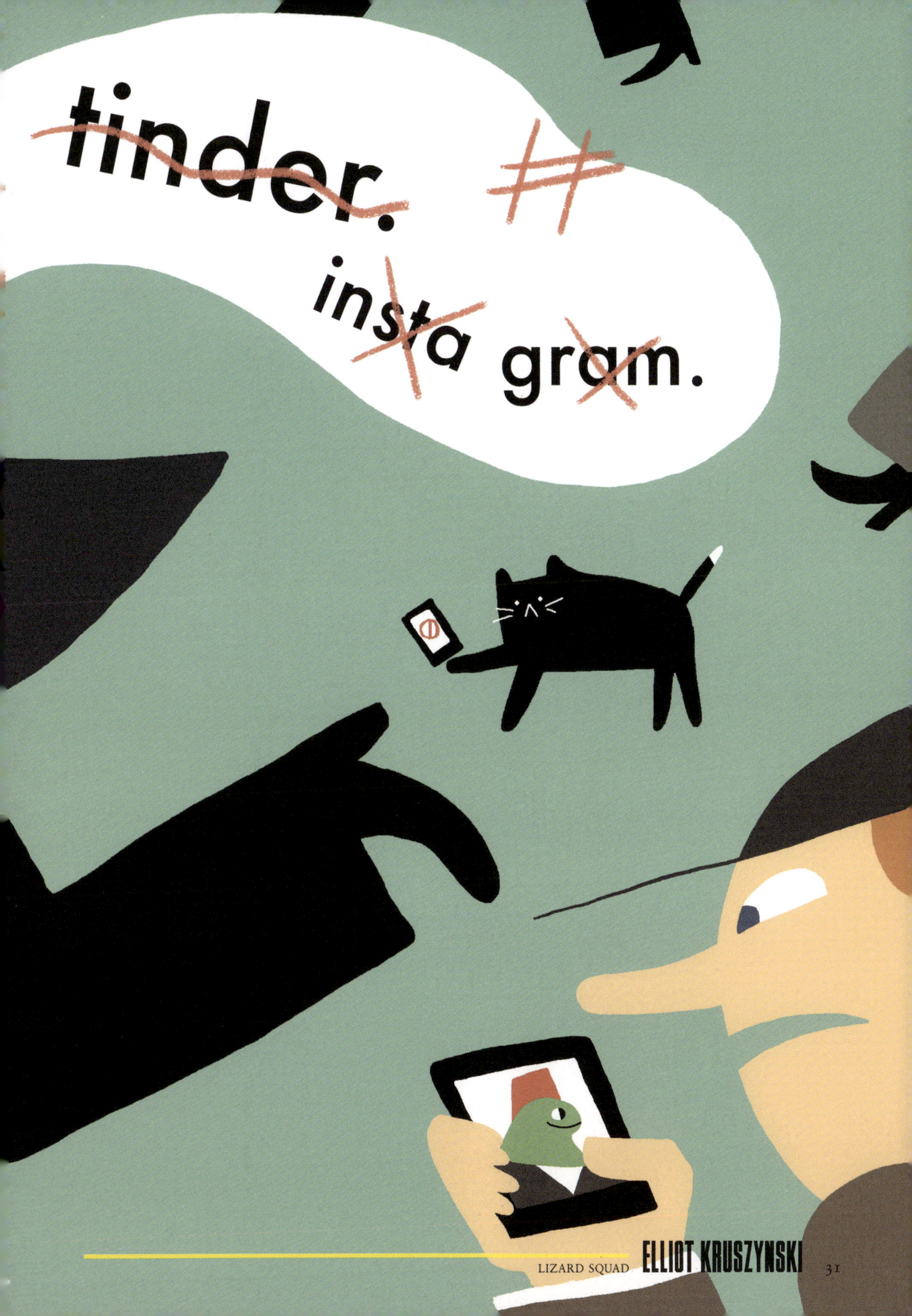
tinder.
insta gram.

SIMPLE DIRECT

BY SUPERMUNDANE

Illustrator and graphic designer

In today's world there's a lot of stuff vying for your attention. A lot of people have got important messages to shout about, but it's very easy to get lost in the noise. Because of that, the approachable nature of illustration makes it an interesting art form for tackling big, difficult ideas. Illustration is at the same time very graphic and very simple, which allows you to get a complex point across quickly and directly. That speed at which illustration can communicate an idea means that people don't question it too rigorously – they're not challenged by it and so don't pull away. With bigger, more 'serious' art the viewer might first have to take it all in, decode it and then work out the message – and in that time they might've built some resistance to it. With illustration the idea is right upfront, forcing you to consider it.

Illustration can be looked down upon by the art world, but I find it all bizarre really. Maybe it's paranoia, like they want to keep it to themselves, or maybe they think we're going to discover that some of their world isn't as important as they think it is.

For a long time illustration has been seen as a bit twee. Artists I know use the term 'illustration' almost as an insult, as if it's not as valid as so-called 'fine art'. I suppose part of that confusion comes from the fact that a lot of illustration is used in throwaway material. Inside newspapers and magazines, cartoons and illustrations come and go. People accept that they're everyday, just something that you look at once, whereas 'serious' art is supposed to be revered and returned to.

The beauty of illustration is its simplicity. There's an idea and an image and that's about it, it should all be there at first glance. That's kind of the point. Now, more than ever before, there's a responsibility for illustrators to use their craft to communicate in ways that other art forms either can't or won't. Illustration can help important ideas cut through the white noise, which is a pretty powerful thing when you come to think about it.

CRISPIN FINN

TO SEQUEL A MOCKINGBIRD / 2–8 FEBRUARY

"News broke that Harper Lee was to publish a sequel to her seminal work *To Kill A Mockingbird* 55 years since it was published. Amid both hype and controversy over whether she was complicit in the decision to publish, the promise of a second *Mockingbird* is a hugely unexpected and exciting prospect."

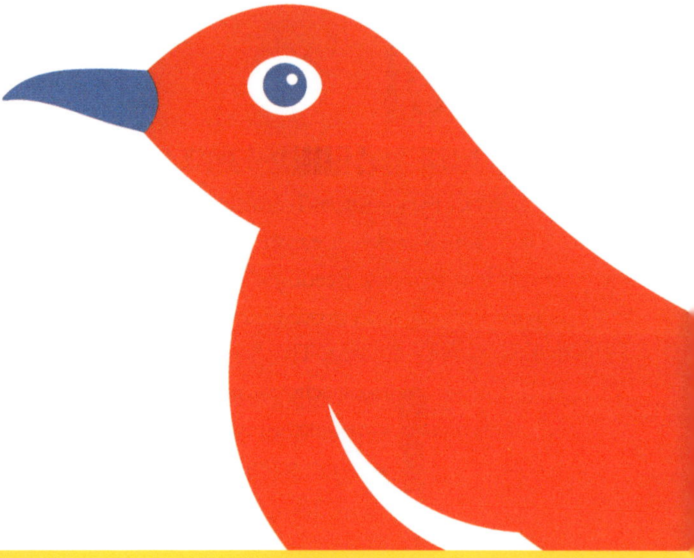

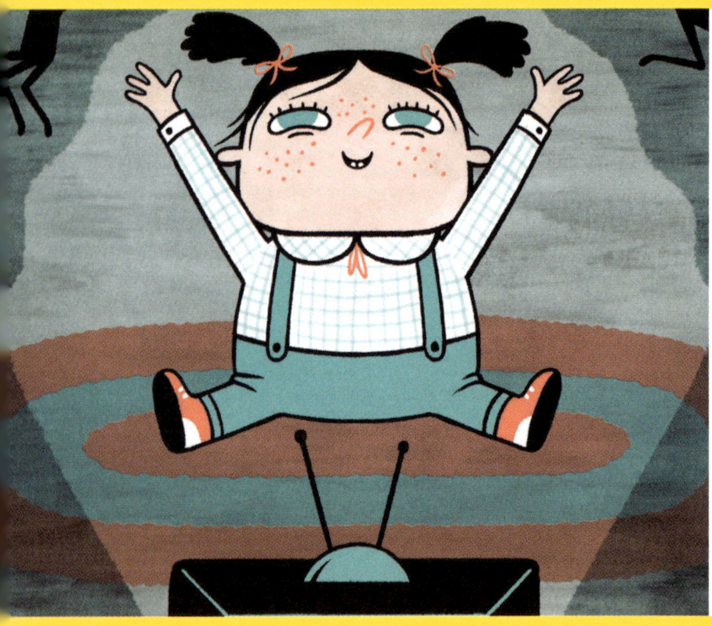

KRISTYNA BACZYNSKI

SPIDER PROPAGANDA / 9–15 FEBRUARY

"*Peppa Pig* featuring 'Mister Skinnylegs' was banned in Australia as it encouraged children to overcome their fear of spiders. As many of their native spiders are venomous, this was a dangerous piece of entertainment. Our instinct is often to pacify concerns and undo phobias, but maybe we should be scared?"

BEN STEERS

CHELSEA FANS / 16–22 FEBRUARY

"On 18 February, Chelsea fans in Paris was the big headline and something that seemed worthy of documenting. I wanted to place the viewer in the shoes of Frenchman Souleymane Sylla, who was repeatedly refused access onto the Metro train by a wall of racist Chelsea football fans."

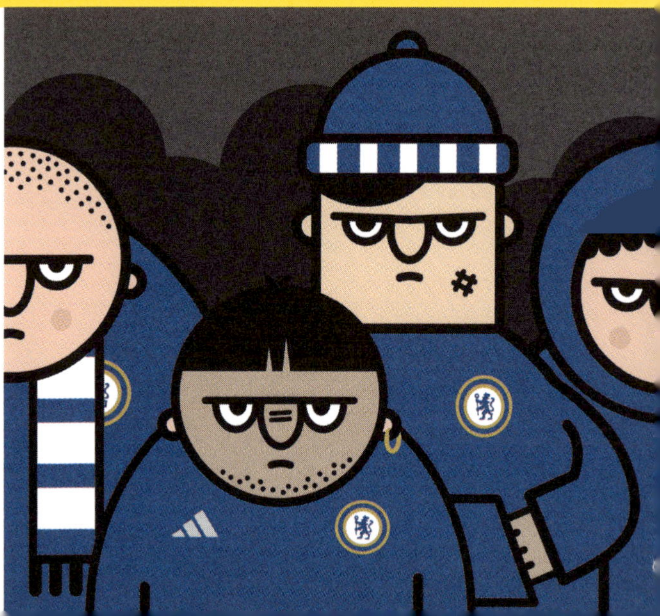

SOFIA NIAZI

COUNTER-TERROR MEASURES / 23 FEBRUARY–1 MARCH

"My piece is about the *Counter-Terrorism and Security Act*, which makes it easier for the Government to restrict the freedoms of British citizens without having to prove that an individual is guilty of a crime. The Act makes it a legal duty upon colleges, schools, prisons, GPs and councils to prevent extremism."

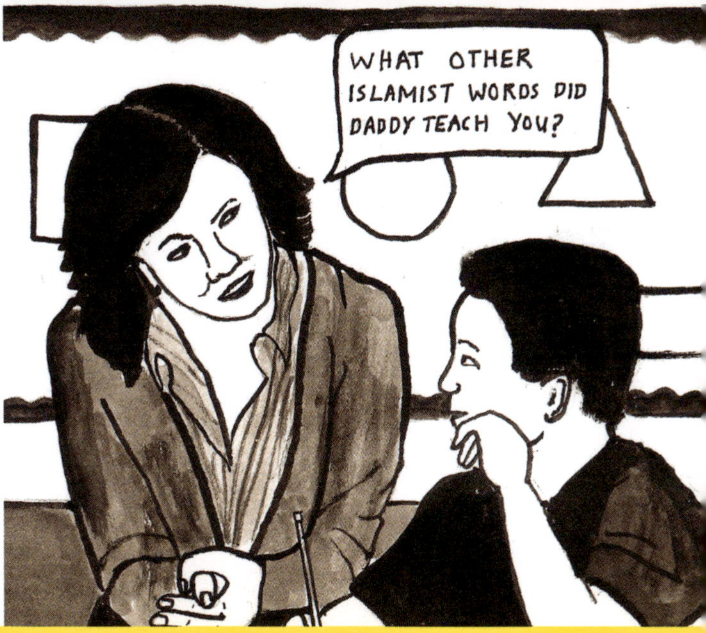

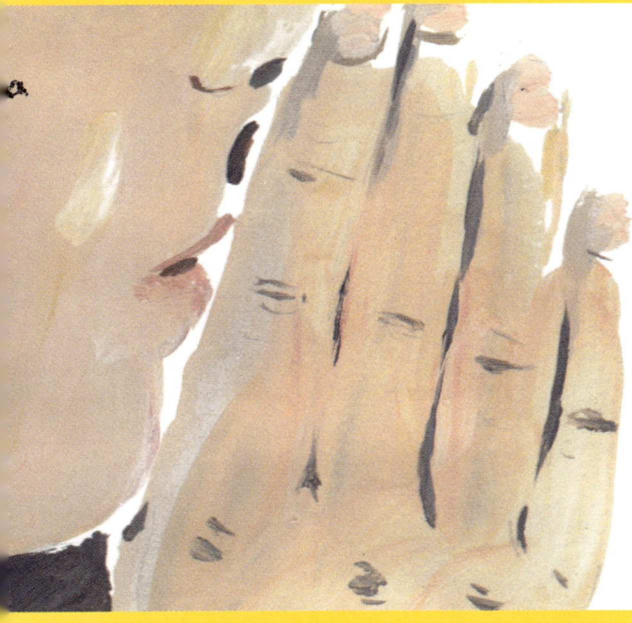

CHARLOTTE MEI

SPY SCHOOL / 2–8 MARCH

"In light of the hounding of Edward Snowden and the NSA spying scandal, my comic reflects on the encroaching access of US and UK governments to the personal data of its citizens."

NEASDEN CONTROL CENTRE

ENVIRONMENTAL APATHY / 9–15 MARCH

"My illustrations focus on the ongoing narrative and campaign against corporate and political apathy to climate change, which is never really out of the news. On this week *The Guardian*, led by Alan Rusbridger, focused on this topic in a series of front page articles."

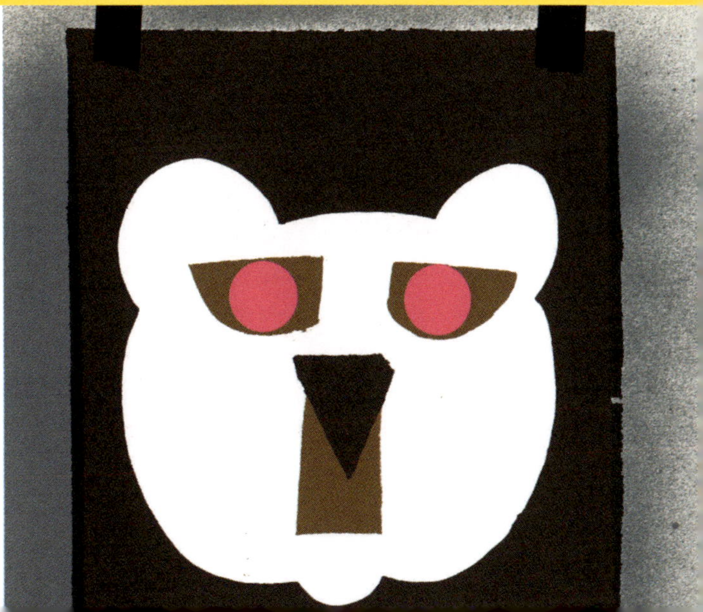

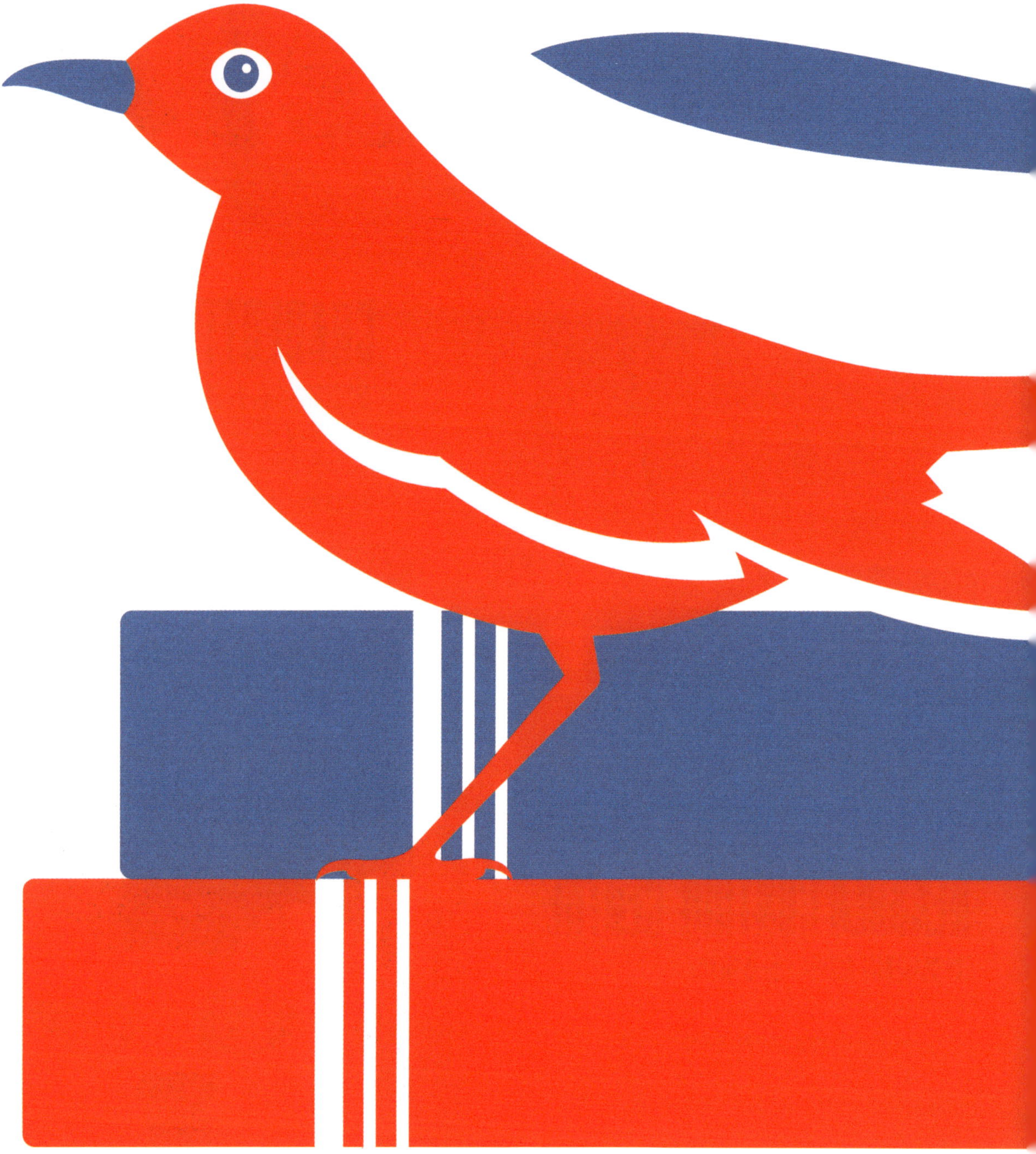

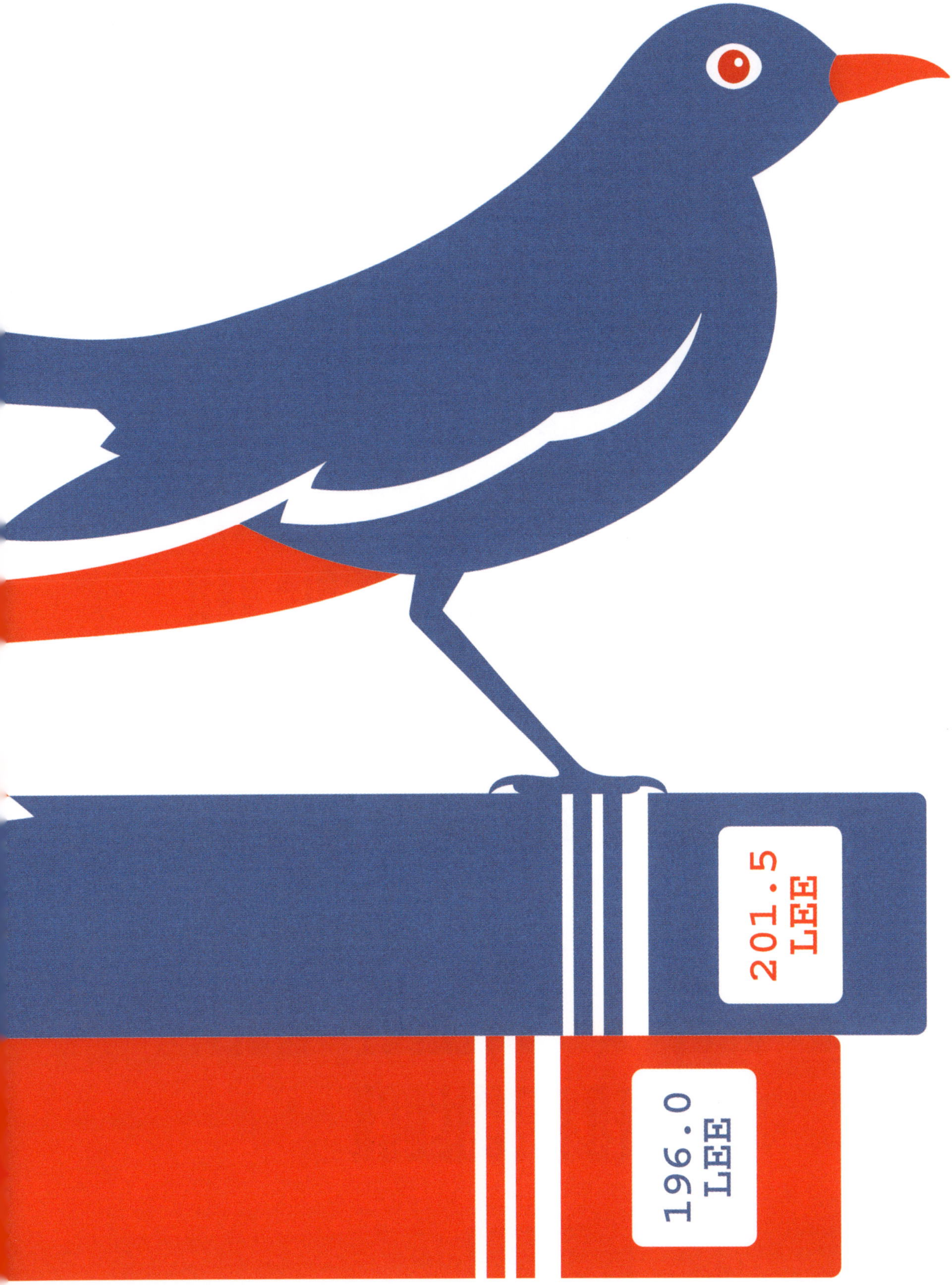
201.5
LEE
196.0
LEE

"FEAR ISN'T SO DIFFICULT TO UNDERSTAND. AFTER ALL, WEREN'T WE ALL FRIGHTENED AS CHILDREN? NOTHING HAS CHANGED SINCE LITTLE RED RIDING HOOD FACED THE BIG BAD WOLF. WHAT FRIGHTENS US TODAY IS EXACTLY THE SAME SORT OF THING THAT FRIGHTENED US YESTERDAY. IT'S JUST A DIFFERENT WOLF."

ALFRED HITCHCOCK

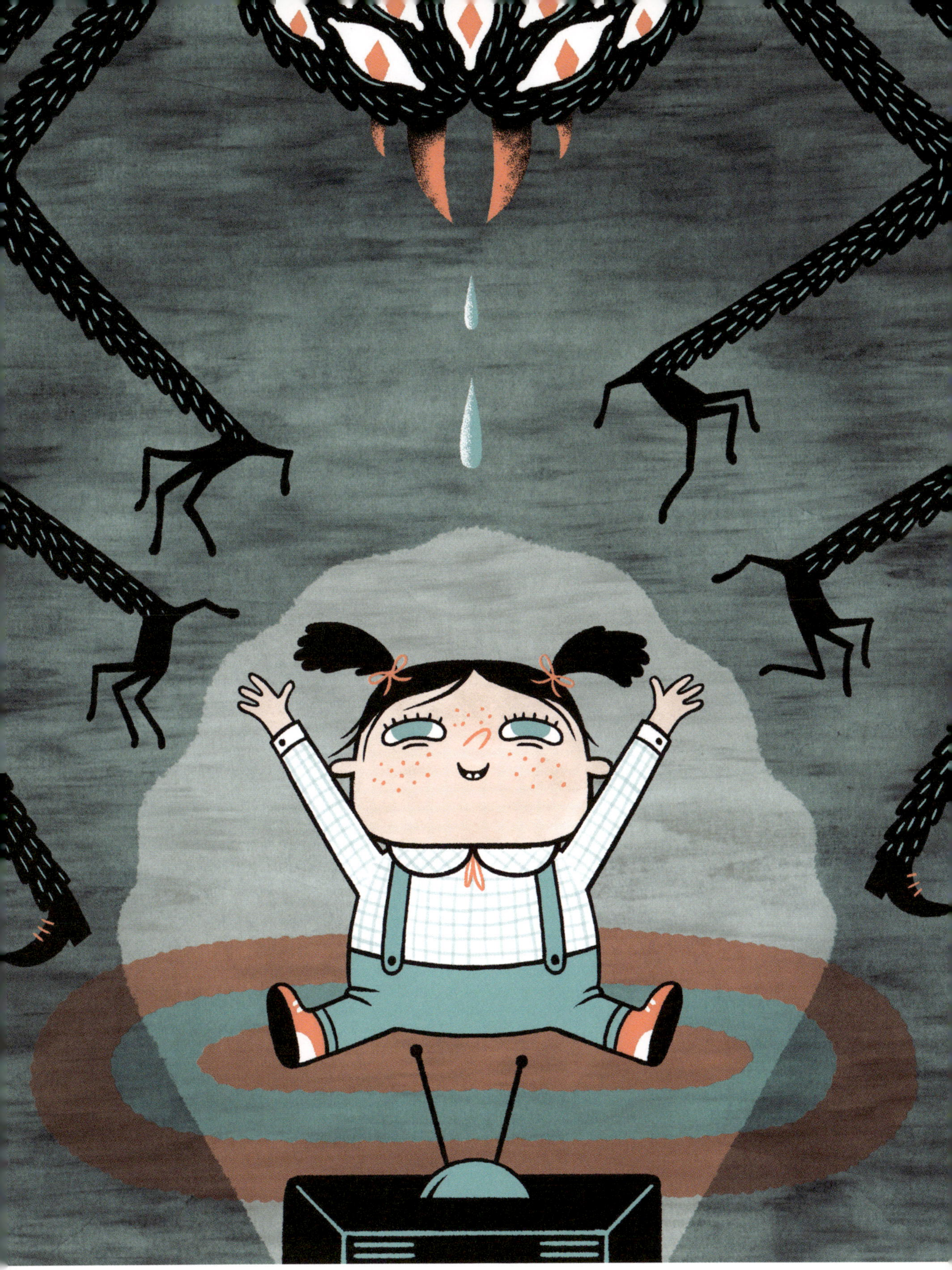

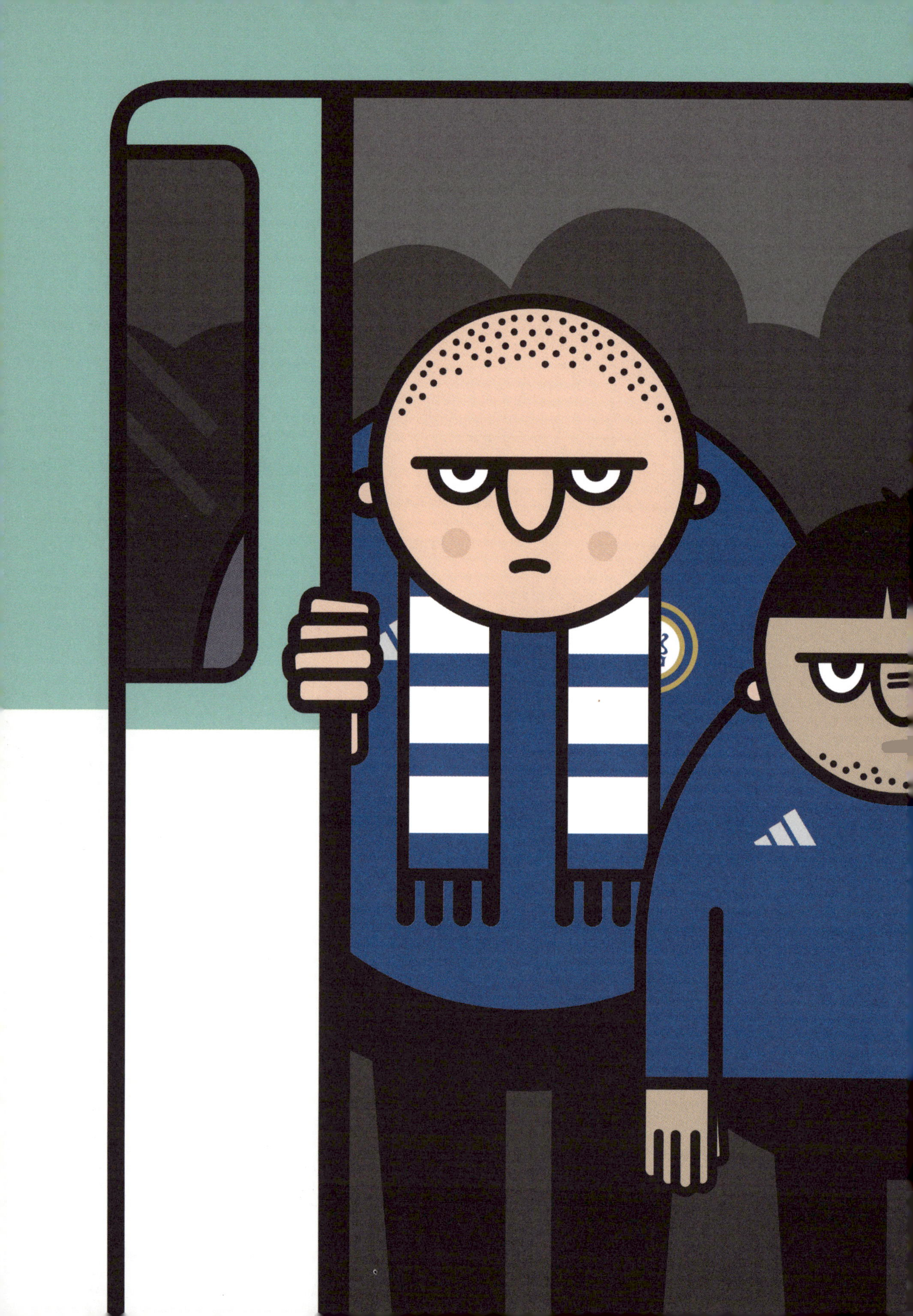

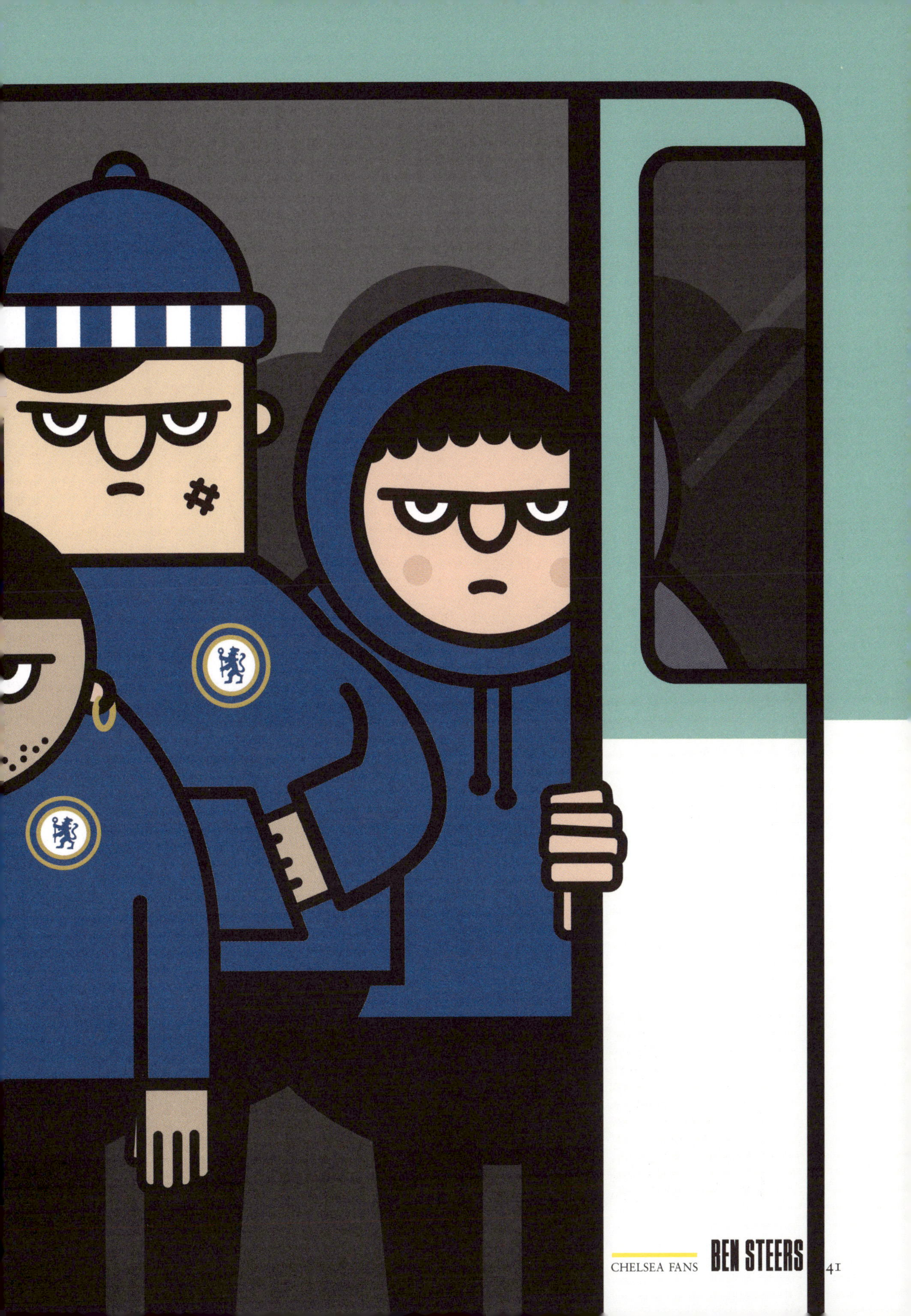

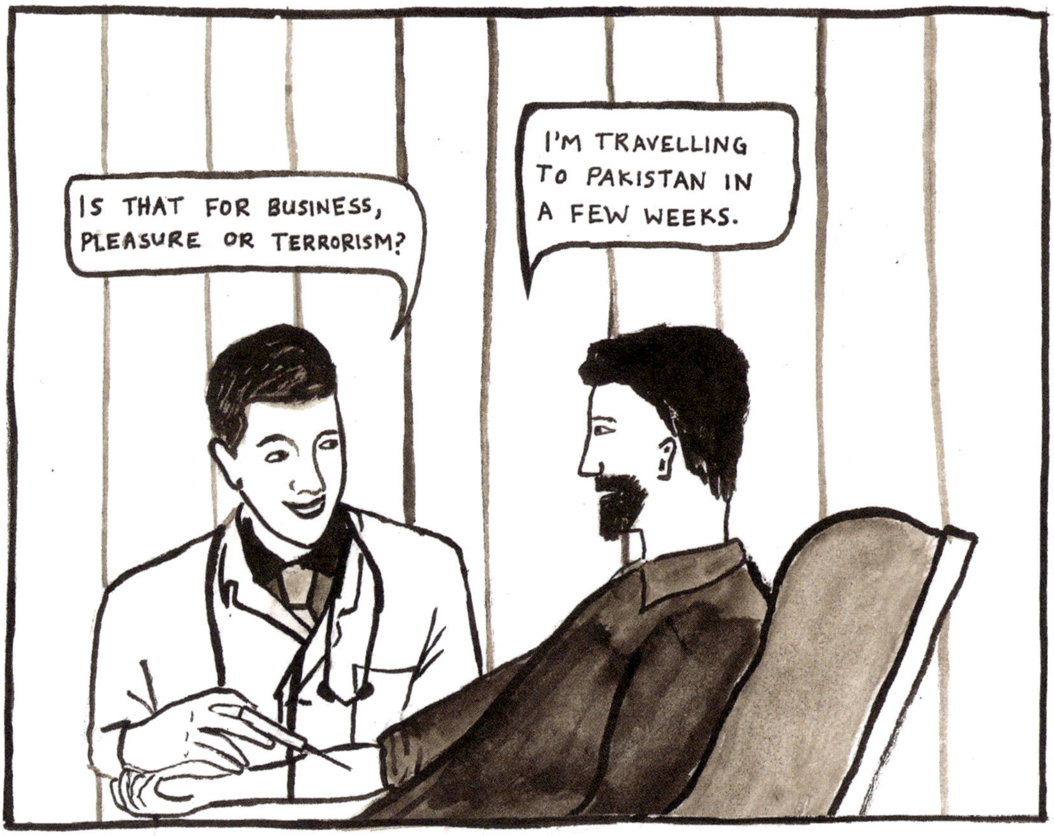
I'M TRAVELLING TO PAKISTAN IN A FEW WEEKS.
IS THAT FOR BUSINESS, PLEASURE OR TERRORISM?

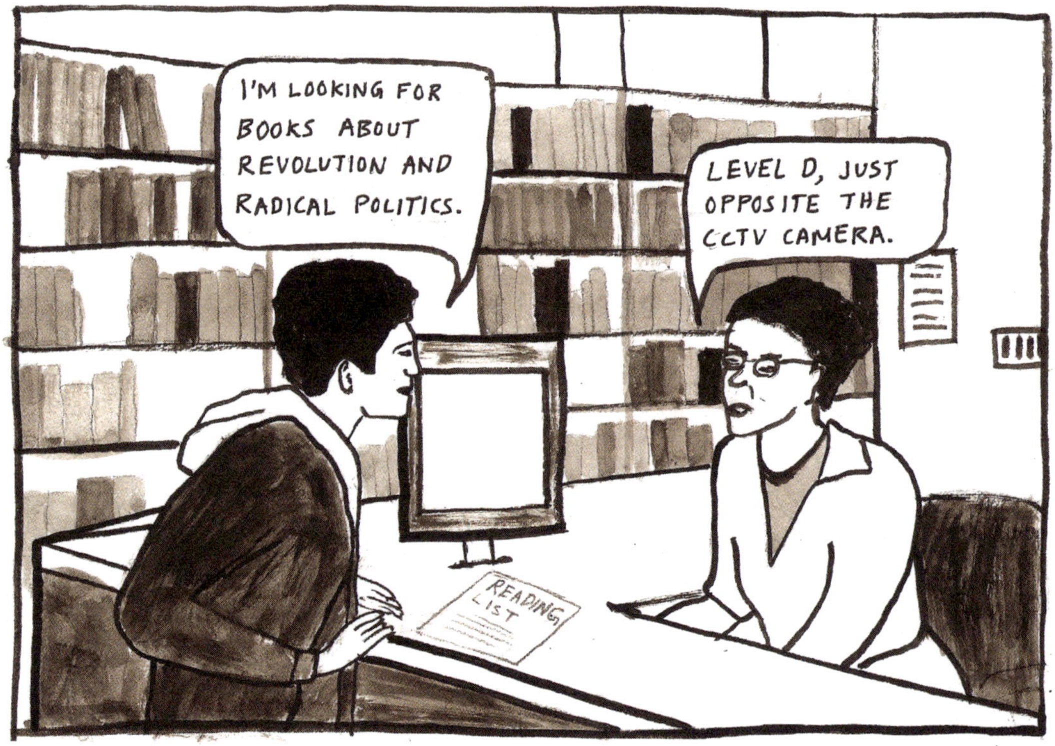
I'M LOOKING FOR BOOKS ABOUT REVOLUTION AND RADICAL POLITICS.
LEVEL D, JUST OPPOSITE THE CCTV CAMERA.
READING LIST

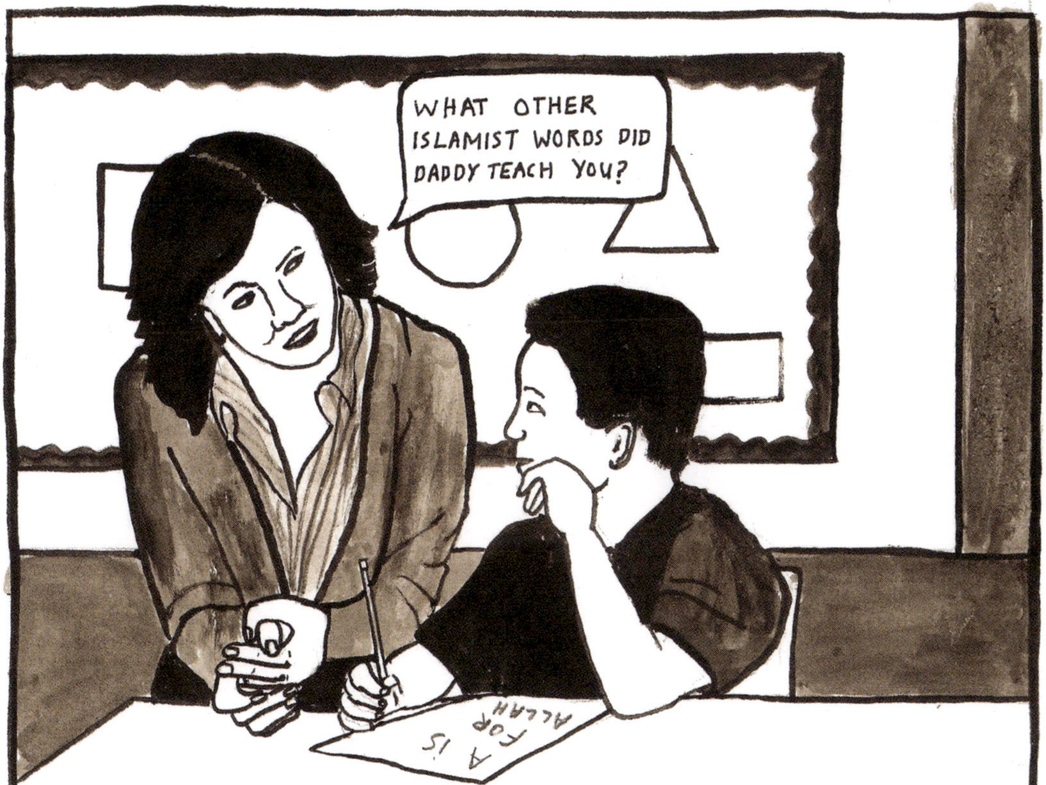
WHAT OTHER ISLAMIST WORDS DID DADDY TEACH YOU?
A IS FOR ALLAH

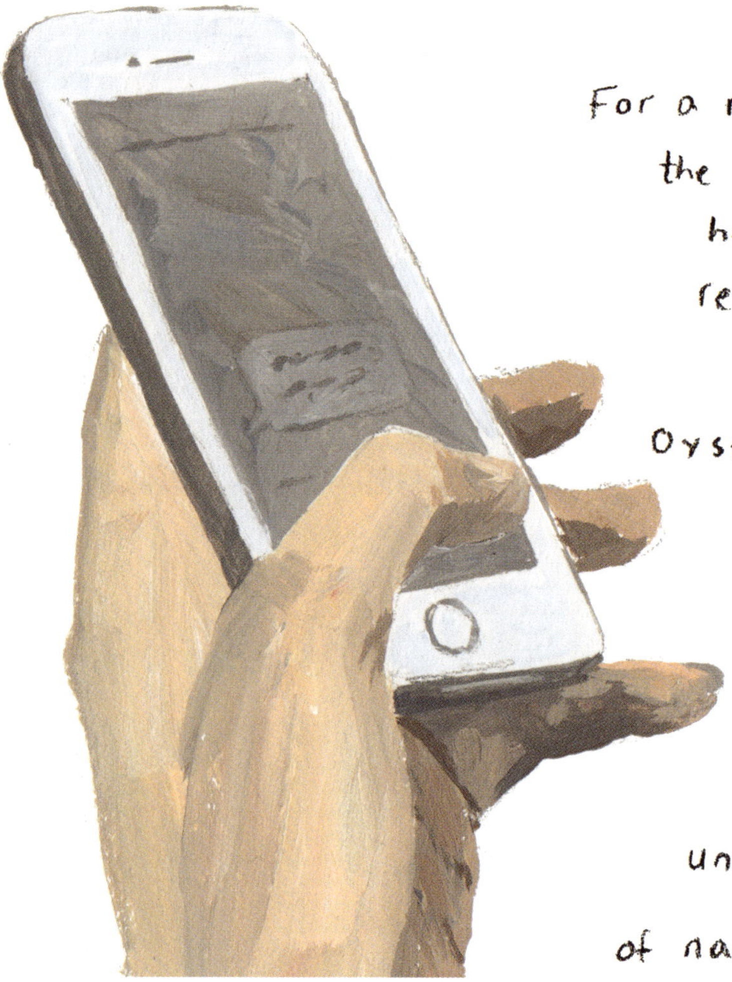

For a number of years
the NSA and GCHQ
have been making
records of your
private messages
Oyster card data
Google searches
emails
and calls
both meta data
and content.
under the pretense
of national security.

Historically, governments
have used recorded data
to incriminate those who
resist changes
or try to protest.

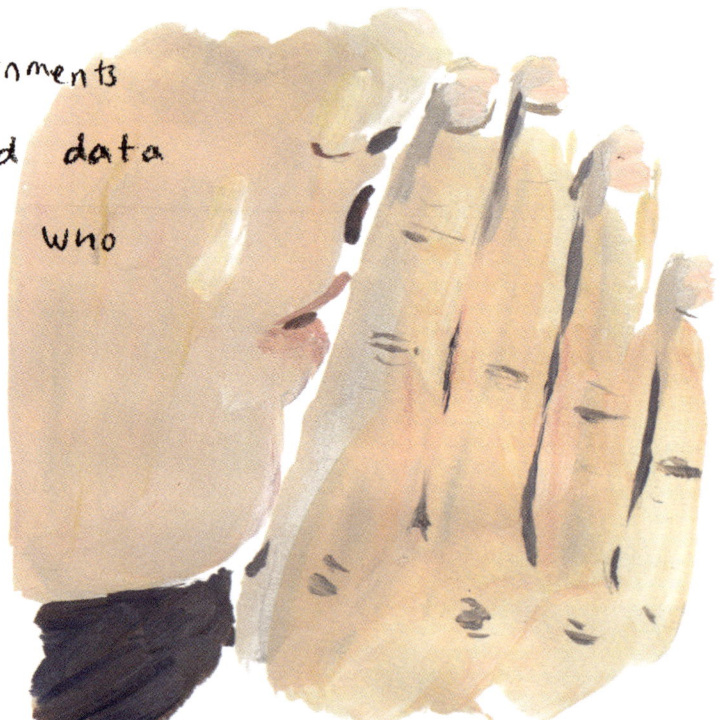

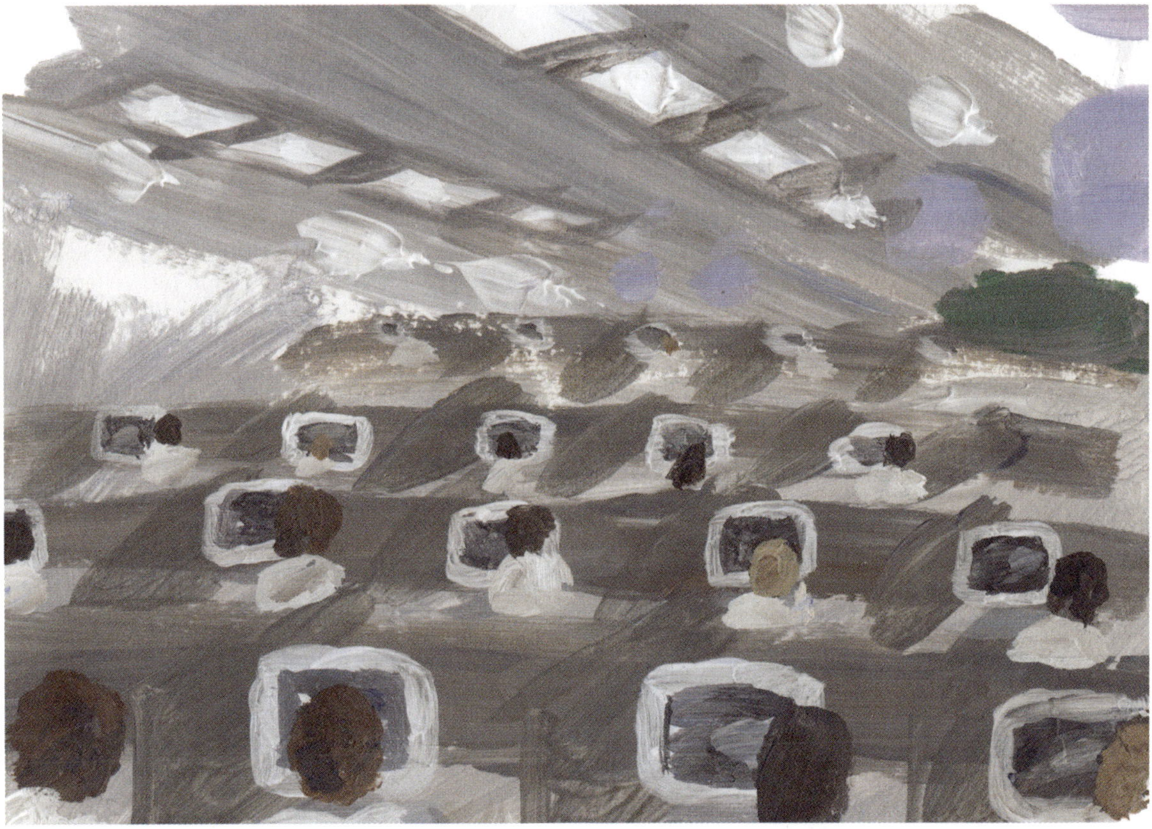

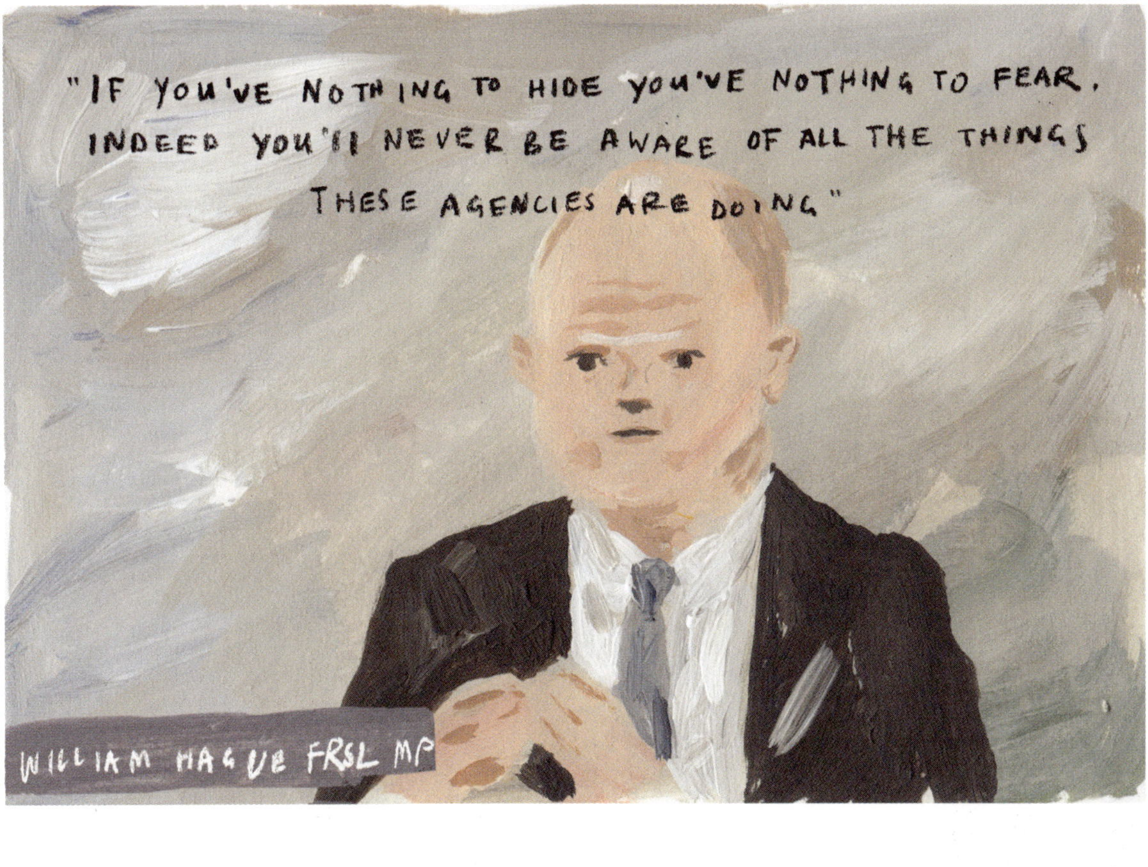
"IF YOU'VE NOTHING TO HIDE YOU'VE NOTHING TO FEAR. INDEED YOU'll NEVER BE AWARE OF ALL THE THINGS THESE AGENCIES ARE DOING"
WILLIAM HAGUE FRSL MP

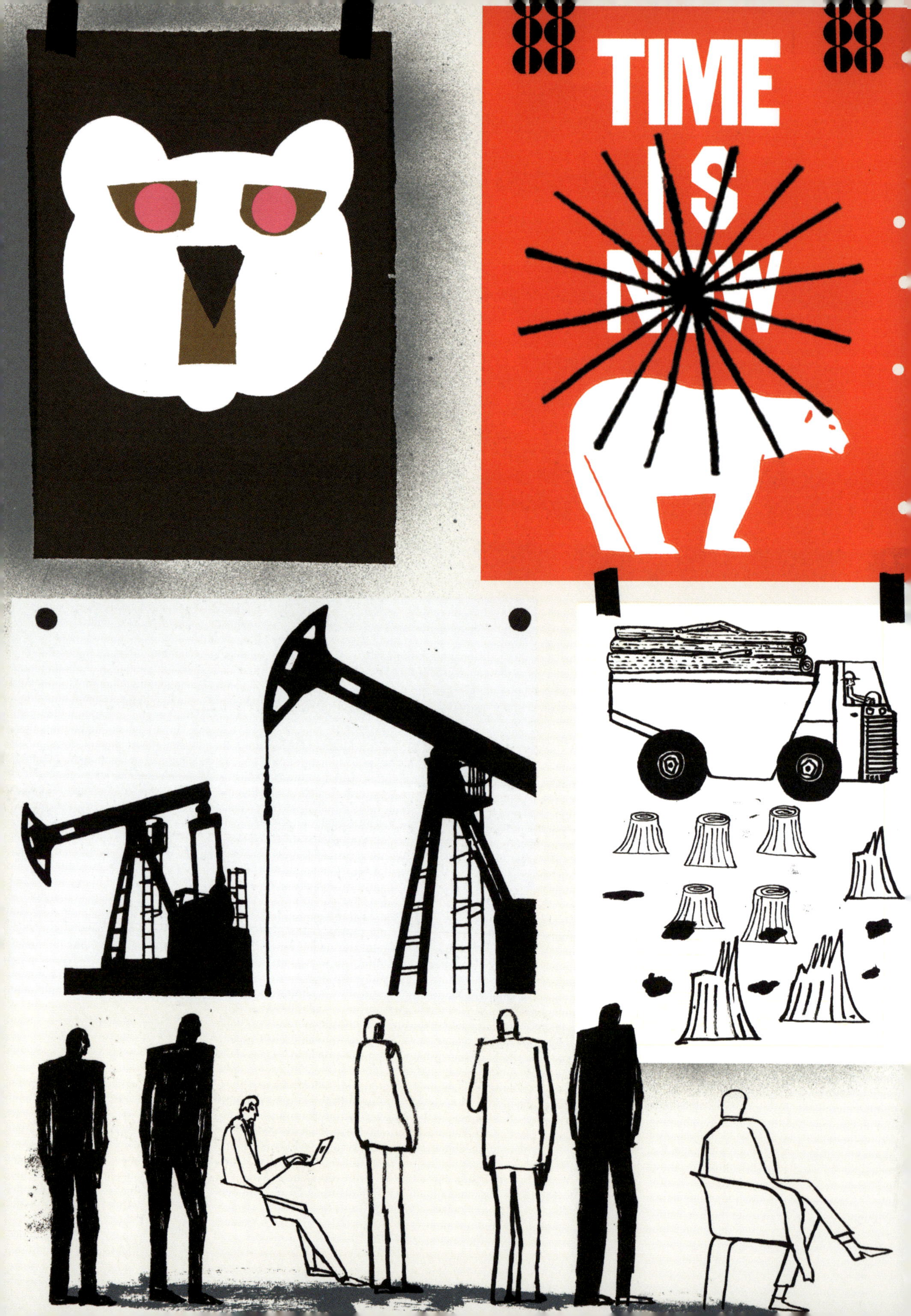
TIME
IS
NOW

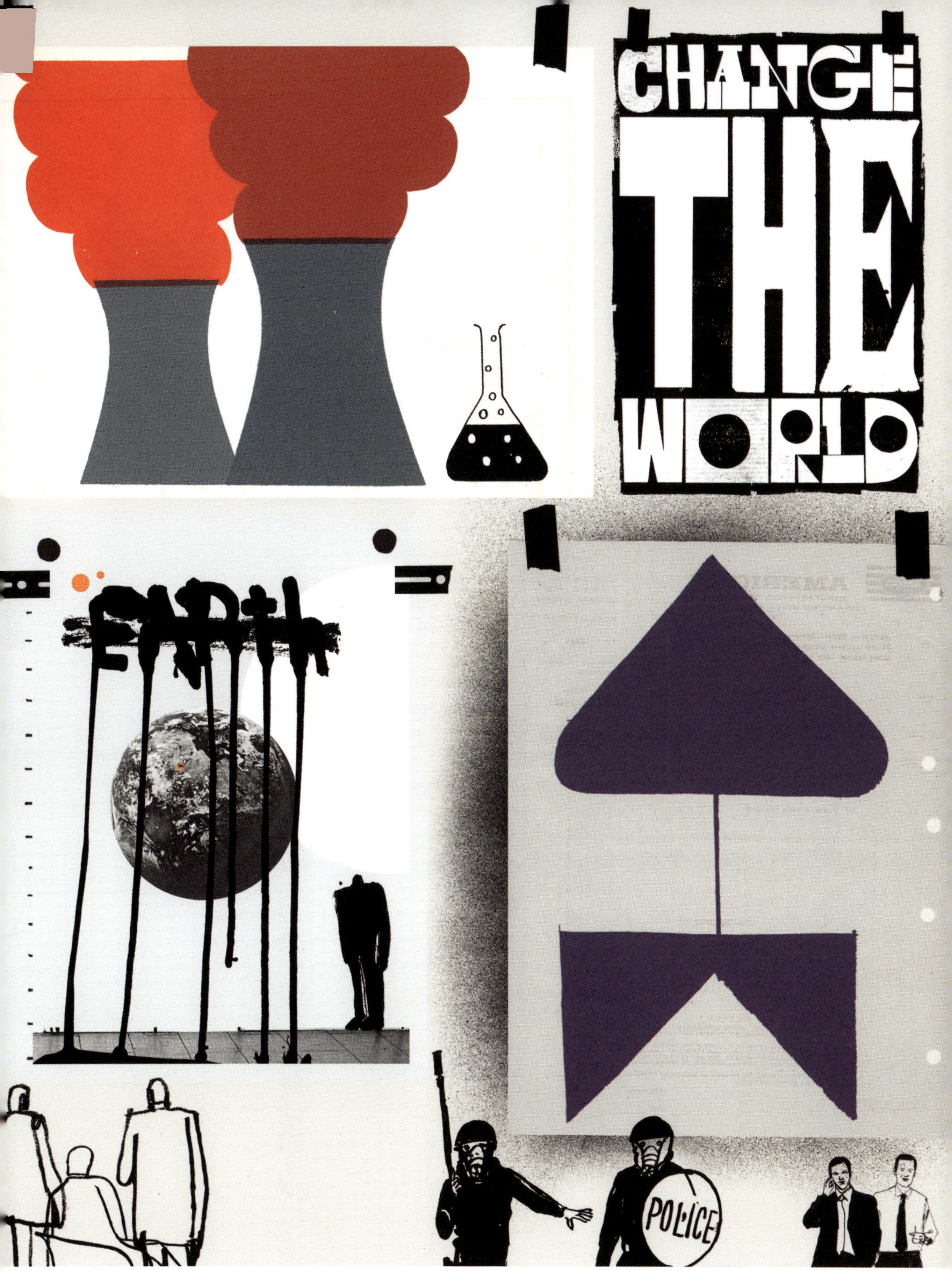
CHANGE
THE
WORLD
EARTH
POLICE

GUNS FOR HIRE

Illustration is a universal language that doesn't necessarily need words. In that sense it doesn't matter what age you are or where you are from, you can get an idea of what's happening in an illustration whoever you are. I could probably illustrate the answer to a question better than actually using words, which gives you an idea of how good a medium illustration can be. Illustration is everywhere at the moment, especially in 'serious' magazines and papers alongside 'serious' articles. There are many reasons why. For one, good photographers cost a fortune. Sometimes to create the photo a magazine wants, they'll need to pay the photographer, their travel expenses, the model, the set designer, the stylist, all their expenses for the day... the list of costs can be exhausting.

With an illustration, it's usually just one person required to create the image. That's less hassle and less cost. Also, with illustration the art director and illustrator can manipulate an image to however they want. With photography, when the photo is taken, creatively you are bound within that photograph, whereas in illustration, if you have the right illustrator the possibilities are endless.

I get a lot of my work from *The New Yorker*, and for all of the *New Yorker*'s 90-year history they have always favoured illustration over photography. I've also worked for *Time* magazine and the *New York Times*, and the illustrations I did for them probably wouldn't have worked if they were photos.

When it comes to magazines, the illustrator and the photographer seem to be perceived completely differently. My theory is that it has to do with celebrity. Most illustrators are stuck at home or in a studio on their own, with only their pet cat to talk to and maybe an art director on the end of the phone. Most lauded photographers spend their time taking pictures of people, and successful photographers will be assigned to take photos of celebrities and the famous. The fact that the photographer has a one-to-one relationship with the celebrity makes them a celeb by association. Celebrity and credit go hand-in-hand in many cases.

But, that doesn't mean that as an illustrator I feel any responsibility to show what my art form can do. During art school and for most of my career, my 'philosophy' was 'all style and no substance'. I tried to make a point that the illustration had to look good first and foremost, and whatever idea there was behind it was secondary.

I guess this was just me trying to be anti-establishment. The art course I was on mainly focused on ideas and concepts and less about technique and aesthetics. Essentially, we illustrators are guns for hire. From my experience we don't have much of a say on our output. It's dependent on what the art director or client wants.

What you can do, of course, is choose what you work on. Now that I'm more politically aware I've stopped working for *The Mail*, *The Telegraph* and *The Sun*, who were fairly regular clients when I was younger. Ultimately it's a choice, not a responsibility, whether illustrators want to produce work that is more than just a pretty picture.

BY STANLEY CHOW

Illustrator

ROBBIE PORTER

SOLAR ECLIPSE / 16–22 MARCH

"I've always been intrigued and terrified of space. My brother took me on an introduction to astrophysics course at Greenwich Observatory, so I've had space on the brain. I couldn't resist doing a piece on the eclipse. Space looks pretty friendly in this picture… more cosmic cuddle than terrifying abyss."

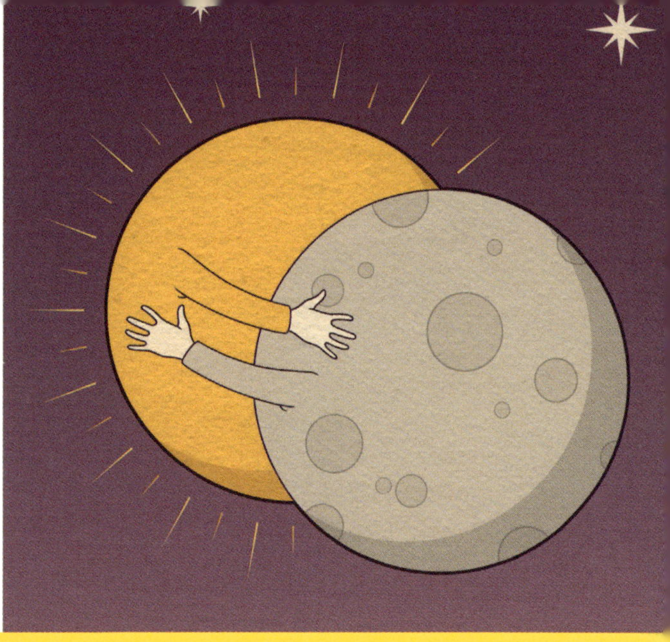

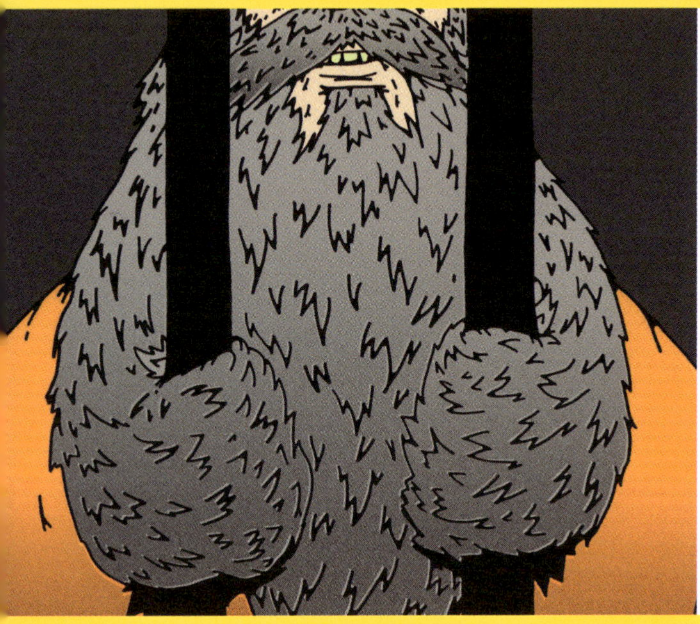

CHRIS MARTIN

BEARD JAIL / 23–29 MARCH

"I tried to find a subject that was ridiculous and serious at the same time. The story of a Chinese man being locked away because of his beard jumped out at me as a story to visualise, something you can explain in the image alone."

SUPERMUNDANE

GAY PIZZA / 30 MARCH–5 APRIL

"I'm not sure how many gay couples would have pizza at their wedding, but this statement sparked a huge backlash. The idea of not serving someone pizza based on their sexual orientation – something that religious people seem to spend far too much time thinking about – is ridiculous and I want to show that."

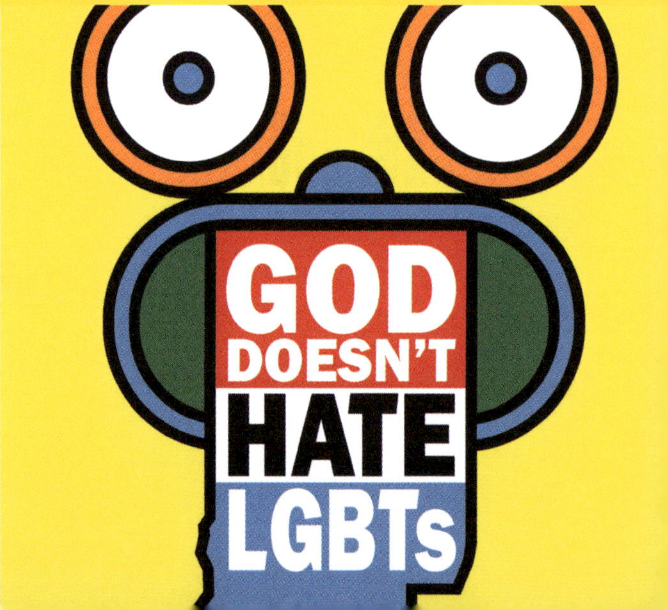

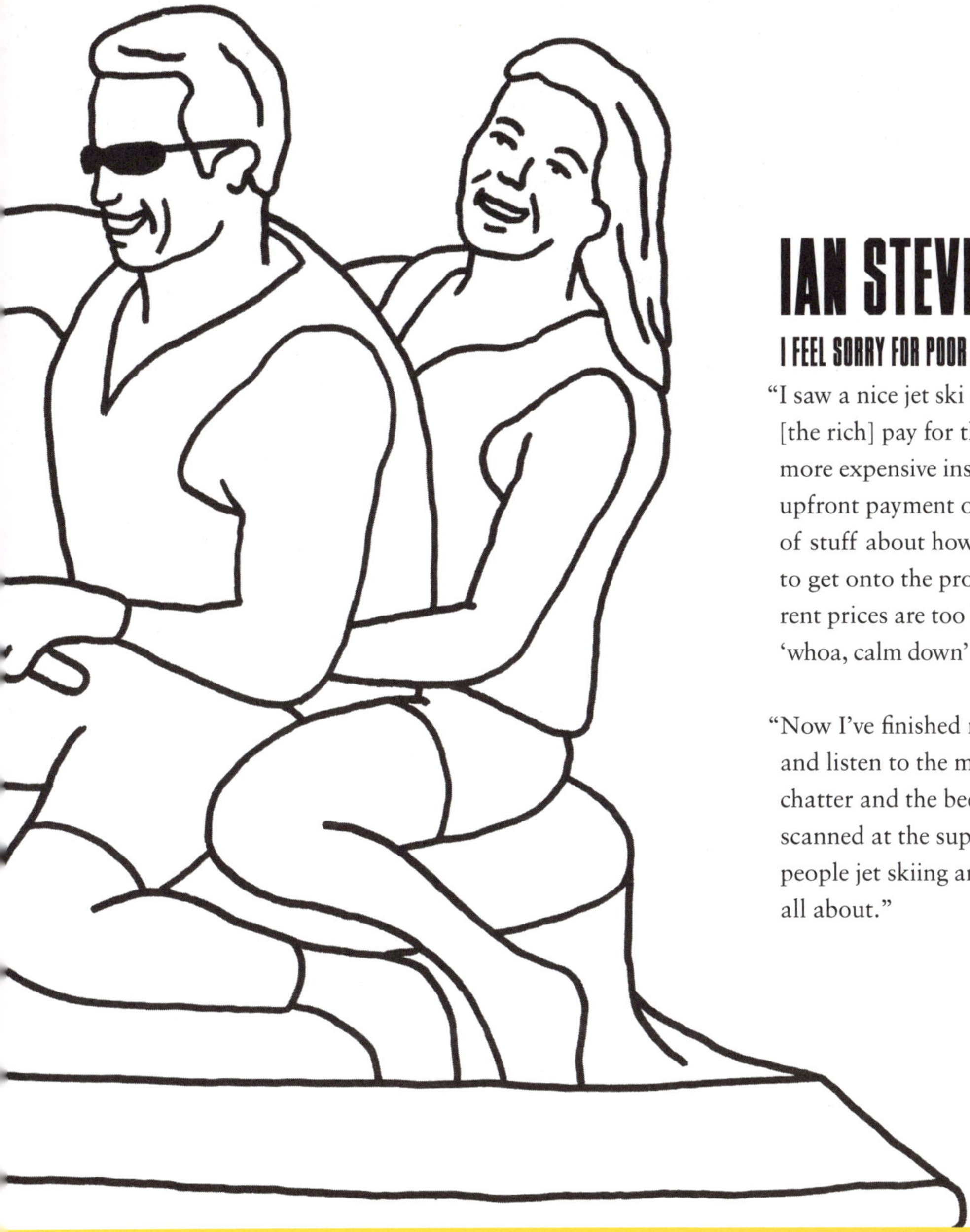

IAN STEVENSON

I FEEL SORRY FOR POOR PEOPLE / 6–12 APRIL

"I saw a nice jet ski and I wondered if they [the rich] pay for things in four slightly more expensive instalments or the cheaper upfront payment option. I wrote a load of stuff about how hard it is for people to get onto the property ladder and that rent prices are too high, and then thought 'whoa, calm down' and deleted it.

"Now I've finished my artwork, I will go and listen to the modern symphony of chatter and the beeps of the items being scanned at the supermarket, thinking of people jet skiing and wondering what it's all about."

WOODROW PHOENIX

CRUSHED / 13–19 APRIL

"I was amazed to see a headline about a person dying in a cycling collision. Inadequacy of the law around fatal collisions is due, in part, to a legal system that is weighted in favour of people who drive. If every death on the roads was treated like Moira Gemmill's in April then people might begin to think differently."

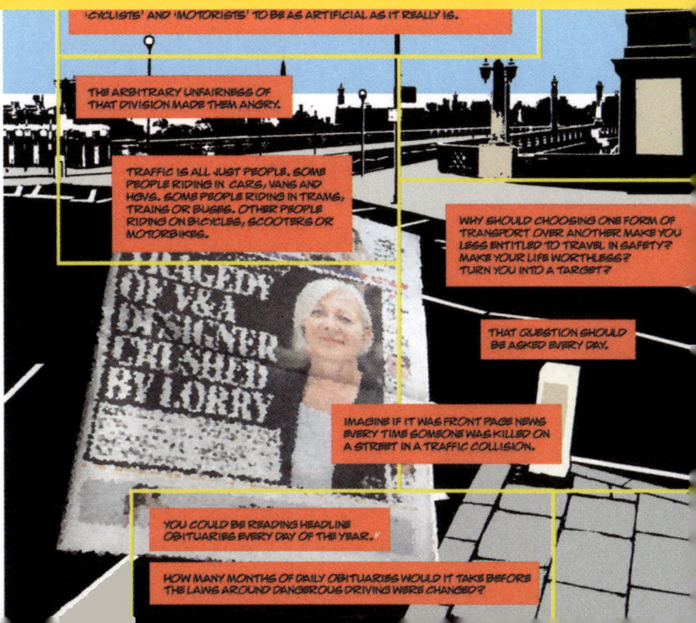

ECLIPSING ILLUSTRATION

When working on books and magazines, it can be very easy to look at illustration as a sort of plaster; something that can be stuck anywhere to heal broken articles.

In putting this book together we've heard countless illustrators lament how publications use their work. One artist told us how sometimes they feel their artwork sits 'like a gargoyle' above dense chunks of copy, while another explained how they'll create an image from the brief, only for a sub-editor to place a title over it and change the meaning entirely.

Too often illustration is seen as a pretty aside; a decoration for the weight of the written word. Our rush to 'brighten', 'lift' or 'punch up' a page of copy eclipses the thought process behind artwork.

Our intention for *Yellow* was to give illustration the spotlight and, for once, have words play the role of back-up dancer. For the first time in my career I had to plan how articles might fill gaps, rather than the other way around. Looking at how an article might fit around an existing illustration is an interesting exercise that I'd recommend to any other editors. Theme soon trumps topic or narrative, and subsequently articles become more conceptual – you're forced to explore the idea behind an illustration and the relationship between word and image.

I never thought that illustration would teach me a different way to think about copy, but then, if us editors are completely honest, we've probably not given our artist friends the chance before.

BY DANIEL HUMPHRY

Editor of *Yellow*

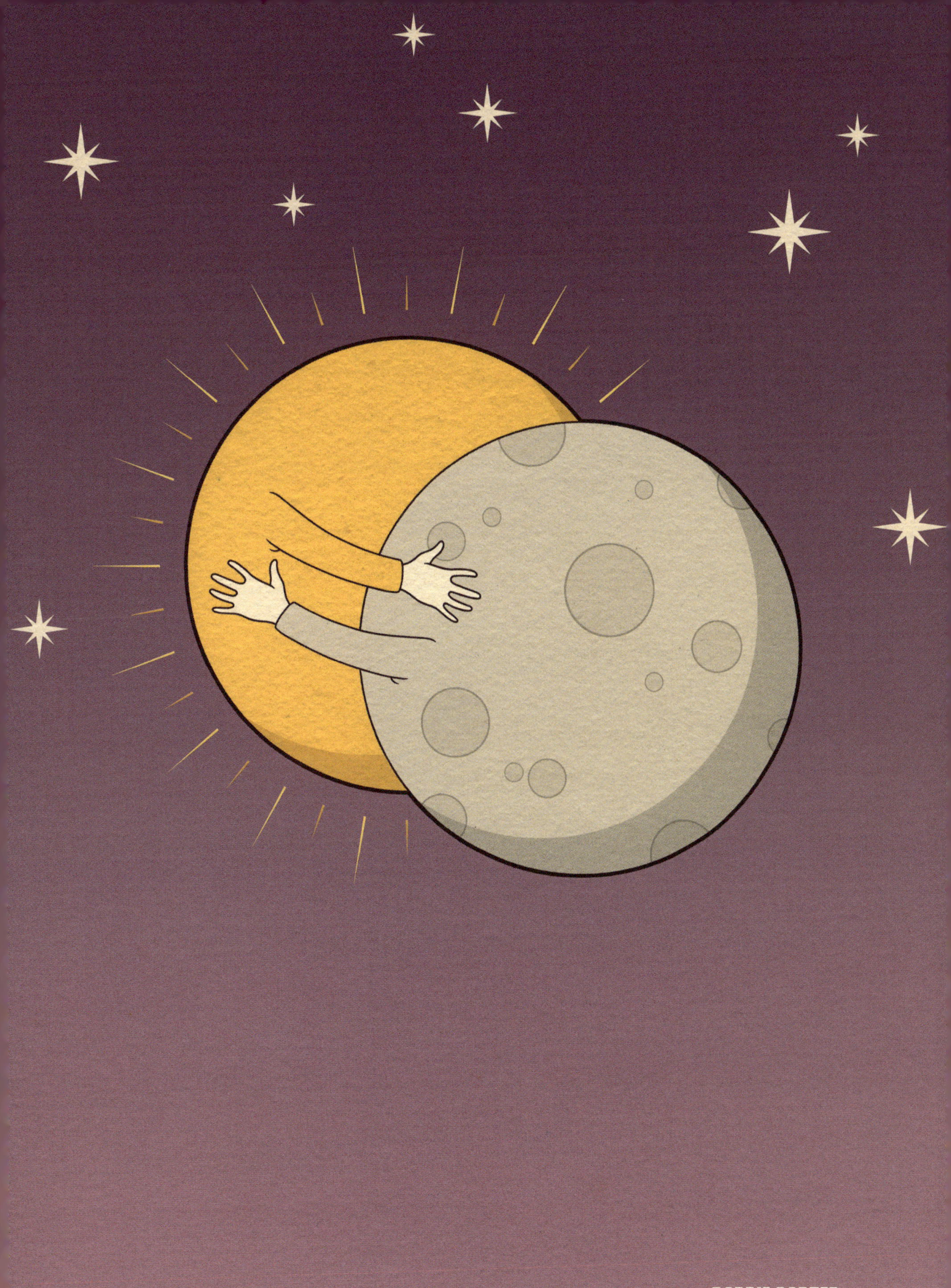

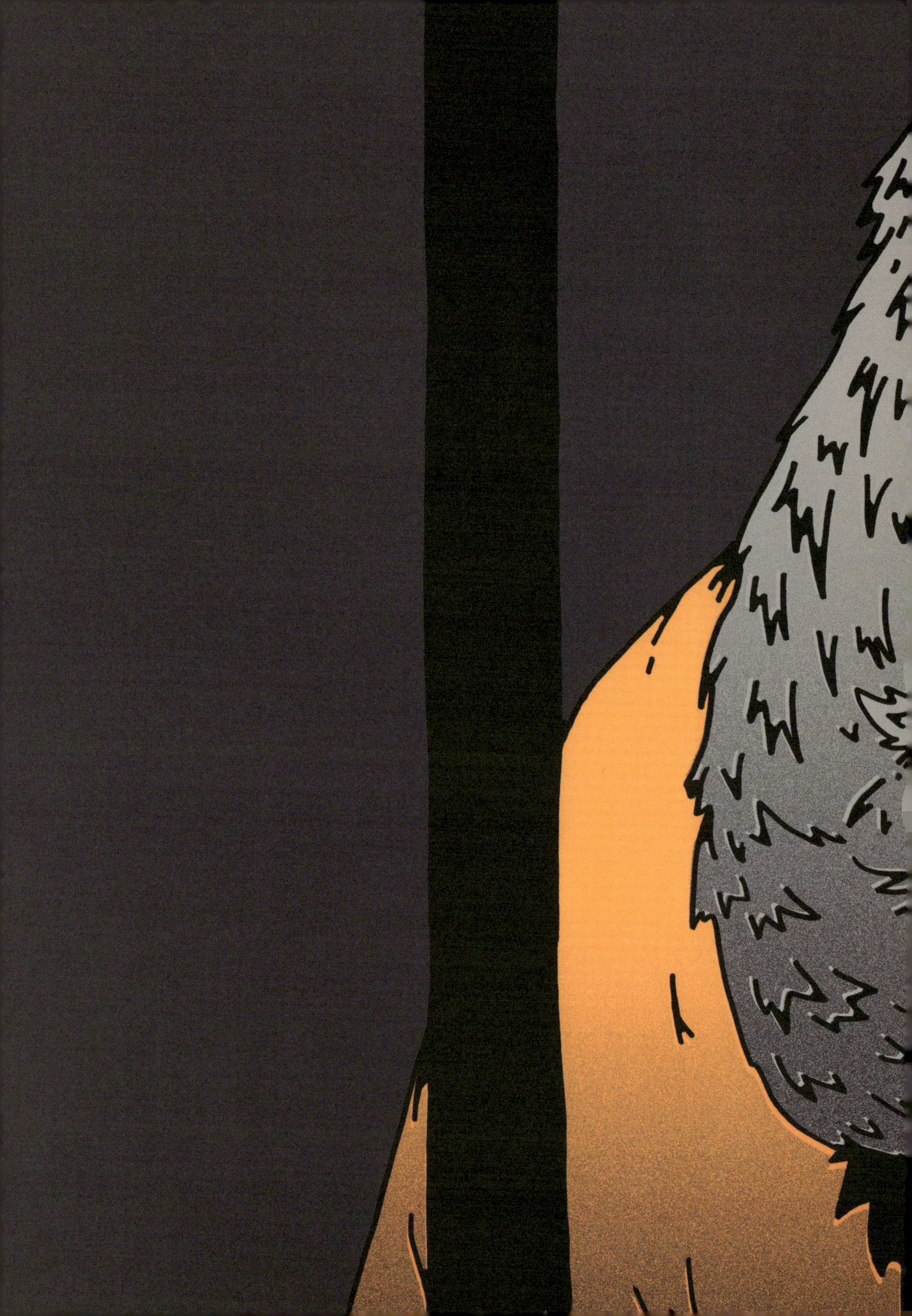

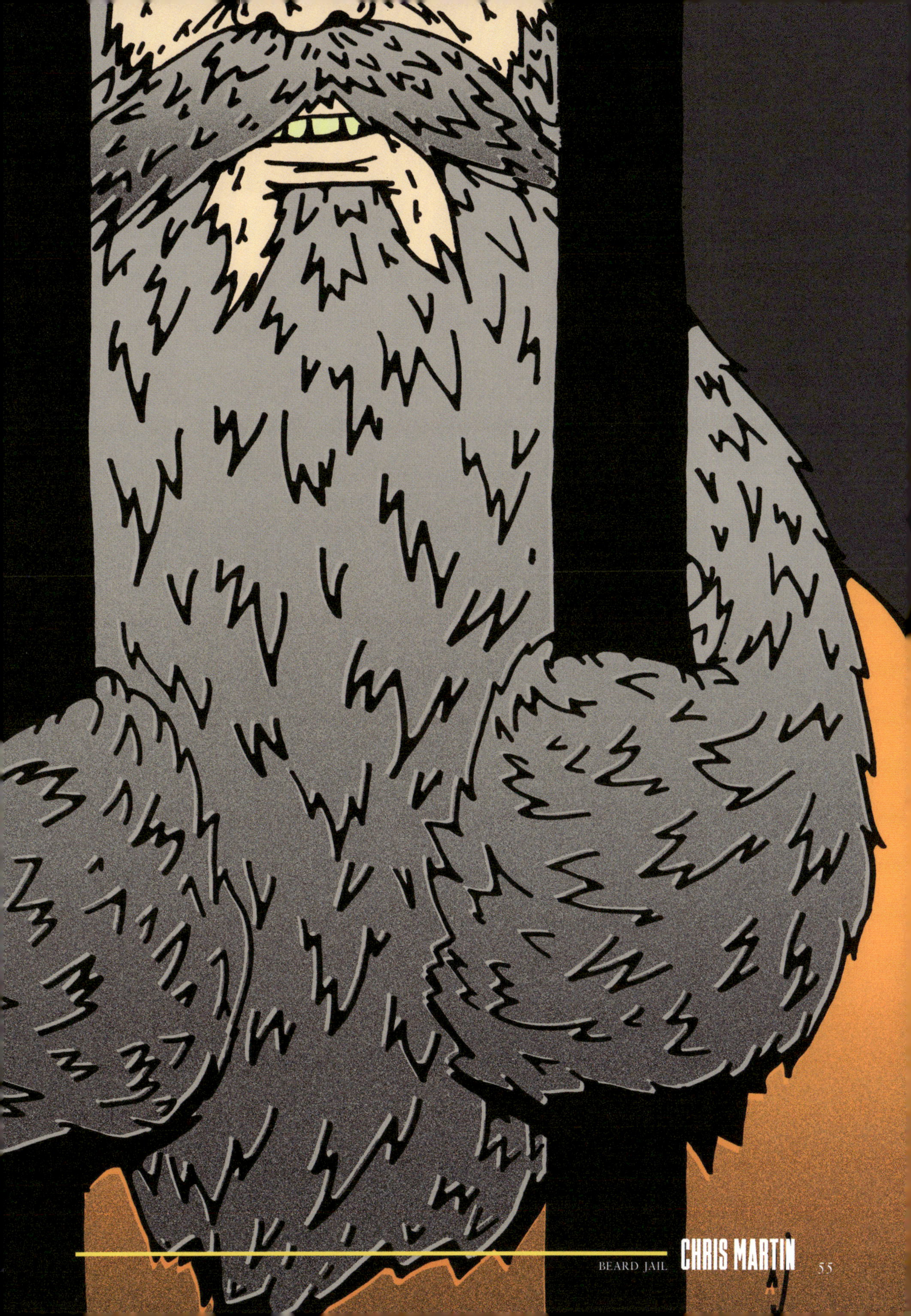

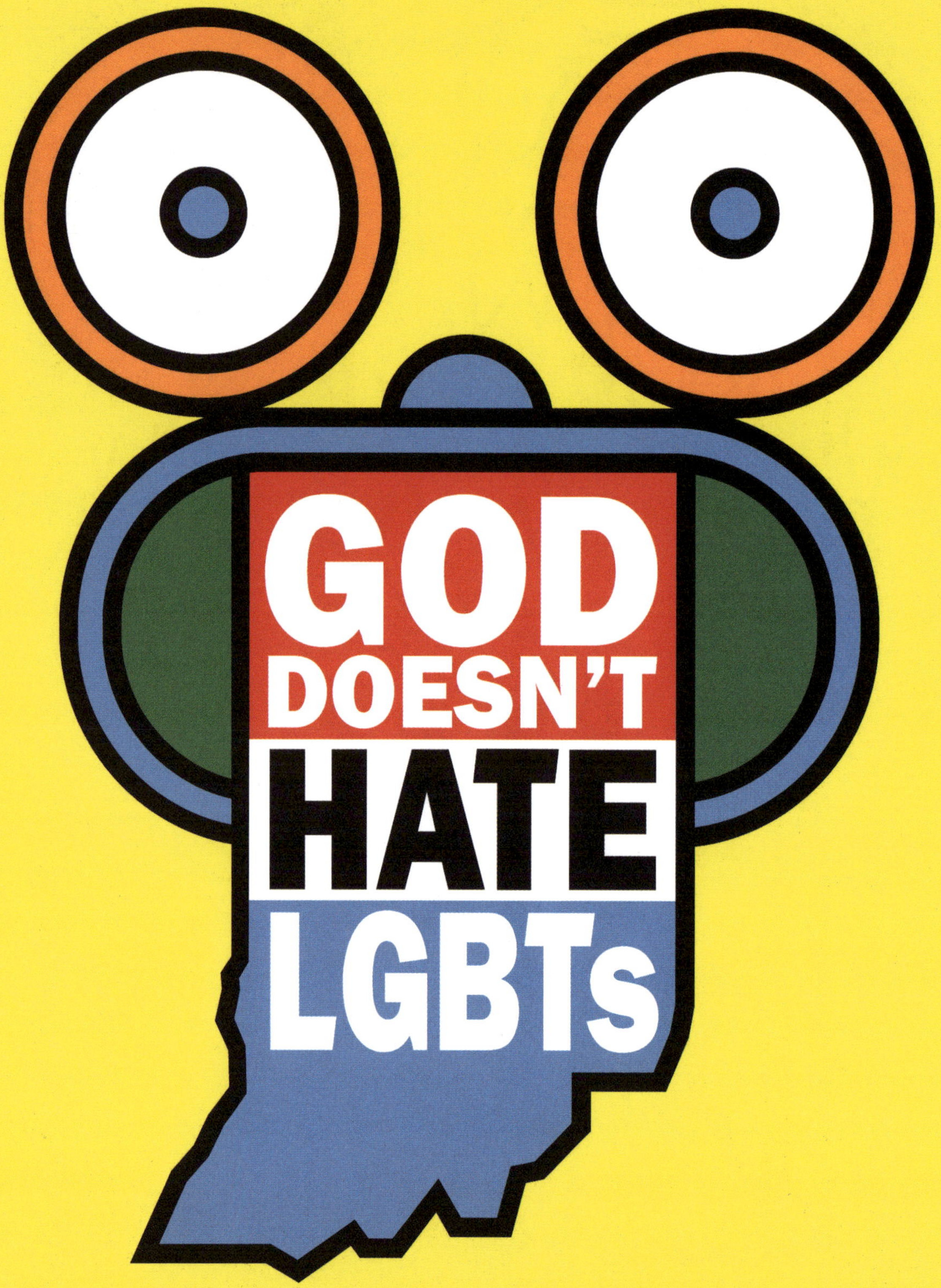
GOD
DOESN'T
HATE
LGBTs

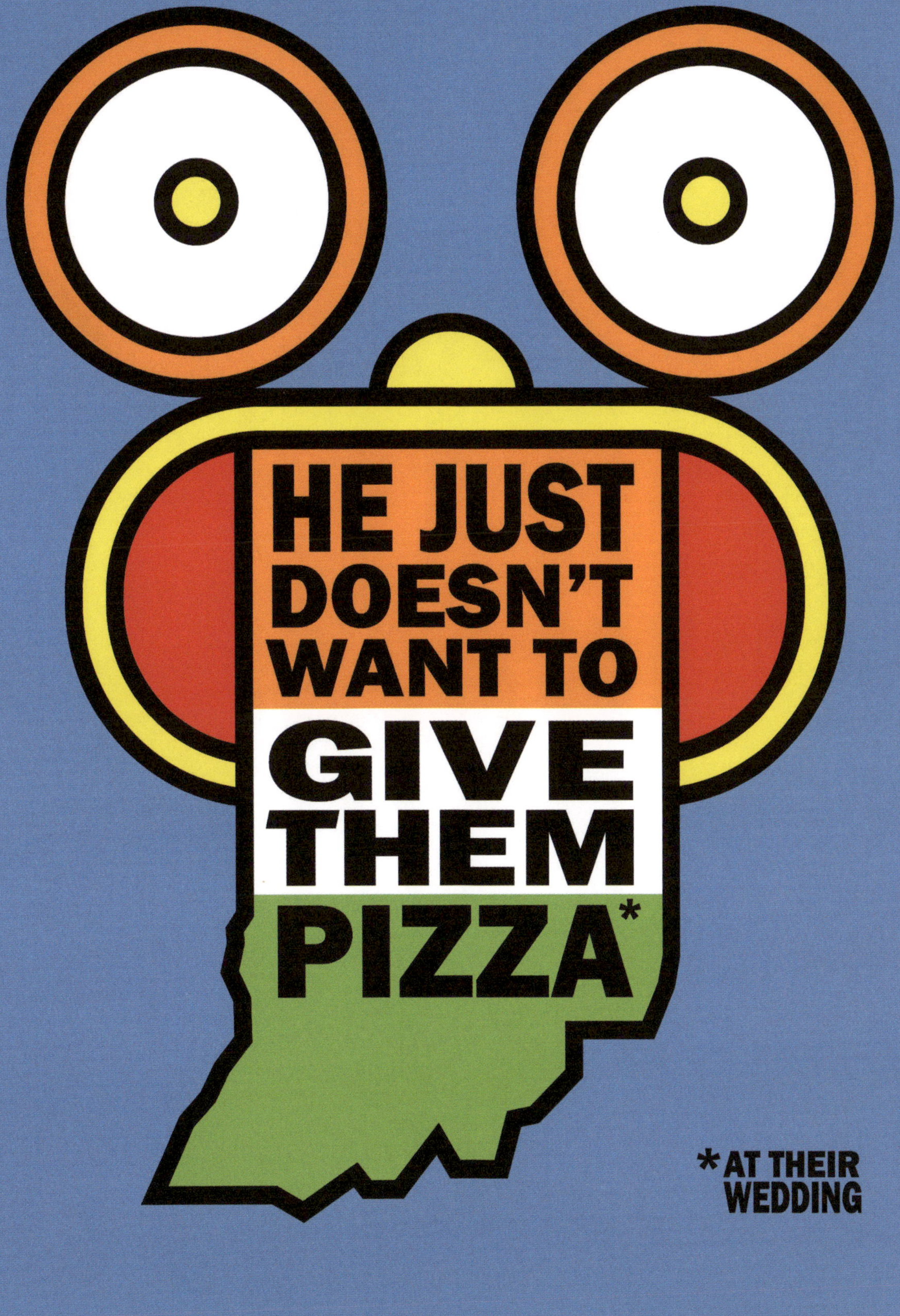
HE JUST DOESN'T WANT TO GIVE THEM PIZZA*
*AT THEIR WEDDING

WEALTH_GAP

The wealth of the rich has roughly doubled in the last few years, during one of the great economic traumas of modern history. At the same time, working people have suffered the longest fall in pay packets since Queen Victoria sat on the throne back in the 19th Century.

If you look at London, it's obviously a city of great wealth, where Russian oligarchs snap up new build properties in the centre and leave them vacant, while one-in-four kids who actually live here grow up in an overcrowded home. You have to ask why are more people not up in arms? I fall back to this quote by Tony Benn, who said, "The way you get change is the burning flame of anger and the burning flame of hope for a better world." There's no shortage of anger, but there's not very much hope.

What's happened recently, particularly since this Government's been in power, people's justifiable anger at their situation has been redirected from those at the top of society to those down the street. Low paid workers have their wages cut, their in-work benefits cut and then they're told not to be angry with their boss or the Government... but to be envious of the unemployed so-called 'scrounger' down the road, living in a mansion made out of wide-screen television sets.

They say to private sector workers whose pensions have been ransacked – don't be angry that your pensions have been slashed by your boss, be angry at the public sector worker whose pension is still intact. They say to people who can't get a secure job with a proper pay packet – don't be angry at the people setting your wages, envy instead the immigrant getting the job that should be yours. It's like telling people – don't be angry at the person who mugged you, be angry at your neighbour who hasn't been mugged quite as much as you have.

But there is an alternative. Injustice is not like the weather, you can complain about it raining but there's nothing you can do to stop it. Injustice is consciously created by people and can be consciously removed by people. It's our choice.

BY OWEN JONES

Columnist and author of *The Establishment: And How They Get Away With It*

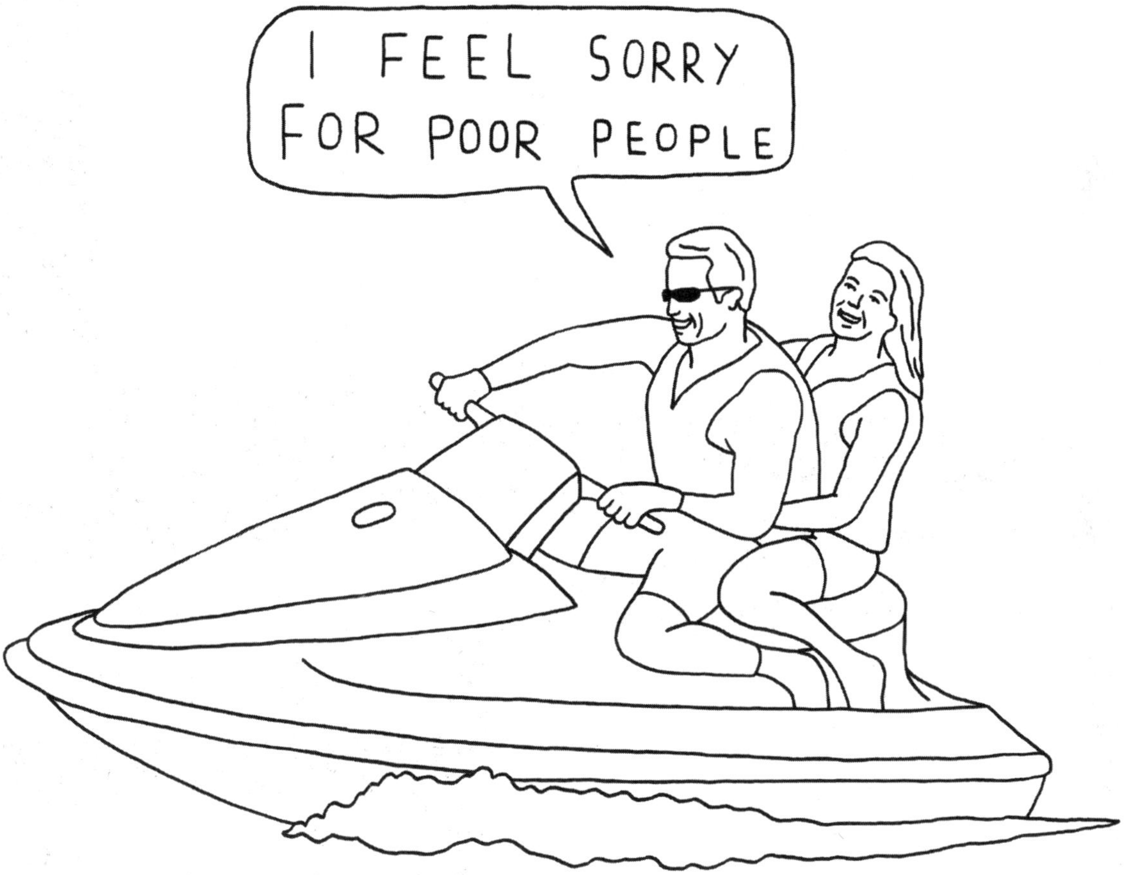
I FEEL SORRY FOR POOR PEOPLE

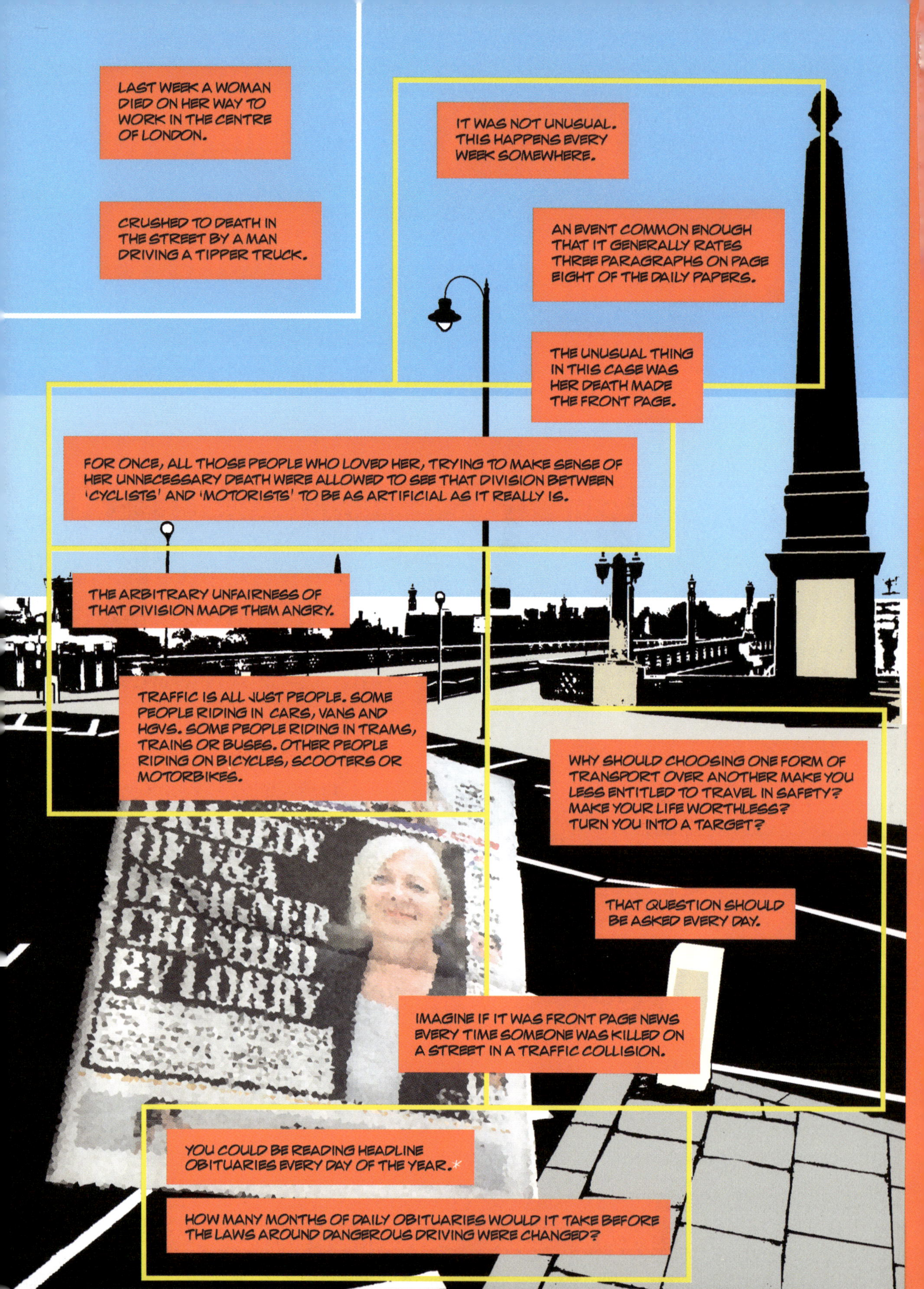

* 13 PEOPLE USING BICYCLES WERE KILLED IN THE UK DURING THE FIRST TWO WEEKS OF 2015.

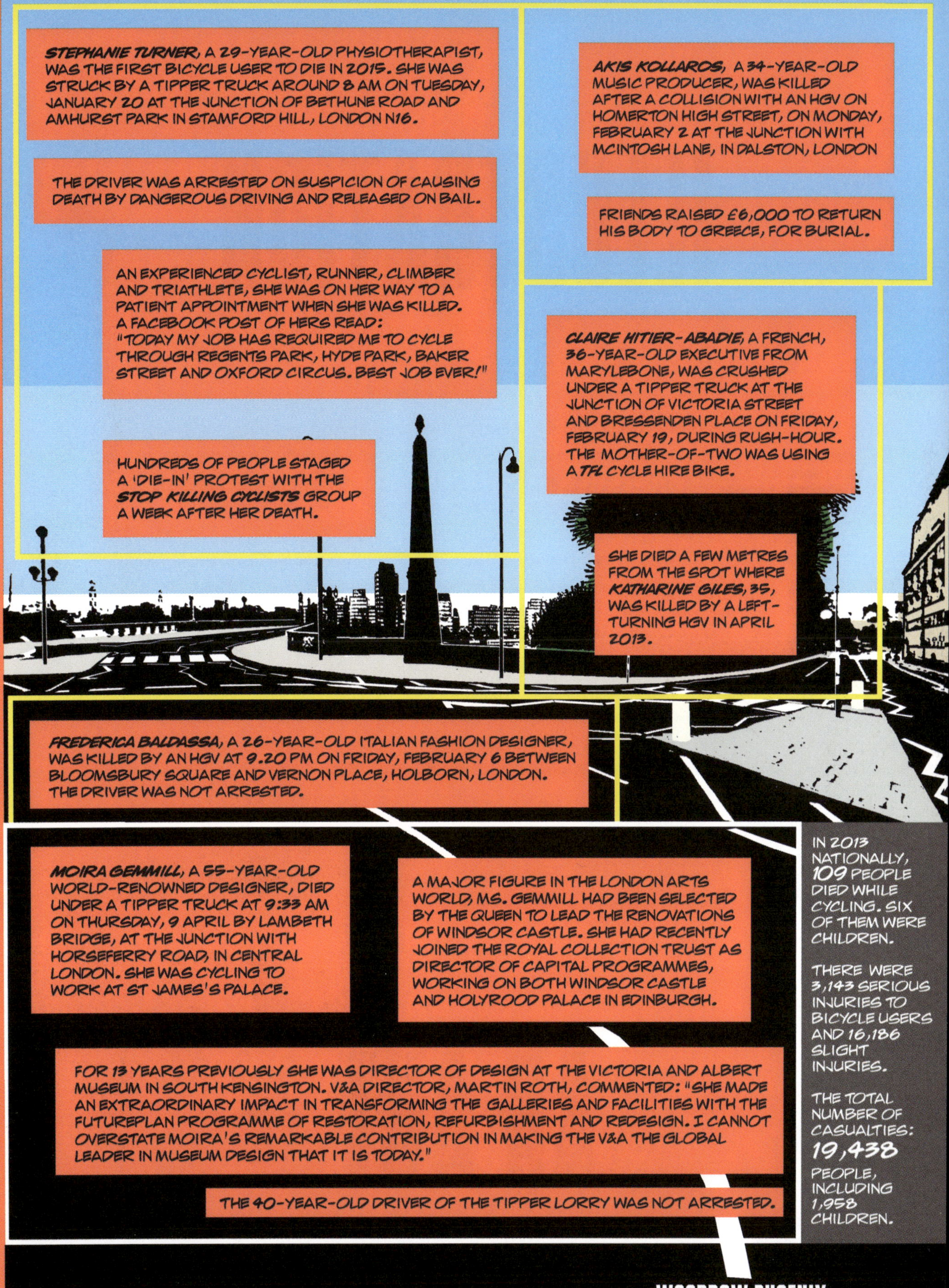
STEPHANIE TURNER, A 29-YEAR-OLD PHYSIOTHERAPIST, WAS THE FIRST BICYCLE USER TO DIE IN 2015. SHE WAS STRUCK BY A TIPPER TRUCK AROUND 8 AM ON TUESDAY, JANUARY 20 AT THE JUNCTION OF BETHUNE ROAD AND AMHURST PARK IN STAMFORD HILL, LONDON N16.
THE DRIVER WAS ARRESTED ON SUSPICION OF CAUSING DEATH BY DANGEROUS DRIVING AND RELEASED ON BAIL.
AN EXPERIENCED CYCLIST, RUNNER, CLIMBER AND TRIATHLETE, SHE WAS ON HER WAY TO A PATIENT APPOINTMENT WHEN SHE WAS KILLED. A FACEBOOK POST OF HERS READ: "TODAY MY JOB HAS REQUIRED ME TO CYCLE THROUGH REGENTS PARK, HYDE PARK, BAKER STREET AND OXFORD CIRCUS. BEST JOB EVER!"
HUNDREDS OF PEOPLE STAGED A 'DIE-IN' PROTEST WITH THE STOP KILLING CYCLISTS GROUP A WEEK AFTER HER DEATH.
AKIS KOLLAROS, A 34-YEAR-OLD MUSIC PRODUCER, WAS KILLED AFTER A COLLISION WITH AN HGV ON HOMERTON HIGH STREET, ON MONDAY, FEBRUARY 2 AT THE JUNCTION WITH MCINTOSH LANE, IN DALSTON, LONDON
FRIENDS RAISED £6,000 TO RETURN HIS BODY TO GREECE, FOR BURIAL.
CLAIRE HITIER-ABADIE, A FRENCH, 36-YEAR-OLD EXECUTIVE FROM MARYLEBONE, WAS CRUSHED UNDER A TIPPER TRUCK AT THE JUNCTION OF VICTORIA STREET AND BRESSENDEN PLACE ON FRIDAY, FEBRUARY 19, DURING RUSH-HOUR. THE MOTHER-OF-TWO WAS USING A TFL CYCLE HIRE BIKE.
SHE DIED A FEW METRES FROM THE SPOT WHERE KATHARINE GILES, 35, WAS KILLED BY A LEFT-TURNING HGV IN APRIL 2013.
FREDERICA BALDASSA, A 26-YEAR-OLD ITALIAN FASHION DESIGNER, WAS KILLED BY AN HGV AT 9.20 PM ON FRIDAY, FEBRUARY 6 BETWEEN BLOOMSBURY SQUARE AND VERNON PLACE, HOLBORN, LONDON. THE DRIVER WAS NOT ARRESTED.
MOIRA GEMMILL, A 55-YEAR-OLD WORLD-RENOWNED DESIGNER, DIED UNDER A TIPPER TRUCK AT 9:33 AM ON THURSDAY, 9 APRIL BY LAMBETH BRIDGE, AT THE JUNCTION WITH HORSEFERRY ROAD, IN CENTRAL LONDON. SHE WAS CYCLING TO WORK AT ST JAMES'S PALACE.
A MAJOR FIGURE IN THE LONDON ARTS WORLD, MS. GEMMILL HAD BEEN SELECTED BY THE QUEEN TO LEAD THE RENOVATIONS OF WINDSOR CASTLE. SHE HAD RECENTLY JOINED THE ROYAL COLLECTION TRUST AS DIRECTOR OF CAPITAL PROGRAMMES, WORKING ON BOTH WINDSOR CASTLE AND HOLYROOD PALACE IN EDINBURGH.
FOR 13 YEARS PREVIOUSLY SHE WAS DIRECTOR OF DESIGN AT THE VICTORIA AND ALBERT MUSEUM IN SOUTH KENSINGTON. V&A DIRECTOR, MARTIN ROTH, COMMENTED: "SHE MADE AN EXTRAORDINARY IMPACT IN TRANSFORMING THE GALLERIES AND FACILITIES WITH THE FUTUREPLAN PROGRAMME OF RESTORATION, REFURBISHMENT AND REDESIGN. I CANNOT OVERSTATE MOIRA'S REMARKABLE CONTRIBUTION IN MAKING THE V&A THE GLOBAL LEADER IN MUSEUM DESIGN THAT IT IS TODAY."
THE 40-YEAR-OLD DRIVER OF THE TIPPER LORRY WAS NOT ARRESTED.
IN 2013 NATIONALLY, 109 PEOPLE DIED WHILE CYCLING. SIX OF THEM WERE CHILDREN.
THERE WERE 3,143 SERIOUS INJURIES TO BICYCLE USERS AND 16,186 SLIGHT INJURIES.
THE TOTAL NUMBER OF CASUALTIES: 19,438 PEOPLE, INCLUDING 1,958 CHILDREN.

ILLUSTRATION

I started drawing things as a kid and never really saw it as a potential job, so when I got to 'that age' I went in to graphic design. I realised very quickly that it wasn't for me… I wasn't even that good at it to be honest. What I really loved was drawing things, but the problem was that I didn't want to be a struggling artist.

For a long time I saw the difference between illustration and art as the matter of being given a brief. I always liked problem solving and for me being an artist was about coming up with your own brief and your own message. Back then I didn't think I had anything to say.

For years I answered briefs and created editorial pieces, until it gradually dawned on me that I wanted to explore a more personal body of work that expressed my own ideas. I thought that would be some giant leap, but really the boundaries between illustration and art are so blurred these days. It's a complete mix.

One thing you can't argue is that illustration is inherently commercial. It involves a client and having to sell something, whether that's an idea for an article or a product for an advert. From that perspective, I can understand why some people don't consider illustration as art. Those people need to understand that contemporary illustration has evolved though.

AS ART

MALIKA

Now, more and more illustrators balance being an artist who exhibits personal work, along with taking on commissions from clients. The position of the contemporary illustrator is stronger these days, we're not just styling up sketches that an art director sends over. We get more freedom to come up with the ideas and then express them as we see fit, even if that's still quite a new development.

People are slowly waking up to the power of illustration, how you can play tricks with the visual. Illustration doesn't pretend to be reality: it's a much more emotional form of communication in which you can create a mood, an atmosphere, even a complex story – all within a single, sometimes very simple image.

So, if you want to just illustrate a very pretty picture, that's fine. I like looking at pretty pictures! But, for me, when you start adding more layers to a piece and try to really say something, to comment on what's happening around you, that's when things start to get interesting.

It's probably too much unnecessary pressure to say that 'all illustrators should be trying to say something with their work'. It needs to come from within, from a desire to speak out about an issue that's personal, but if you have something to say and the ability to say it, then you probably should.

FAVRE

Illustrator (artist)

NATHANIEL RUSSELL

CAITLYN JENNER / 20–26 APRIL

"I was impressed that someone in a visible position in pop culture could talk about such a private subject. I'm interested in the manufactured 'reality' of reality TV. Nothing seems real anymore, everything seems staged and marketed… even our most private and personal selves."

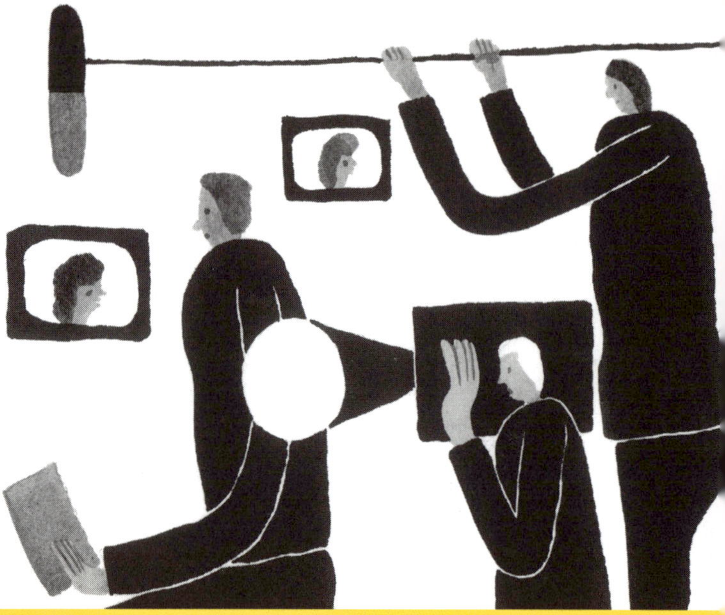

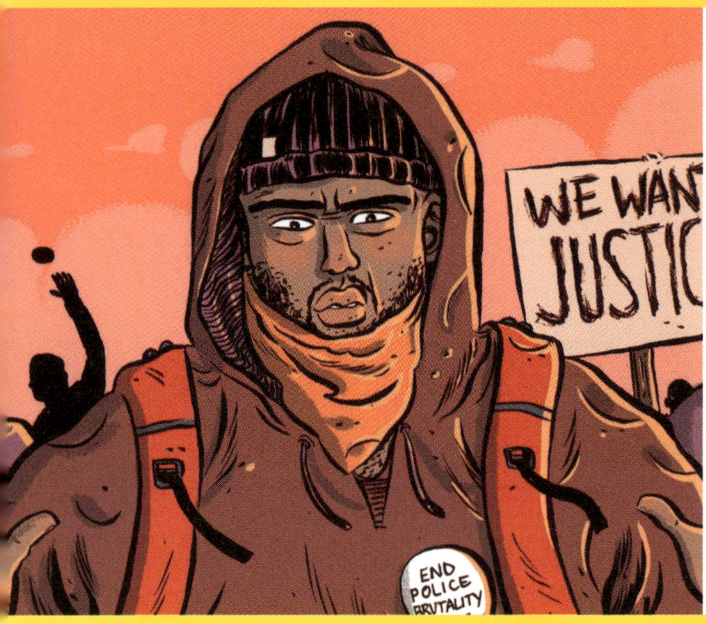

JAMIE COE

BALTIMORE RIOTS / 27 APRIL–3 MAY

"During my week, protests took place in Baltimore after the death of Freddie Gray in police custody. Police brutality, especially towards the African-American community, has always been a problem, but recently there's been many incidents captured on video, bringing more awareness to this very real issue."

MITCH BLUNT

CONSERVATIVE ROUT / 4–10 MAY

"My piece is about the Liberal Democrats' being punished for their part in the Coalition Government and ultimately being chewed up and spat out by the public at the General Election. The foxhound in the artwork relates to the Tories, and a nod to the large possibility of them bringing back fox hunting(!)."

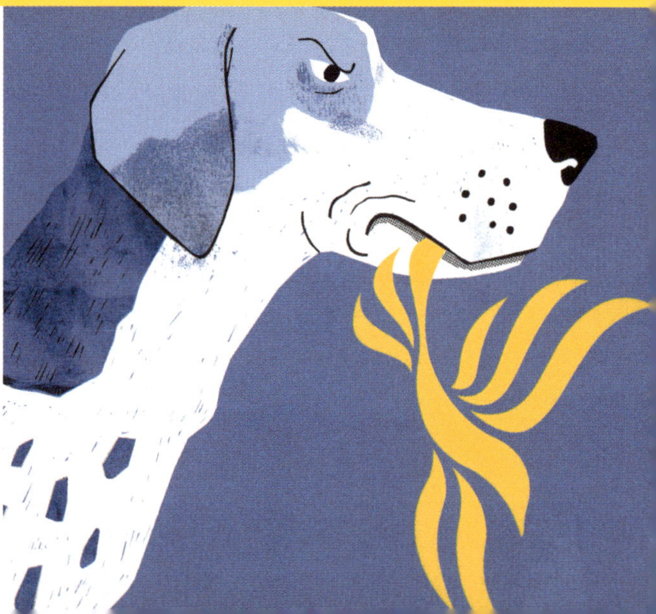

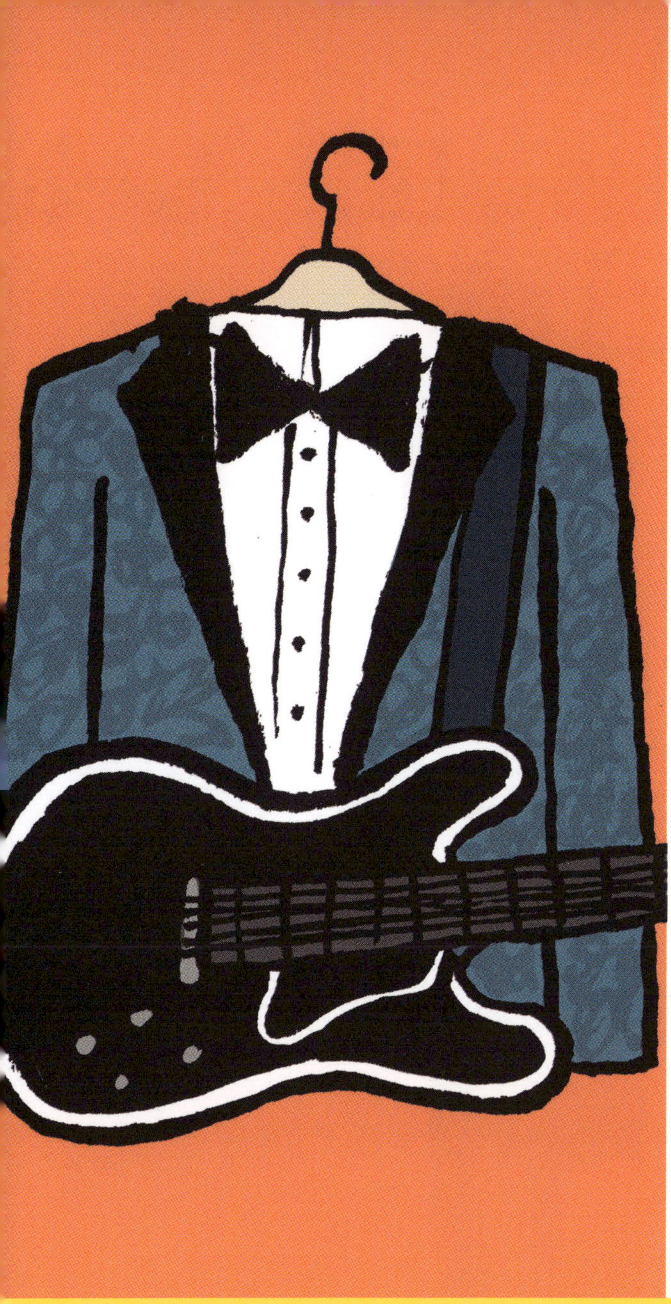

JEAN JULLIEN

BYE BYE KING / 11–17 MAY

"I was really saddened to hear of the passing of B.B. King, the legendary musician. My dad brought me up with his music, so I had that strange feeling you get every year when an iconic figure dies.

"I love how much of a costume he seemed to have been wearing for so many years. Like the black shirt, black trousers, black everything combo of Johnny Cash or the red leather jacket of Michael Jackson. So I wanted to hang that on the wall and have a simple play on words with his initials."

DAVID BISKUP

UNION SPLIT / 18–24 MAY

"In May Len McCluskey, leader of Britain's largest Trade Union, denied his comments about severing ties with Labour unless they show that they're still 'the voice of organised labour'. With the majority of Labour leadership candidates shifting to the right, are the union links with Labour becoming a thing of the past?"

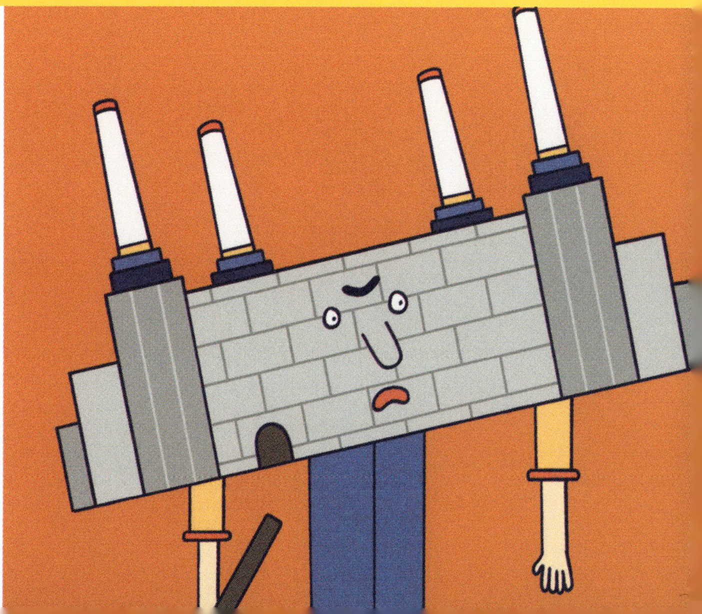

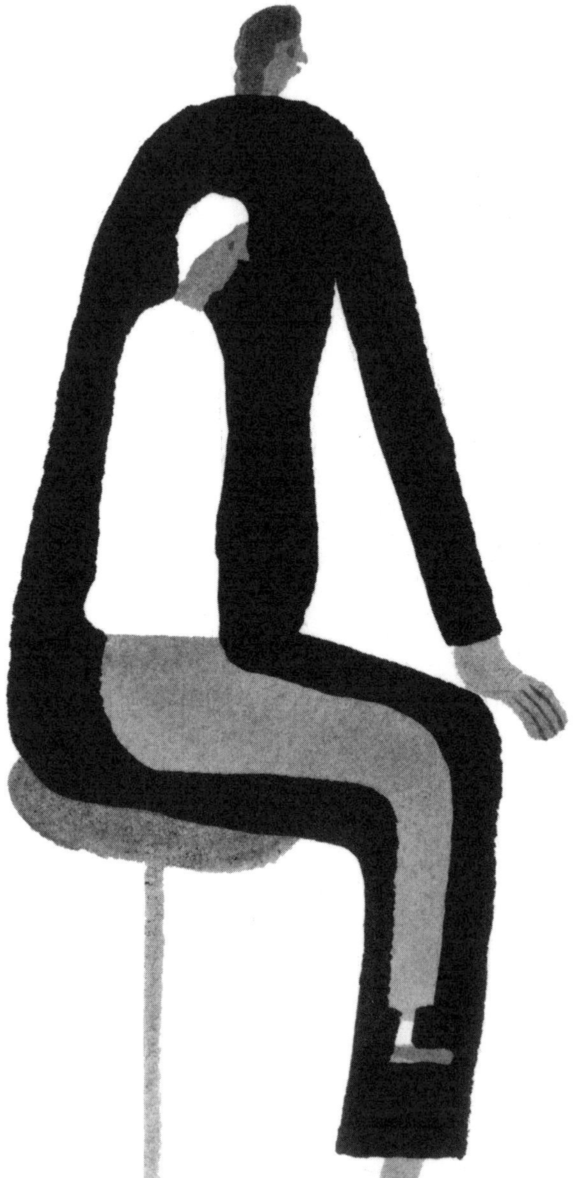

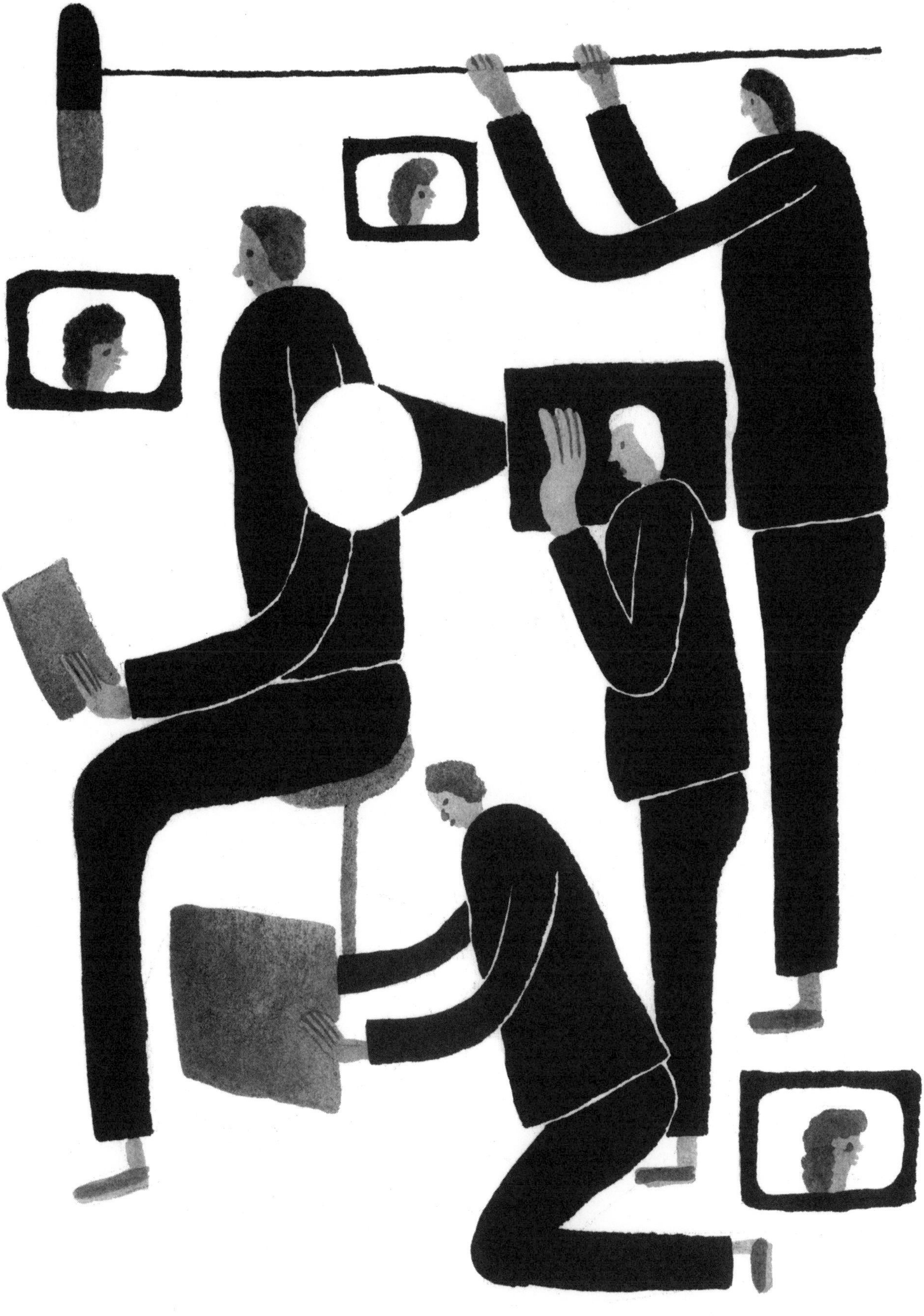

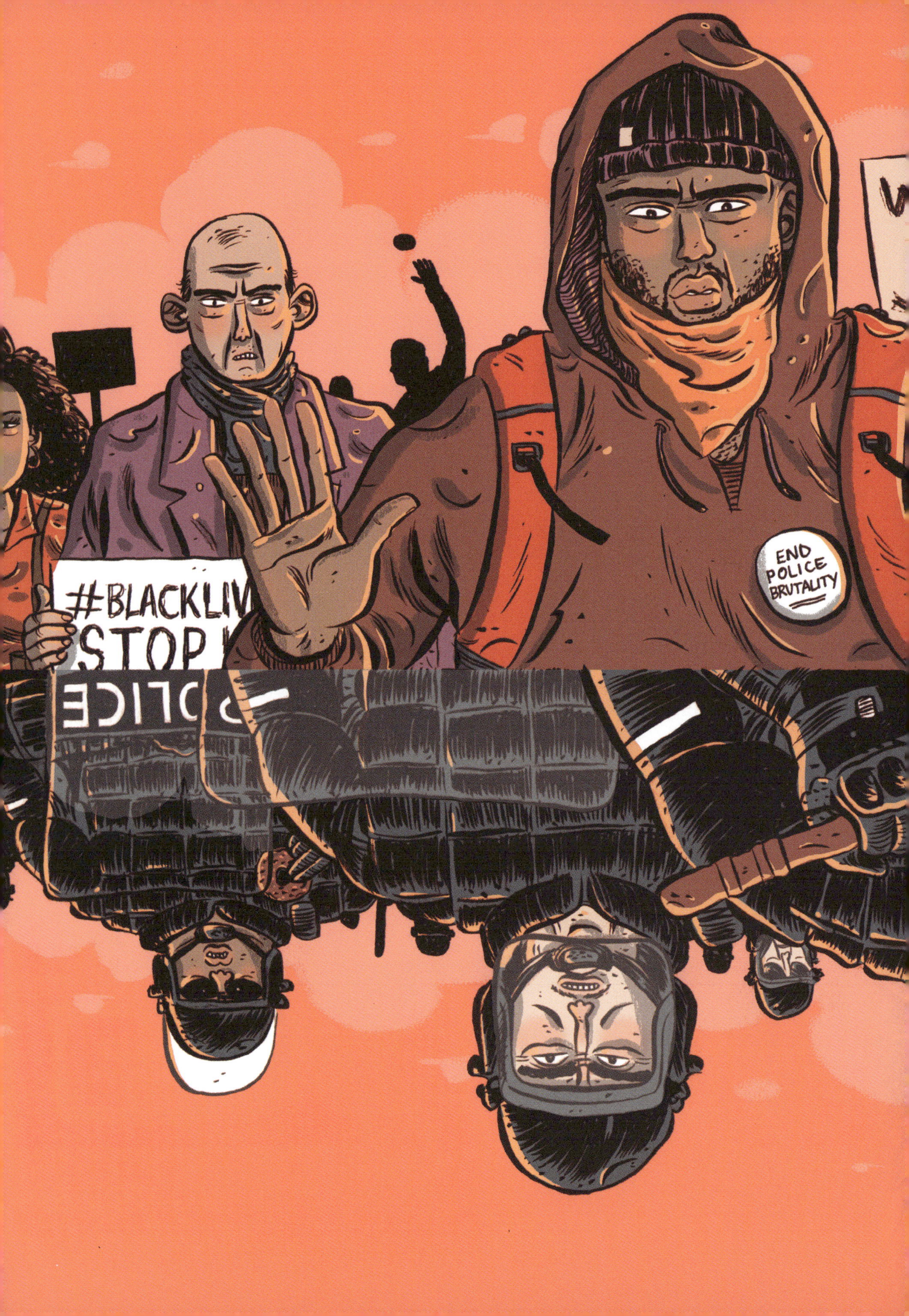
#BLACKLIV
STOP
END POLICE BRUTALITY

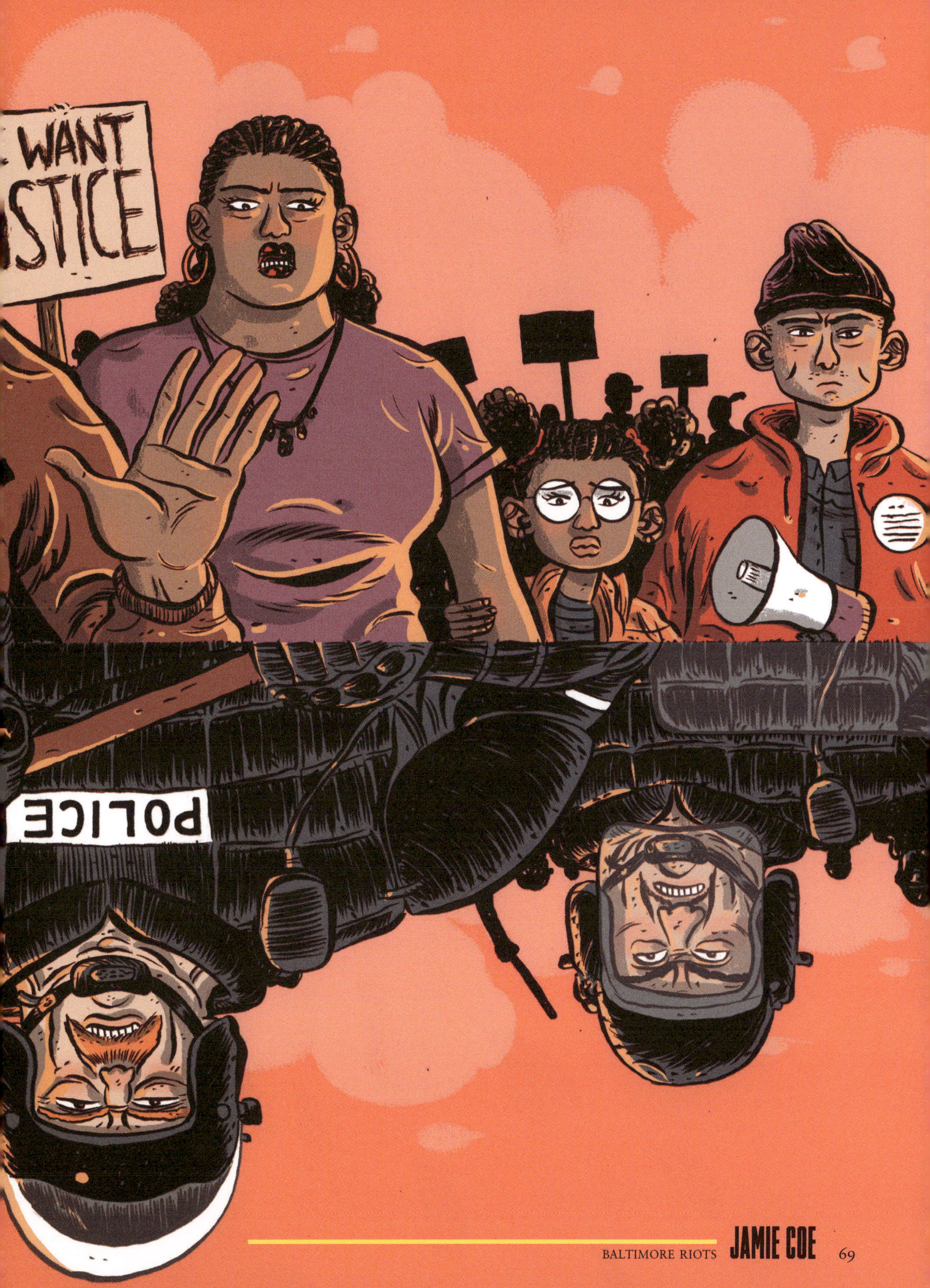
WANT
STICE
POLICE

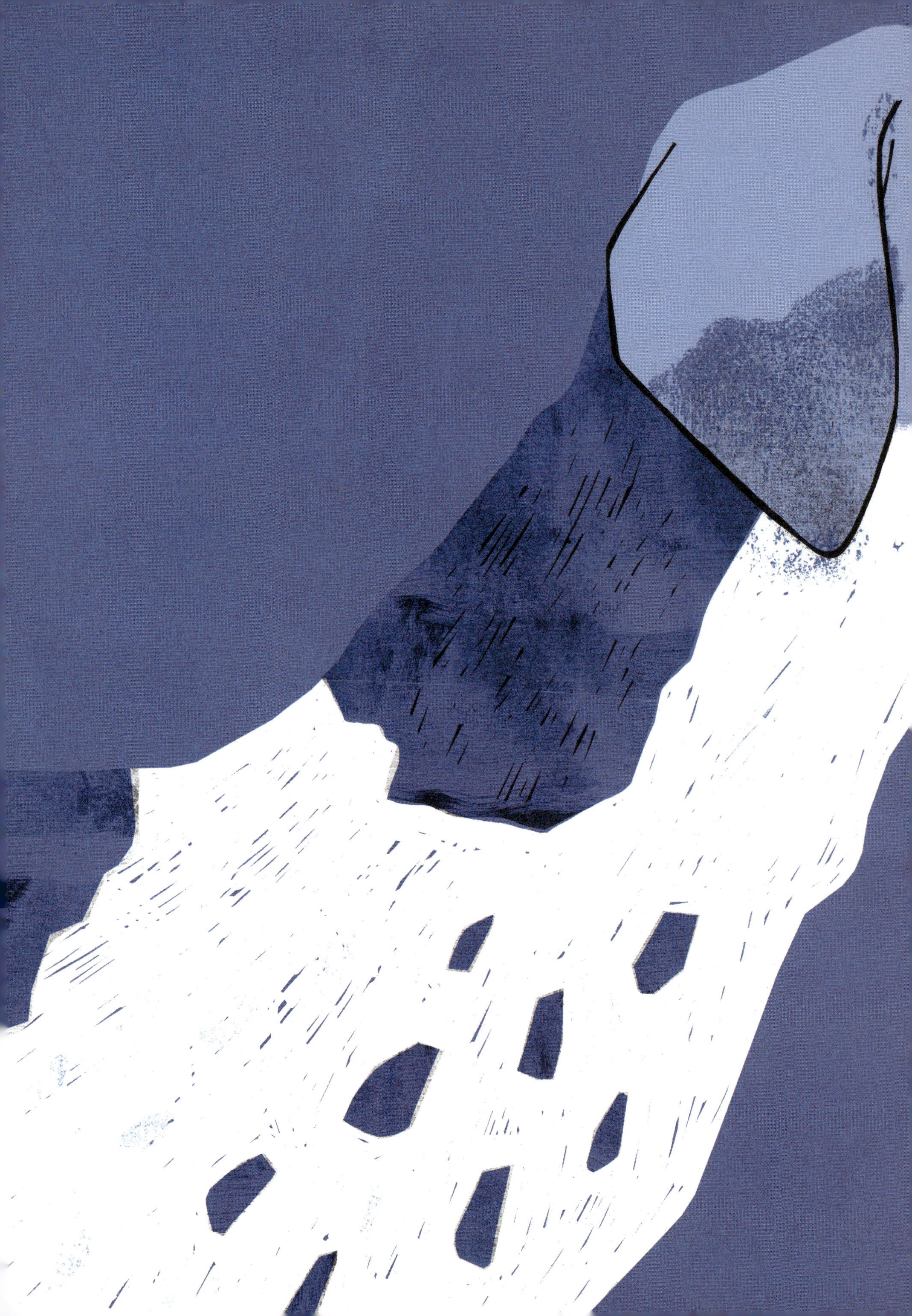

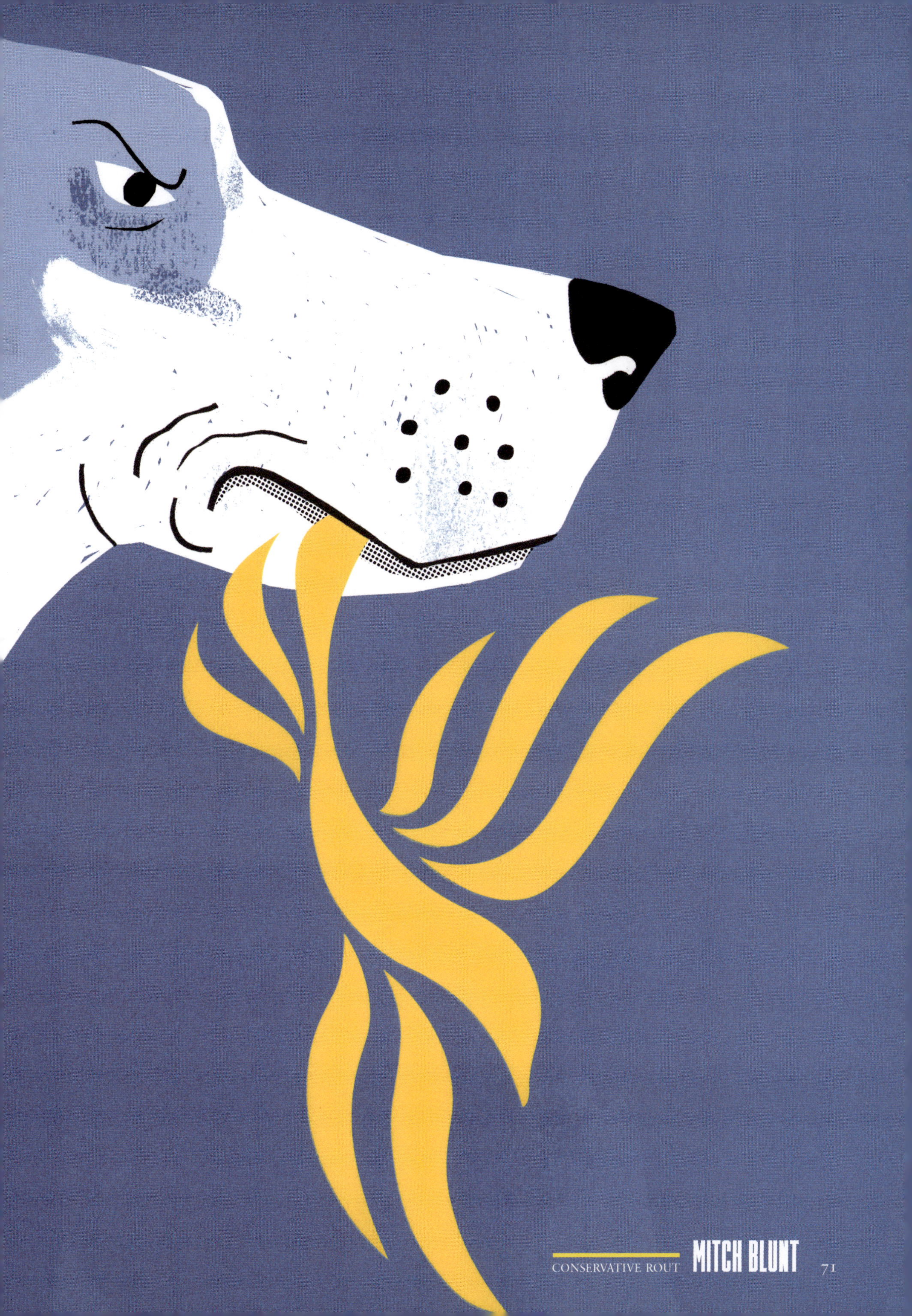

THE UNDERDOG ART FORM

Illustration is not a new thing. Whether it's the Renaissance or some punk album cover, drawing has always been there. But it's not until you use the actual word 'illustration' that people make this childish connotation, or sneer down on it. That used to really bother me, not to be considered an 'Artist' with a big A, just because I illustrate.

Now I see the underdog status as an advantage. You can get away with a lot more and surprise people if they don't expect much from you. By getting no acknowledgement from the traditional art world, illustration becomes less scary to people and that means we can communicate with them more directly. It lets us in the back door.

Illustration is a fantastic medium for commenting on current affairs. It has a graphic quality and a seduction that you don't usually associate with news, it creates a sideways look at the story you're trying to relay.

Even when used in newspapers and magazines, illustration tends to sit as a nice extra to the words – something that brightens the page, but is secondary to the article. But illustration can tell the story on its own, all the information, opinion and context in one powerful image that people understand right away. Not bad for a sneered upon art form.

BY JEAN JULLIEN

Illustrator

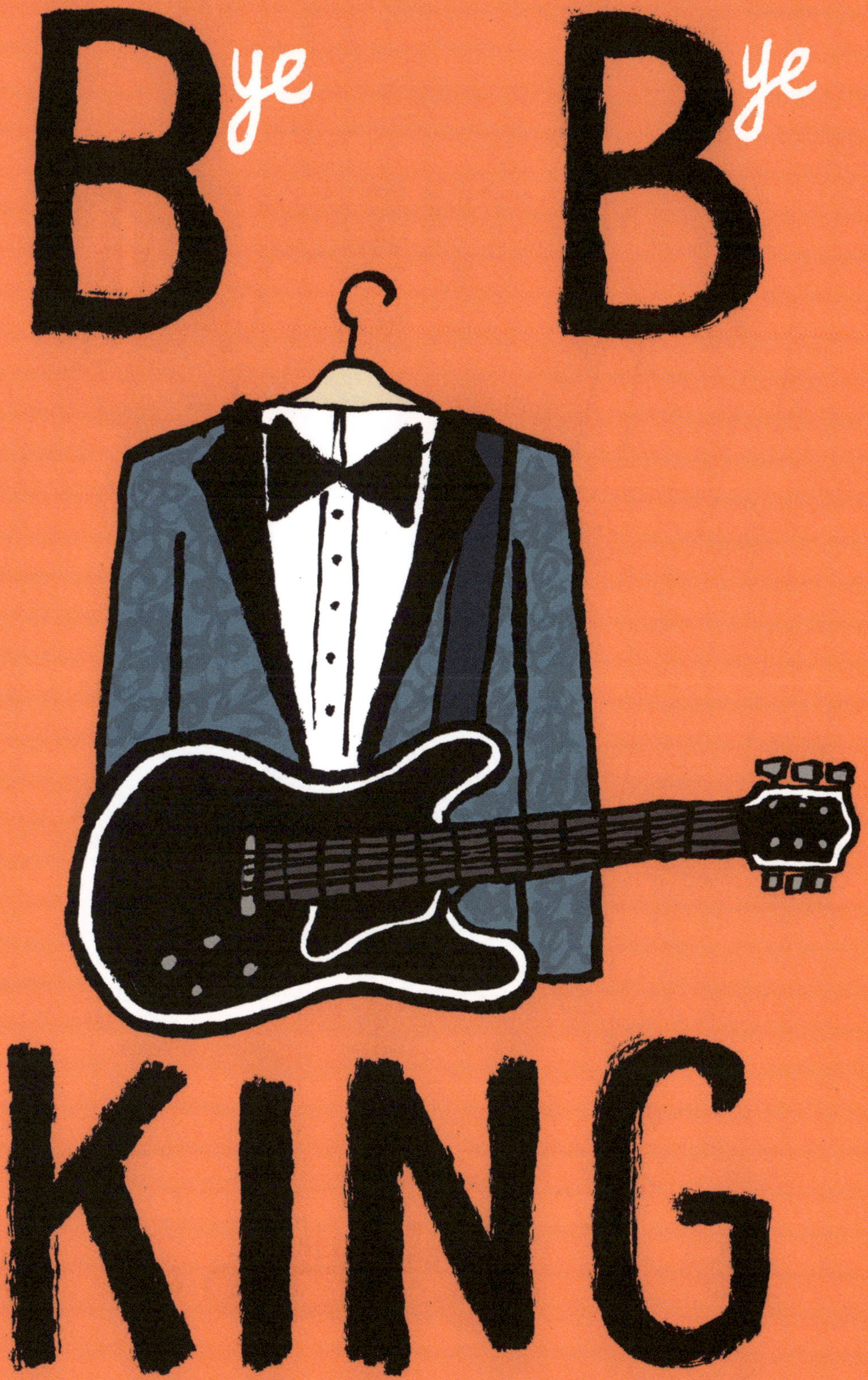
Bye Bye
KING

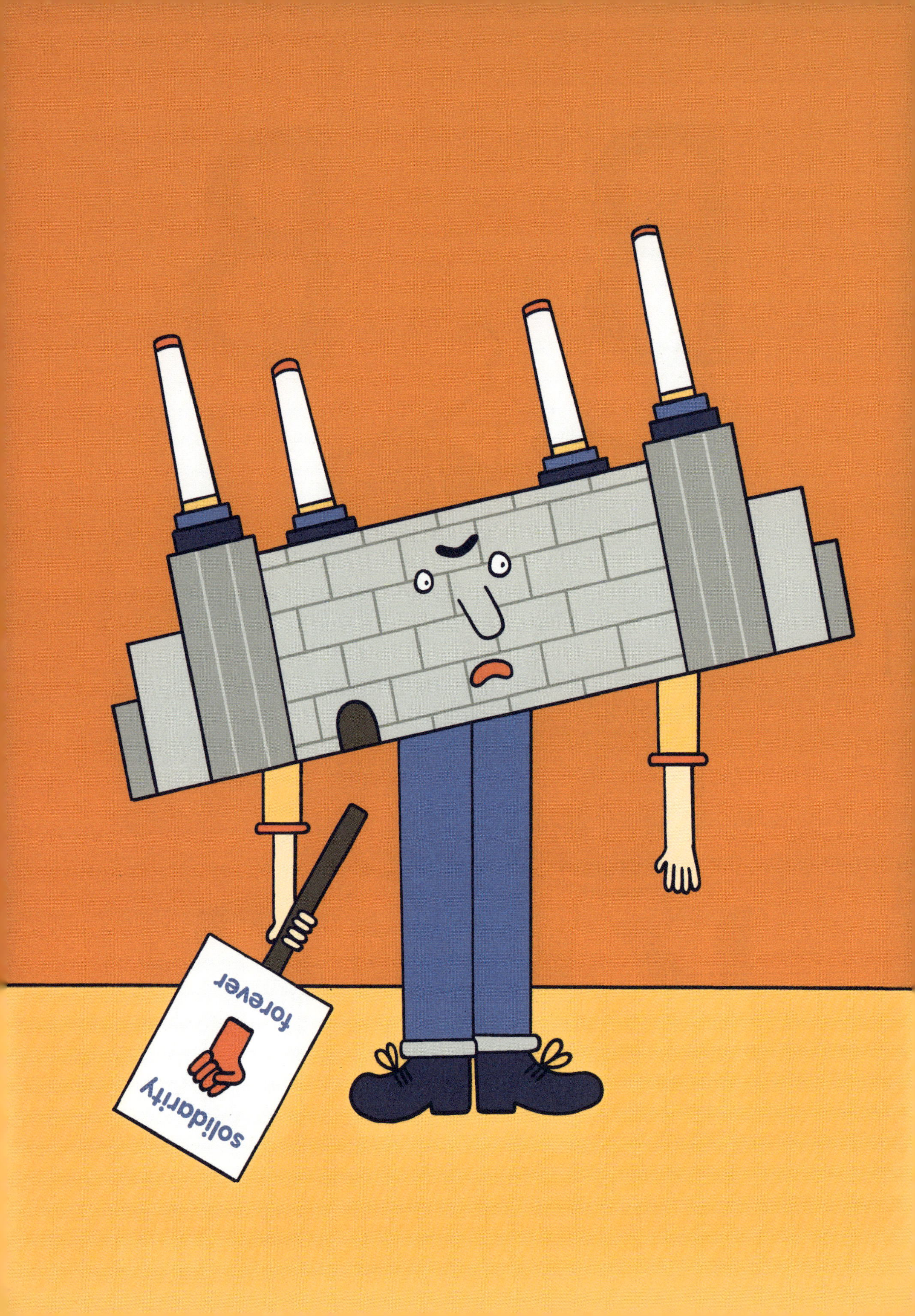
solidarity
forever

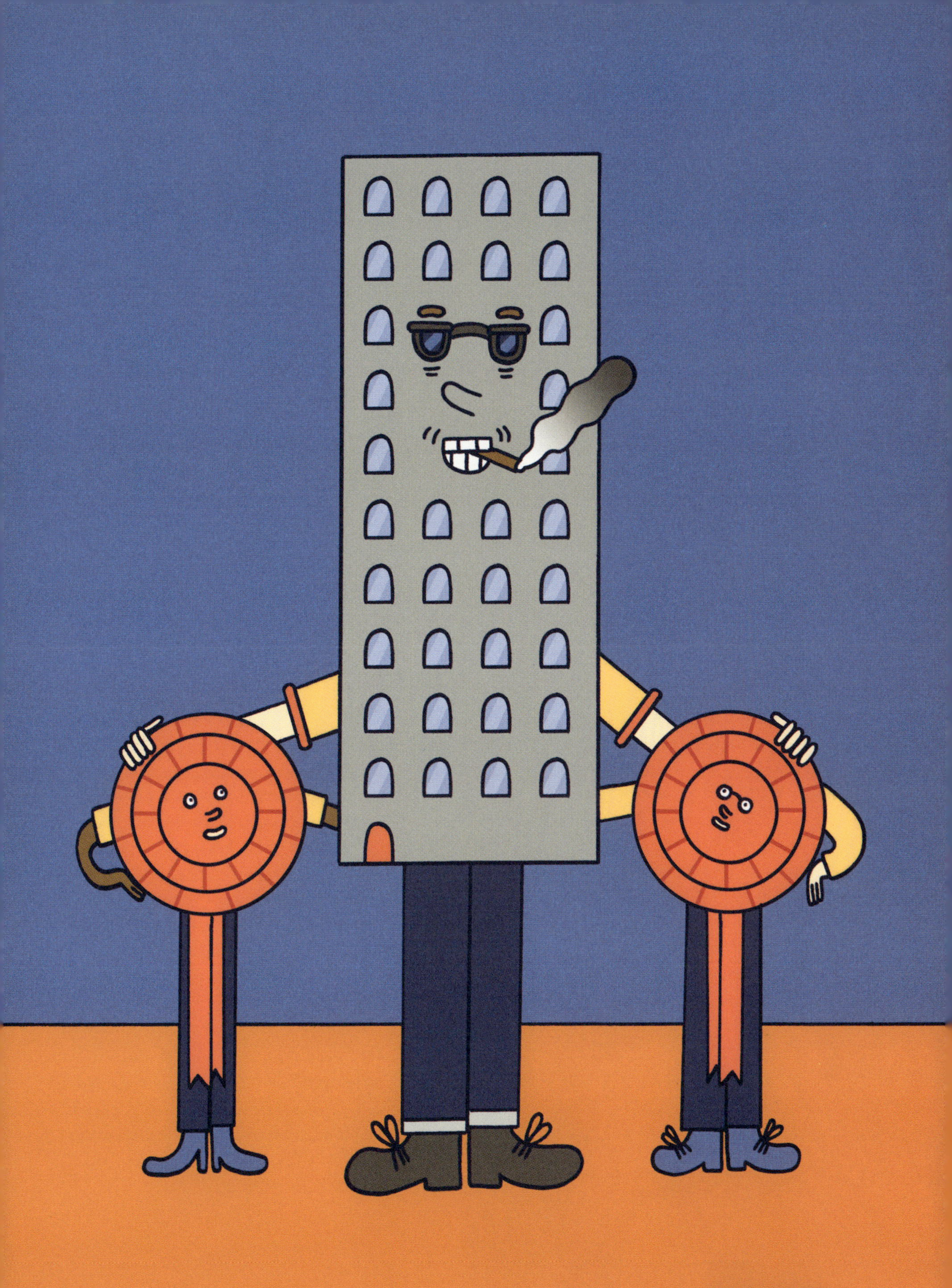

JOE DECIE

SOCIAL MEDIA NEWS / 25–31 MAY

"I chose to access the news exclusively via Facebook and Twitter. The result was extremely blinkered, with a political bias of the little social bubble I live my online life in. I represented the stories through objects that were around my messy house. I don't own an iPhone though, I had to make that up."

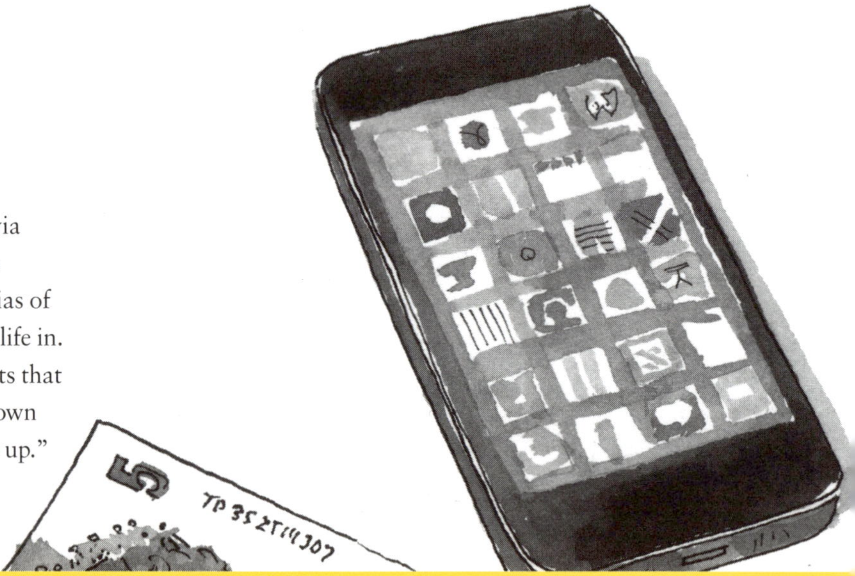

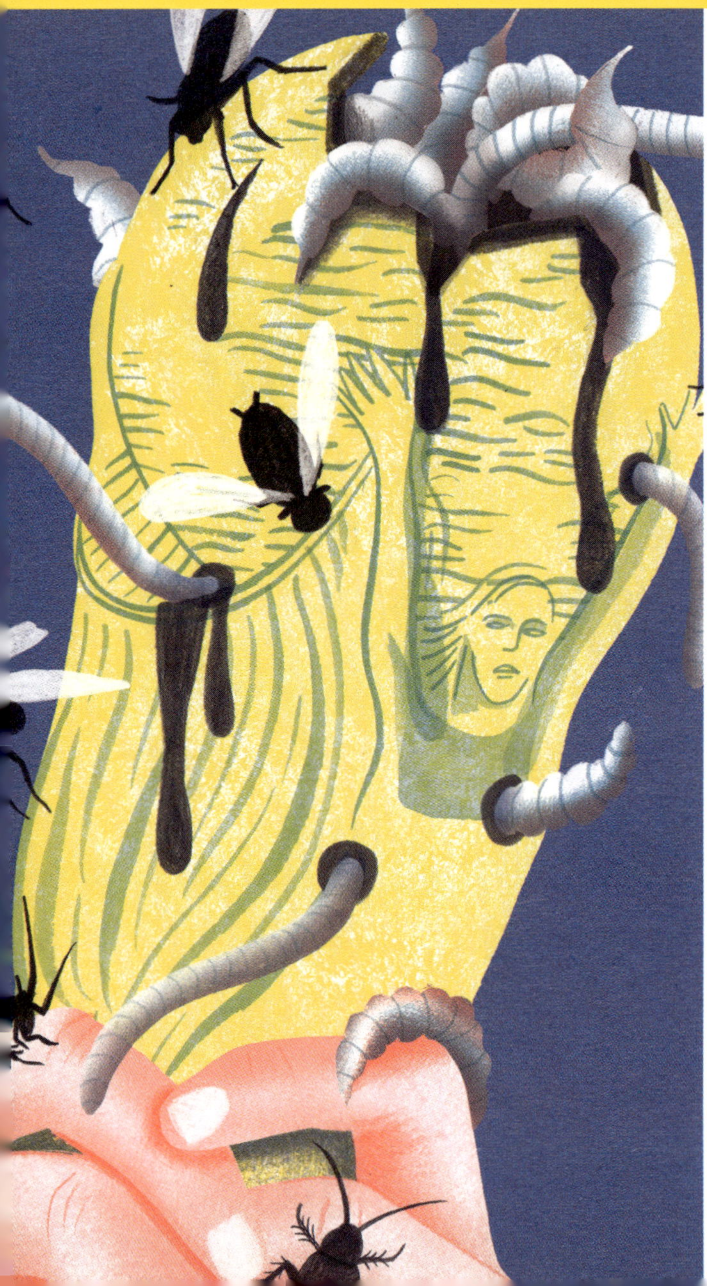

ELEANOR TAYLOR

FIFA CORRUPTION / 1–7 JUNE

"I have absolutely no interest in football and I would never have imagined myself illustrating a piece about it. But, on this week, the FIFA scandal really dominated the news and I felt like it could not be ignored.

"It's less a story about football and more about the pervasive culture of corruption and greed that goes on in the organisation and game.

"This was a challenging but enjoyable piece to illustrate. I must say a big thanks to my partner who patiently discussed the story at length with me as I was slightly despairing – we really hashed it out between us to come up with a good concept."

NATE KITCH

HACK WARS / 8–14 JUNE

"In June *The Times* believed Russia and China had access to the Snowden files, jeopardising operations and safety of US and British agents. It made me think of the threat we face from nations such as Russia, not from physical attack, but the darker, hidden assault of hacking that constantly looms above us all."

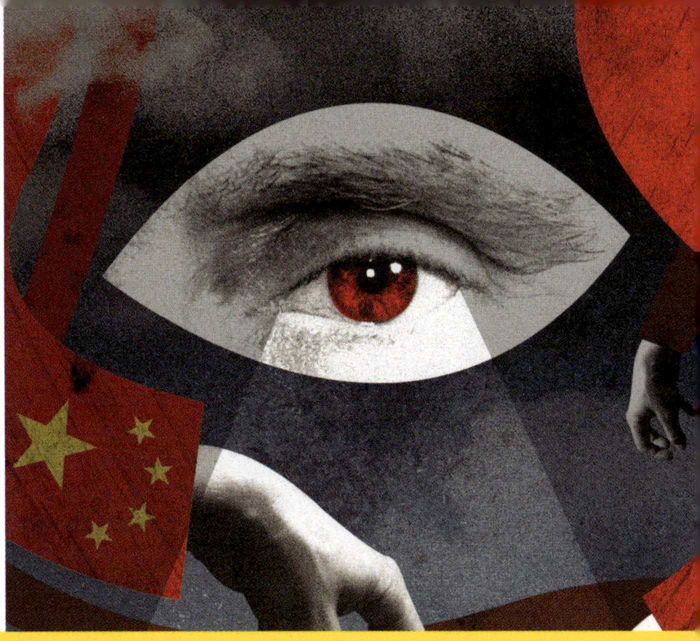

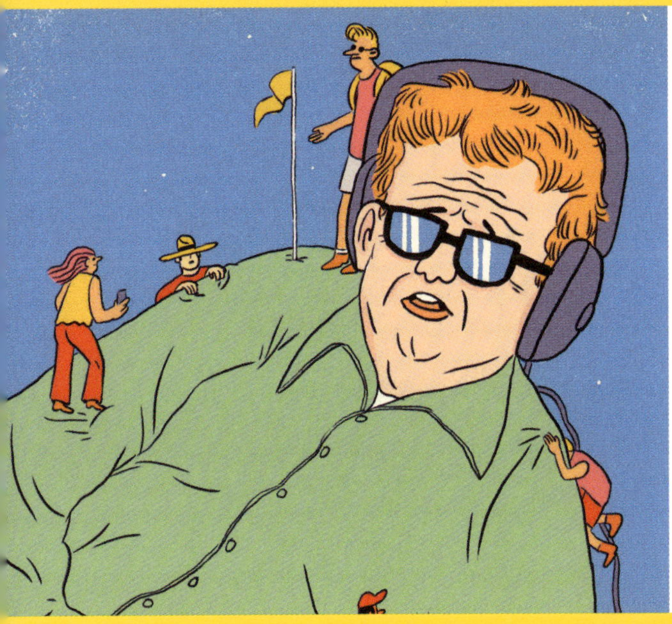

STEPHEN MAURICE GRAHAM

THE INTERIOR BRITPOP THOUGHTS OF CHRIS EVANS / 15–21 JUNE

"After years of exile, murmuring innuendos on *The One Show* and playing the cheery everyman on his radio show, it seemed that a switch flipped and the real Chris Evans was back. The comic came out of this nostalgia and how Chris felt about this return to his glory days."

LOUISE POMEROY

DOG MEAT / 22–28 JUNE

"I chose to respond to China's *Yulin Dog Meat Festival*. There was a lot of public outrage about how cruel it is. It's interesting that generally people don't consider the lives of pigs, cows and chickens, but are completely disgusted by the thought of slaughtering animals we consider domestic."

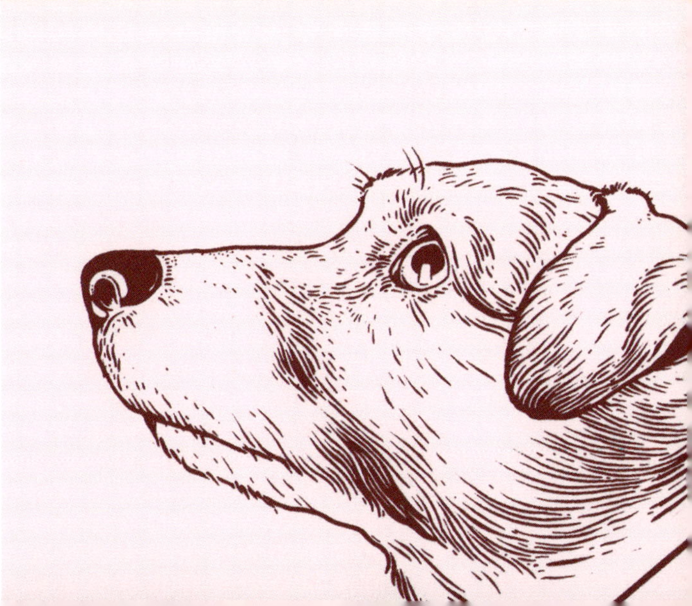

THIS WEEK I'VE ONLY BEEN ACCESSING THE NEWS VIA THE FEEDS OF MY SOCIAL MEDIA ACCOUNTS...

...HERE IS THE NEWS.

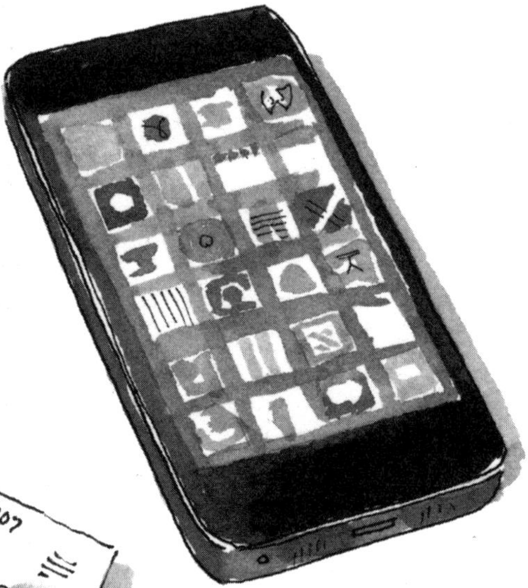

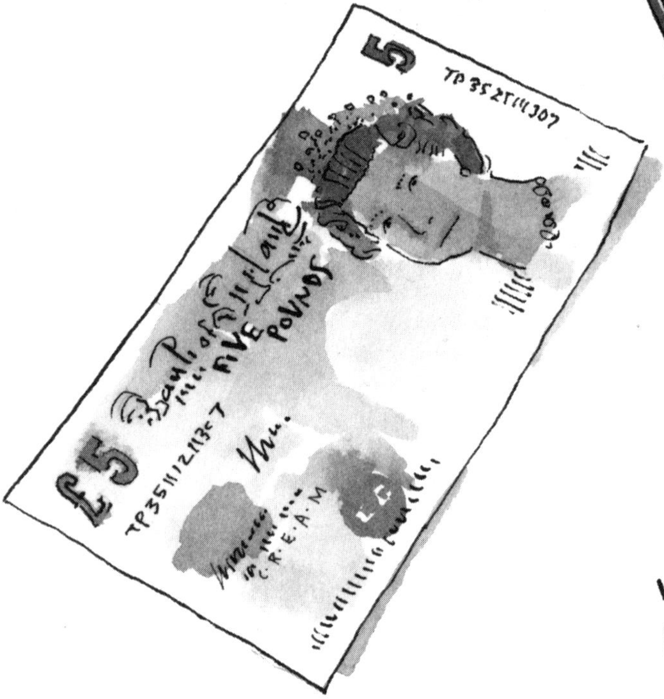

THE QUEEN SAID SOMETHING ABOUT CAPPING BENEFITS AND REQUIRING YOUNG PEOPLE TO LEARN OR EARN.

LOTS OF PEOPLE TALKED ABOUT HER SITTING ON A GOLD THRONE.

THERE WAS SOME ARGUING.

SOME MEN FROM FIFA GOT INTO BIG TROUBLE FOR CORRUPTION

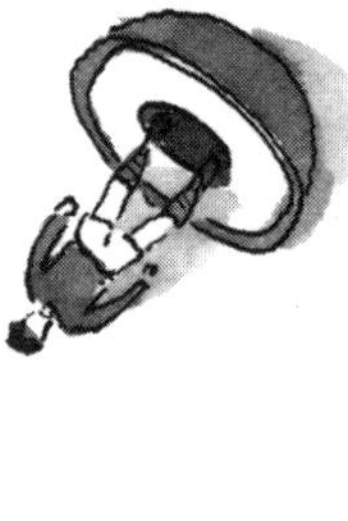

AMERICAN FRIENDS TALKED ABOUT THIS. MOSTLY ASKING "WHAT IS FIFA?"

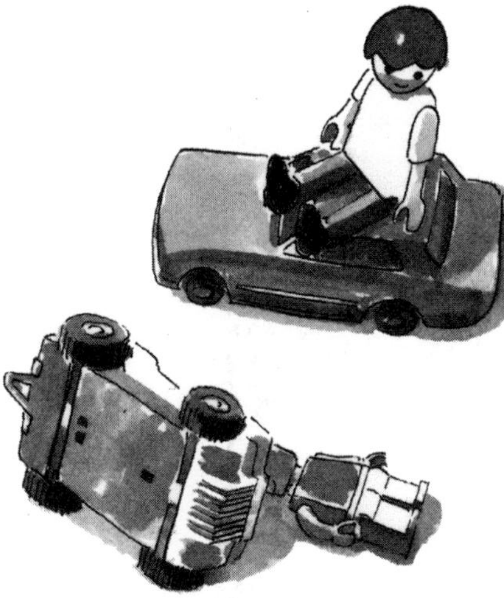

THERE WAS A FILM ABOUT CARS FIGHTING IN THE DESERT. IT HAD STRONG FEMALE CHARACTERS AND LOTS OF ACTION.

ALMOST EVERYBODY LOVED THE FILM.

THERE WAS A CLICKBATE ARTICLE ABOUT ASYLUM SEEKERS RUINING SOMEONE'S HOLIDAY.

EVERYONE AGREED THE ARTICLE WAS TERRIBLE

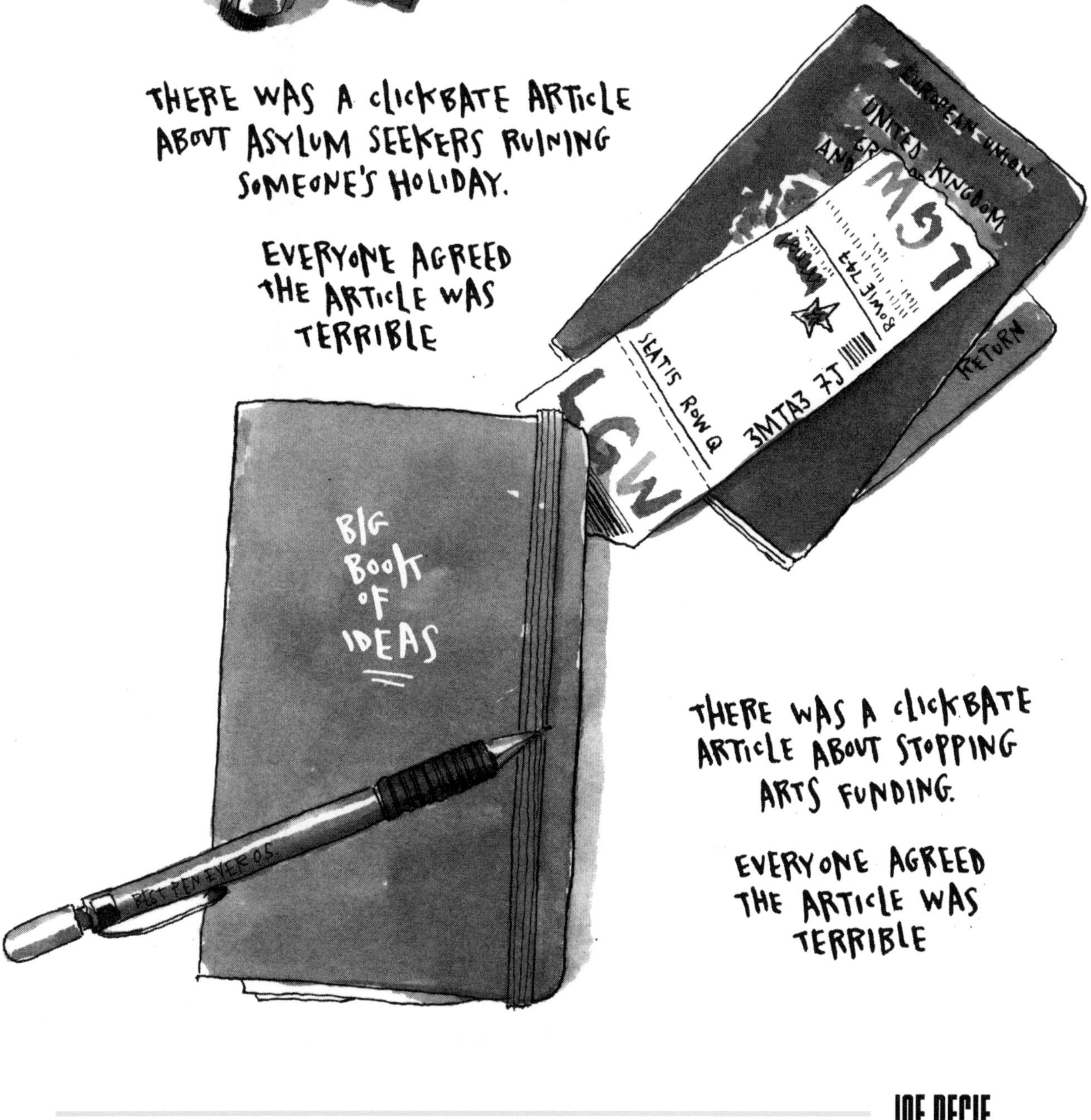

THERE WAS A CLICKBATE ARTICLE ABOUT STOPPING ARTS FUNDING.

EVERYONE AGREED THE ARTICLE WAS TERRIBLE

CORRUPTION. FANDOM. FOOTBALL.

I got into football when I was about eight or nine years old, mostly because all of my friends were. It was a choice of either joining in or hanging out with whichever teacher was unfortunate enough to draw playground duty. The simplicity of the game sucked me in, as it had to millions before and after me the world over. But it was the peripheral stuff around the sport that really hooked me – the kits, the badges, the nicknames, the collectable stickers – all of it catnip to a pre-pubescent boy. At the time my local team, Swindon Town, were enjoying a period of success and ascending through the divisions. It created a real buzz in a town not renowned as the most exciting of places. Once I started going along to games my eyes were opened to a whole new world that seemed to bear very little relation to the sport you watch on television. For starters, it was noticeably more sweary… which I enjoyed greatly.

The first season I started regularly attending live matches was 1984-85, commonly known as the darkest season in English football history. Spectators were still herded into stadiums that hadn't been refurbished since the turn of the century. The disasters that followed were an inevitable consequence of the contempt those in power had for the people who supported the game. There are few people who would want to go back to those days, but for all the positive changes to safety conditions, there have been negative side effects.

The commercialisation of the game accelerated with the formation of the Premier League in the early nineties. It's robbed large sections of the community from access to football. That contempt for supporters survives in the form of inflated ticket prices, fixtures organised for the primary benefit of broadcasters and the various hare-brained schemes to restructure the lower leagues and play league matches overseas.

At a global level, it seems the corruption has been ingrained within the culture of FIFA for generations; it's just become harder for them to keep it hushed. Sepp Blatter is clearly a ridiculous and shameless character, but he alone is not the problem. It's obvious that the organisation needs a complete overhaul, but there appears to be little desire for that to happen amongst its members. The money that sloshes around football has always been a draw for people looking to wet their beaks.

But despite all the commercialisation and the corruption, we're all still fans. Hope is a powerful emotion. Every season, millions of us allow ourselves to dream that this year will be different, that things will finally work out... and for some of us it does. Most football fans have tasted success at some point, whether it be seeing their team win the Champions League Final or the Beazer Homes League, and once you've had a taste of that sweet nectar it's enough to keep you going back.

BY DAVID SQUIRES

Illustrator and football cartoonist for *The Guardian*

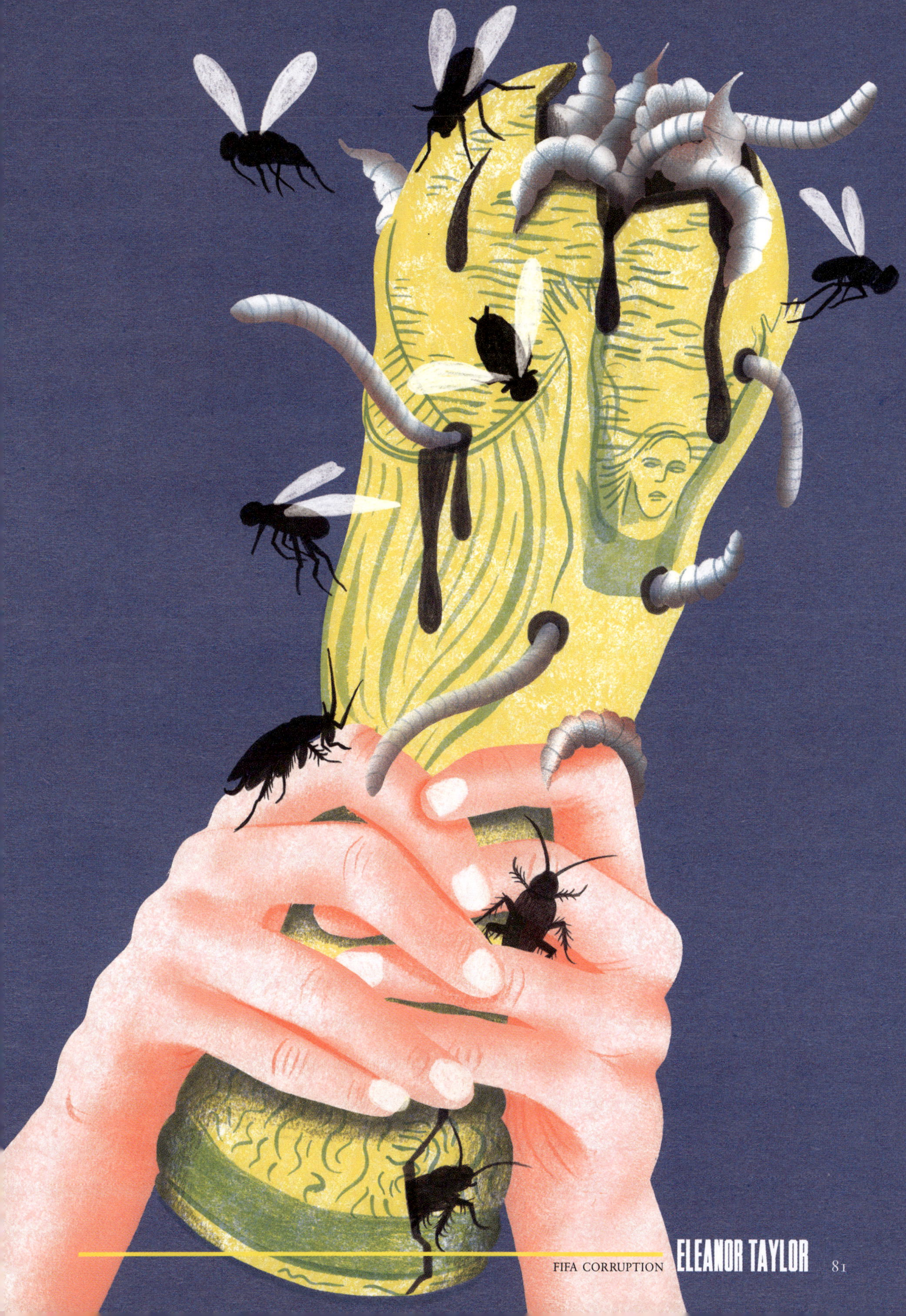

THE GREAT INTERNET SHOOTOUT

There was a time when we believed in 'good' and 'bad' hackers. Like the epic battles from John Wayne Westerns, *Black Hats* and *White Hats* existed in roughly equal balance. *White Hat* hackers protected the innocent against computer vulnerabilities, like slightly geekier Supermen, complete with the latest MacBook – while *Black Hats* tried to expose them, presumably while cackling in an underground lair.

Gone are those days. Now, *White Hats* spend their time jailbreaking smartphones or carrying out the latest productivity 'life hack', leaving their black-hatted counterparts to wage war on users. And what a war it's been! In the last year we saw an astonishing number of hacks against a range of targets. There was a massive cyber-attack on the email network of the Pentagon, which affected 4,000 military and civilian personnel who were working for the Joint Chiefs of Staff. Sony got hacked too, showing us that everyone in Hollywood behaves like they're still in high school, complete with defamatory note passing. The UK internet company TalkTalk was also victimised, resulting in a data breach of approximately four million customers. That was nothing compared to the US however, where the country's second largest health insurance provider, Anthem, had its records 'compromised' by hackers – resulting in the potential leak of everything from names and birthdays to Social Security numbers for up to 80 million past and present customers. Who was to blame for all this anarchy? Suspects range from the Chinese and Russians to North Koreans and bored British teenagers. Or so we're told by the NSA who, of course, have never hacked anyone. What did we learn from it all? Mainly that the people protecting our data may as well be OAPs with their first computer, setting the password as 'PASSWORD' and writing it in large letters on a notebook next to their desk.

As our physical and digital lives become ever more intertwined, we can only expect these kinds of hacks to become more commonplace. Hopefully the *Black Hat–White Hat* shootouts will be a little more even next year.

BY LUKE DORMEHL

Author of *The Formula* and technology writer for *Wired*, *Fast Company* and *The Guardian*

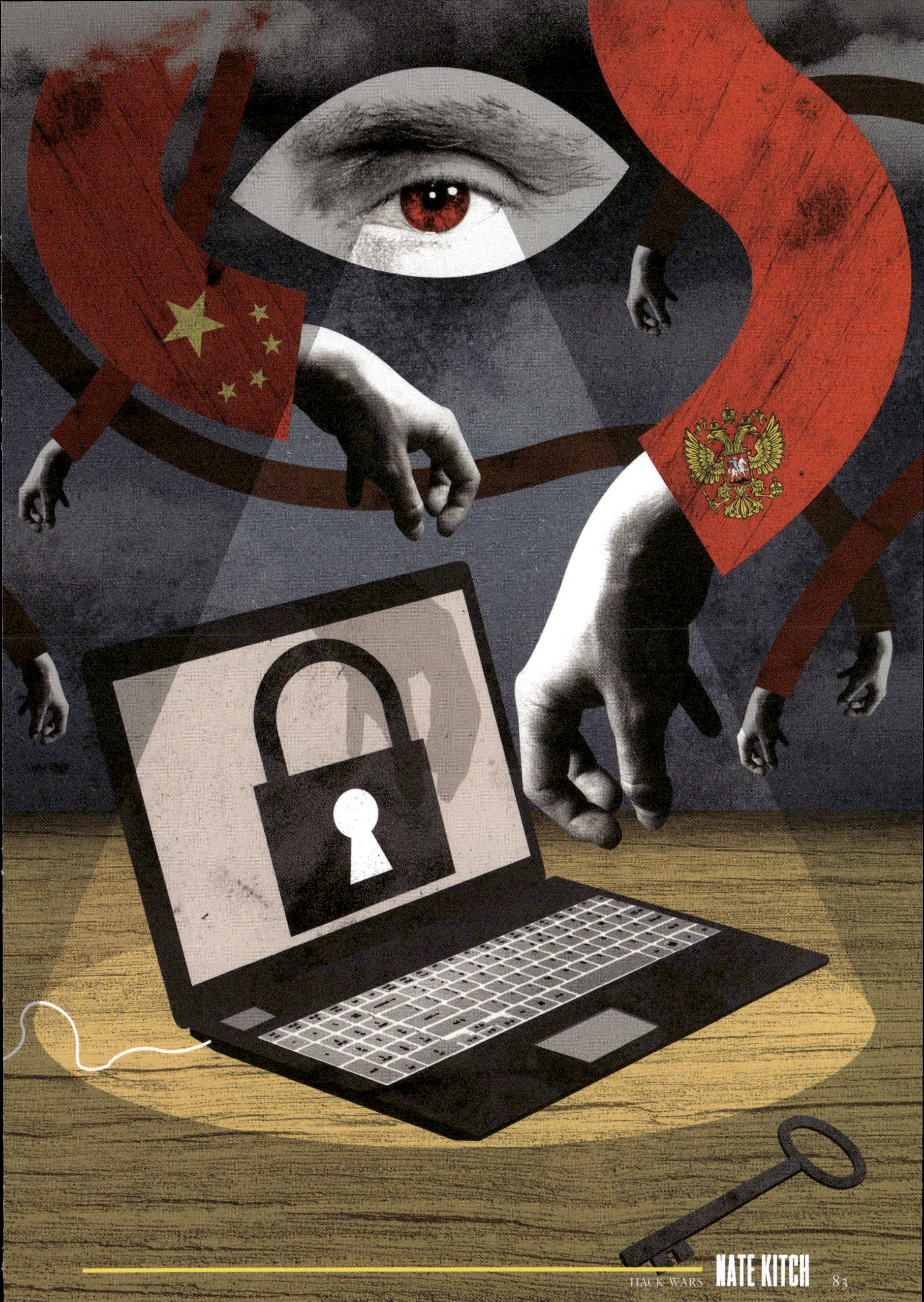
NATE KITCH

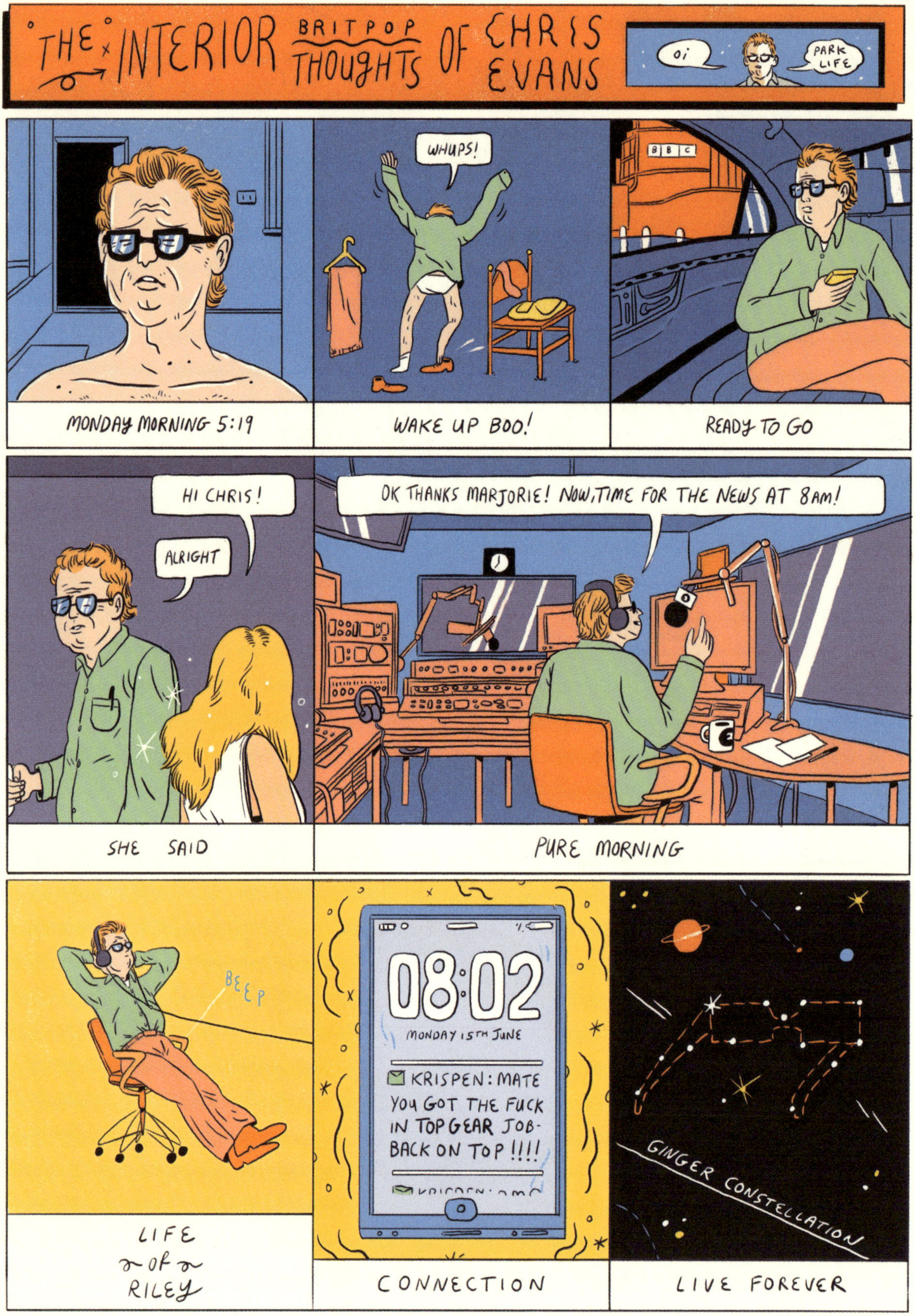
THE INTERIOR BRITPOP THOUGHTS OF CHRIS EVANS
OI
PARK LIFE
MONDAY MORNING 5:19
WHUPS!
WAKE UP BOO!
BBC
READY TO GO
HI CHRIS!
ALRIGHT
SHE SAID
OK THANKS MARJORIE! NOW, TIME FOR THE NEWS AT 8AM!
PURE MORNING
BEEP
LIFE of RILEY
08:02
MONDAY 15TH JUNE
KRISPEN: MATE
YOU GOT THE FUCK IN TOP GEAR JOB- BACK ON TOP !!!!
CONNECTION
GINGER CONSTELLATION
LIVE FOREVER

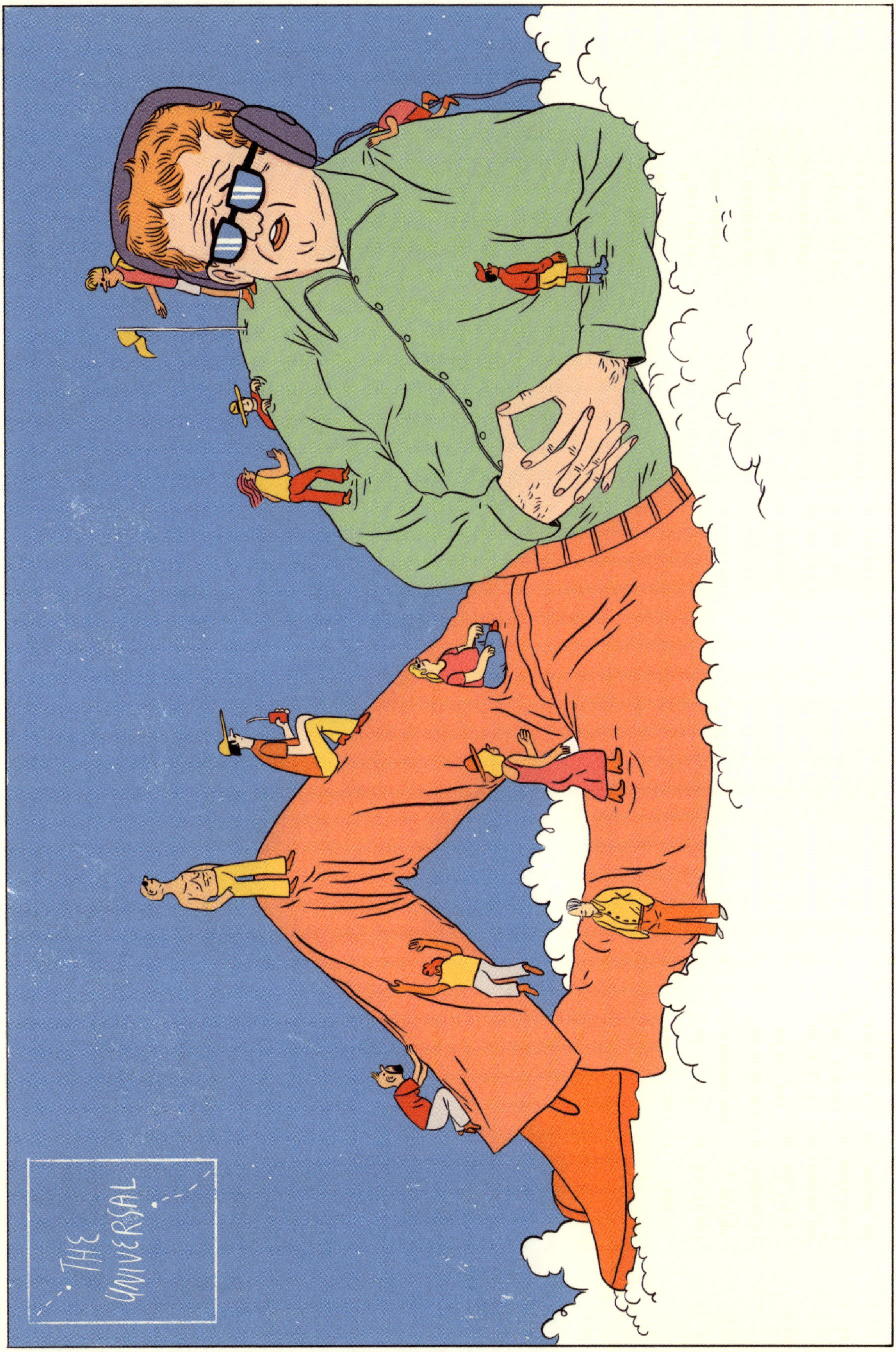
THE UNIVERSAL

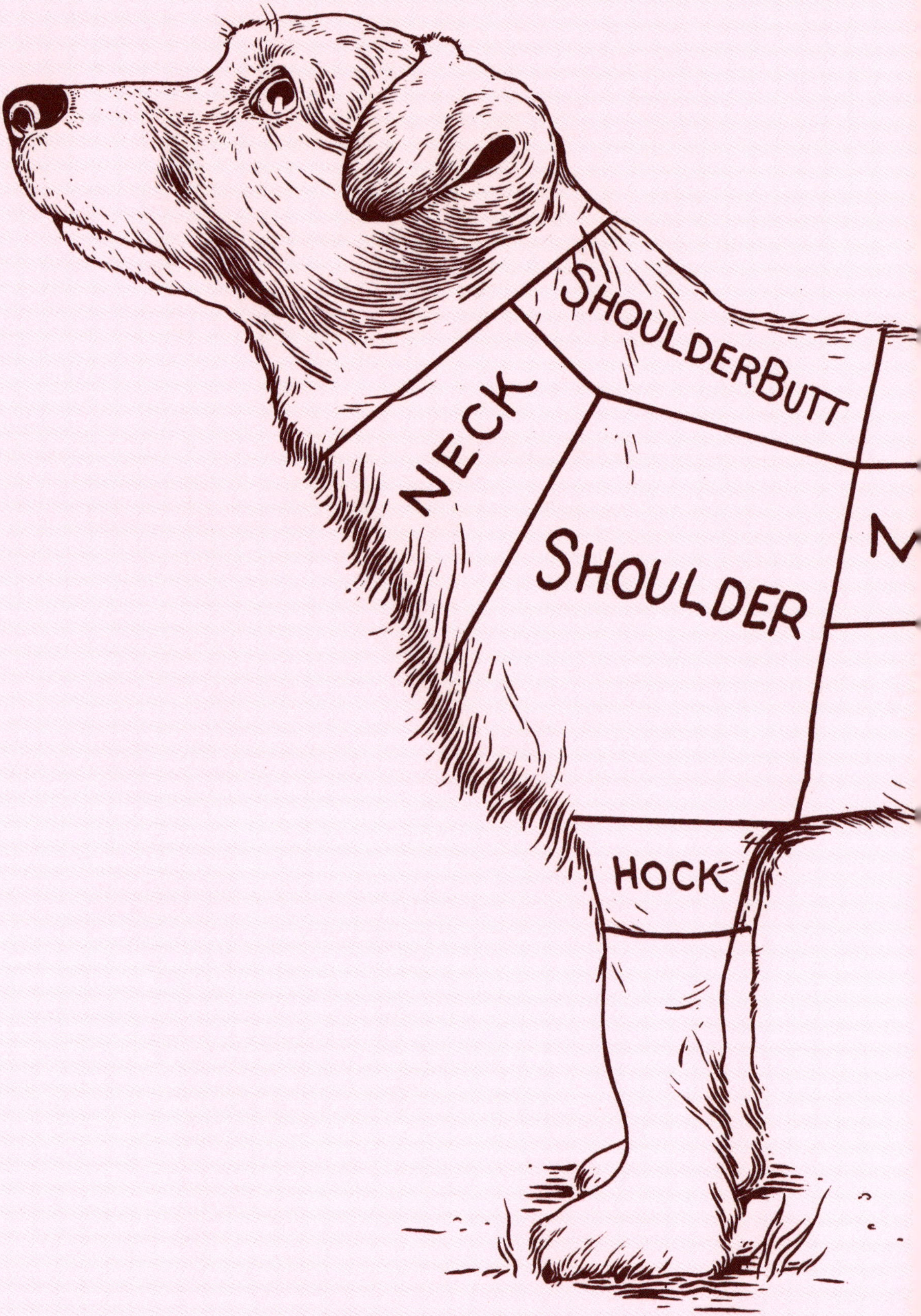
SHOULDERBUTT
NECK
SHOULDER
HOCK

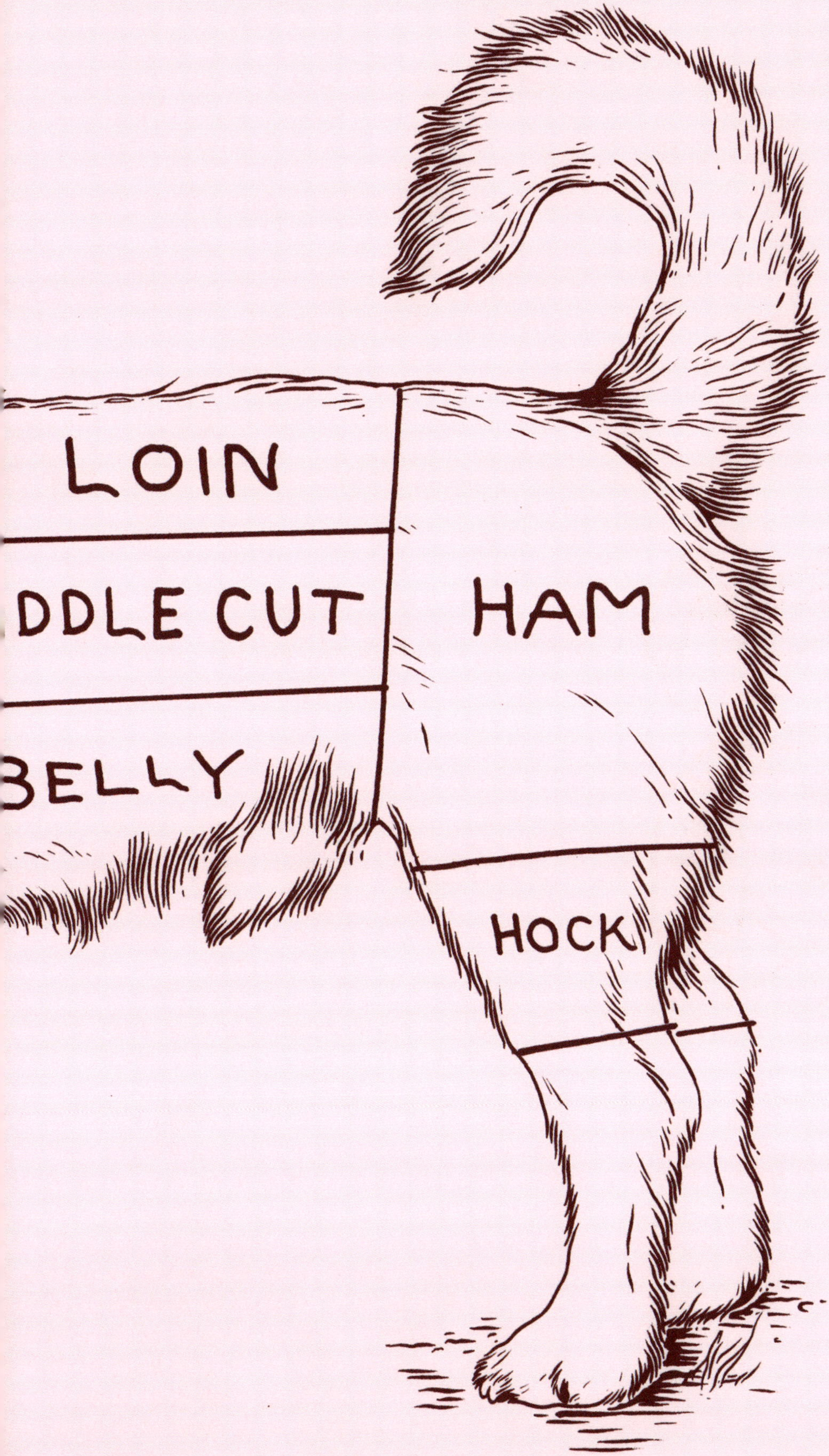
LOIN
DDLE CUT
BELLY
HAM
HOCK

DAVID SQUIRES

REFUGEE DETENTION / 29 JUNE–5 JULY

"I decided to approach a story that emerged in my adopted home of Australia – the introduction of new laws that will make it harder to expose the abuse refugees sometimes face when they arrive here. I feel it's important to tell readers in the UK that they don't have the monopoly on mendacious politicians."

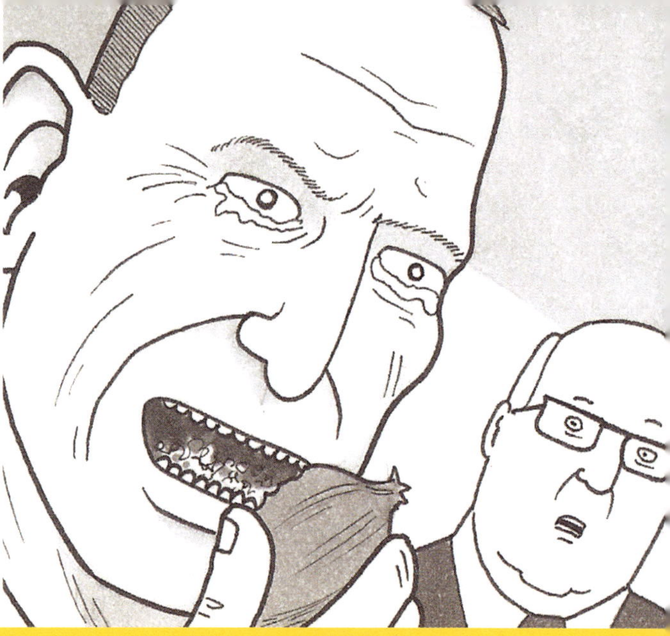

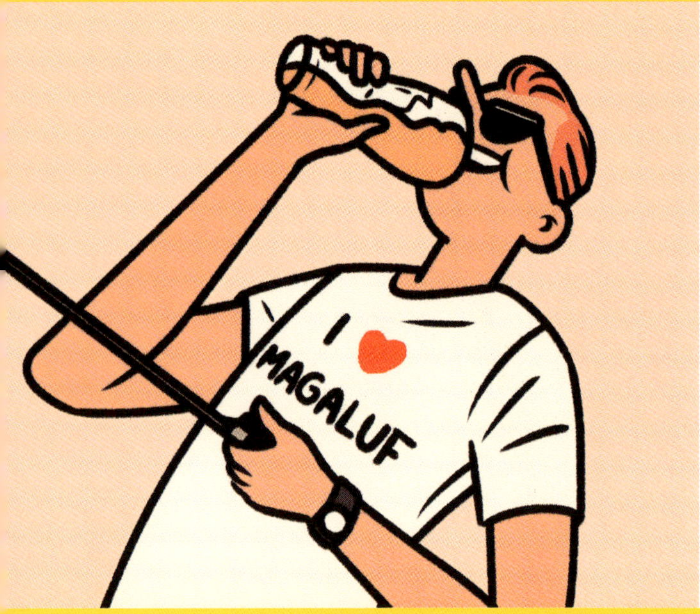

JANNE IIVONEN

SELFIE HAVOC / 6–12 JULY

"Tourists are causing havoc in destinations around the world. From random lewd acts to people climbing on ancient sculptures, just to snap a selfie. What resonated with me was the clash of culture and the extremely self-centred and narcissistic behaviour that has sprung from ever-present social media."

MICHAEL DRIVER

BBC CUTS / 13–19 JULY

"I illustrated the Conservative Party announcement, that they were keen to make further cuts to our dearly beloved BBC. With further cuts made, we shall be waving goodbye to a large number of shows, with many actors and back room staff seeking further employment."

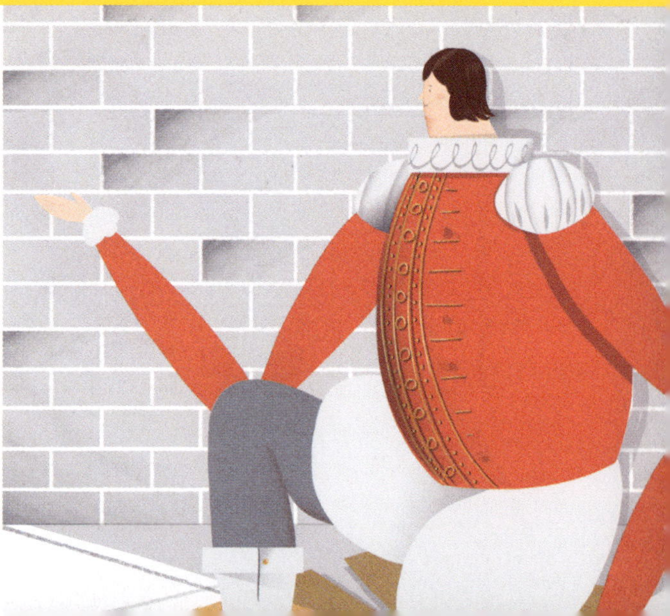

MAT PRINGLE

CORBYN'S RISE / 20–26 JULY

"Our Tory overlords plunged a knife into the have-nots with the *Welfare Reform & Work Bill*, sending Labour into disarray with just 50 MPs including Jeremy Corbyn voting against it. The press have suggested his leadership would usher in the fall of the Labour party. For me, they've been dead for years with their spineless rhetoric."

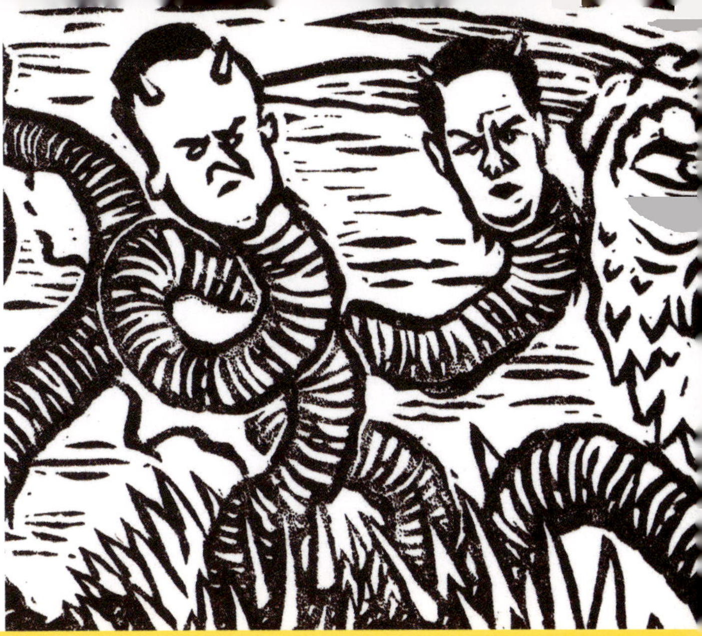

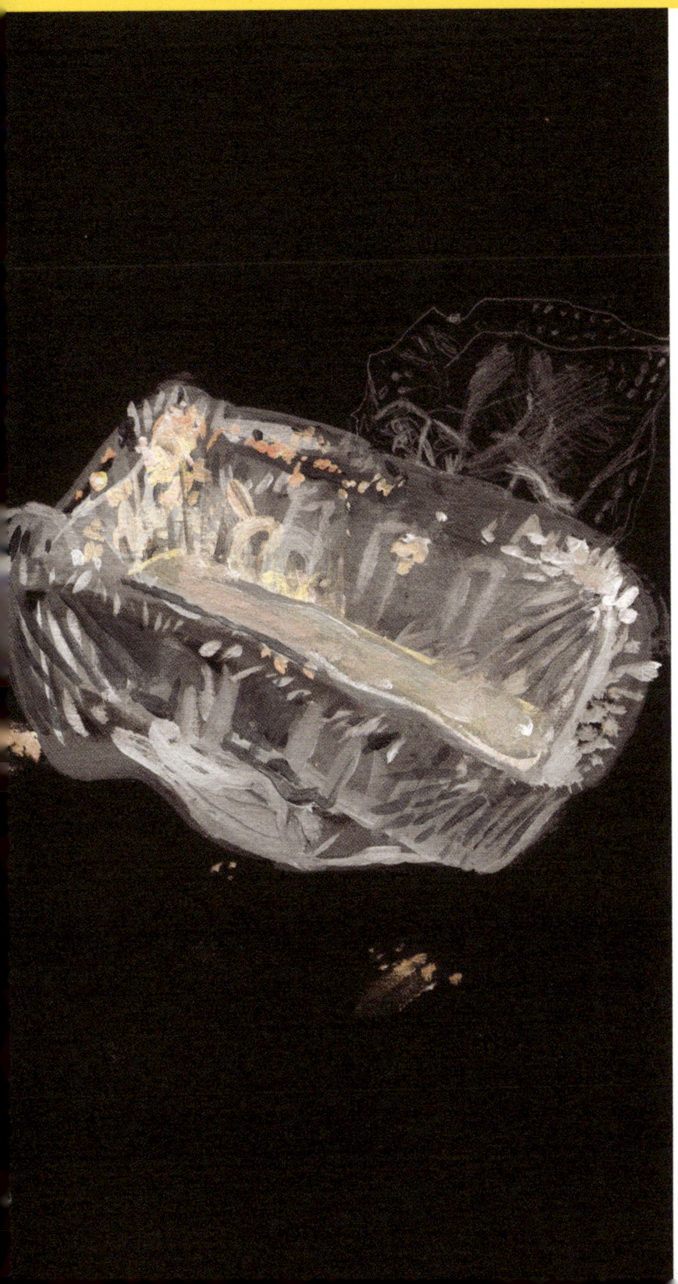

PAUL DAVIS

THE STATE OF IT / 27 JULY–2 AUGUST

"I was drawing away, reflecting on the misery of the news – the hypocrisy, the never-ending bullshit from the media-trained powerful, the disasters, the painful deaths and hopeless determination of folk trying to escape their homeland terribleness, the lies, the back-stabbing and utter ludicrousness of celebrity and selfies – when Sophie Smith (a writer living in East London) showed me a poem she'd written. I loved it, it made me ache. She adapted it very slightly and I painted the foil container. Seemed to sum it up.

"There are elements of contemporary news in there – the lion killer, the air crashes, the immigrant misery, etc – but ends with Helen who tramps the streets trying to stay alive. She dropped through the net and nobody powerful with the means to offer help cares. She's not stupid, she's a good woman, she's simply fucked. It's a news item that never goes away and seems to be getting worse. If only the FTSE 100 paid their corporation tax…"

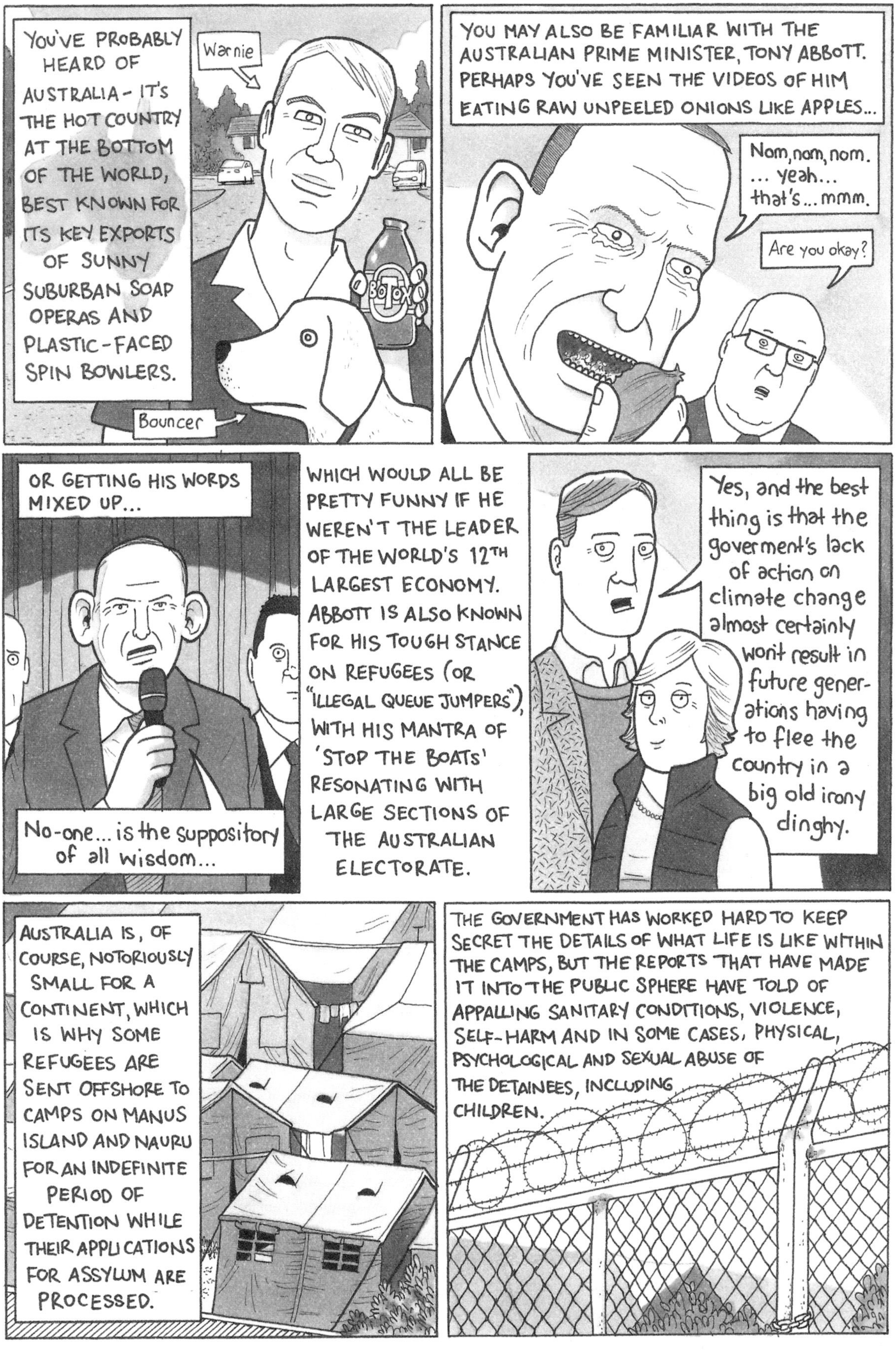

YOU'VE PROBABLY HEARD OF AUSTRALIA - IT'S THE HOT COUNTRY AT THE BOTTOM OF THE WORLD, BEST KNOWN FOR ITS KEY EXPORTS OF SUNNY SUBURBAN SOAP OPERAS AND PLASTIC-FACED SPIN BOWLERS.
Warnie
BOTOX
Bouncer
YOU MAY ALSO BE FAMILIAR WITH THE AUSTRALIAN PRIME MINISTER, TONY ABBOTT. PERHAPS YOU'VE SEEN THE VIDEOS OF HIM EATING RAW UNPEELED ONIONS LIKE APPLES...
Nom, nom, nom. ... yeah... that's... mmm.
Are you okay?
OR GETTING HIS WORDS MIXED UP...
No-one... is the suppository of all wisdom...
WHICH WOULD ALL BE PRETTY FUNNY IF HE WEREN'T THE LEADER OF THE WORLD'S 12TH LARGEST ECONOMY. ABBOTT IS ALSO KNOWN FOR HIS TOUGH STANCE ON REFUGEES (OR "ILLEGAL QUEUE JUMPERS"), WITH HIS MANTRA OF 'STOP THE BOATS' RESONATING WITH LARGE SECTIONS OF THE AUSTRALIAN ELECTORATE.
Yes, and the best thing is that the goverment's lack of action on climate change almost certainly won't result in future generations having to flee the country in a big old irony dinghy.
AUSTRALIA IS, OF COURSE, NOTORIOUSLY SMALL FOR A CONTINENT, WHICH IS WHY SOME REFUGEES ARE SENT OFFSHORE TO CAMPS ON MANUS ISLAND AND NAURU FOR AN INDEFINITE PERIOD OF DETENTION WHILE THEIR APPLICATIONS FOR ASSYLUM ARE PROCESSED.
THE GOVERNMENT HAS WORKED HARD TO KEEP SECRET THE DETAILS OF WHAT LIFE IS LIKE WITHIN THE CAMPS, BUT THE REPORTS THAT HAVE MADE IT INTO THE PUBLIC SPHERE HAVE TOLD OF APPALLING SANITARY CONDITIONS, VIOLENCE, SELF-HARM AND IN SOME CASES, PHYSICAL, PSYCHOLOGICAL AND SEXUAL ABUSE OF THE DETAINEES, INCLUDING CHILDREN.

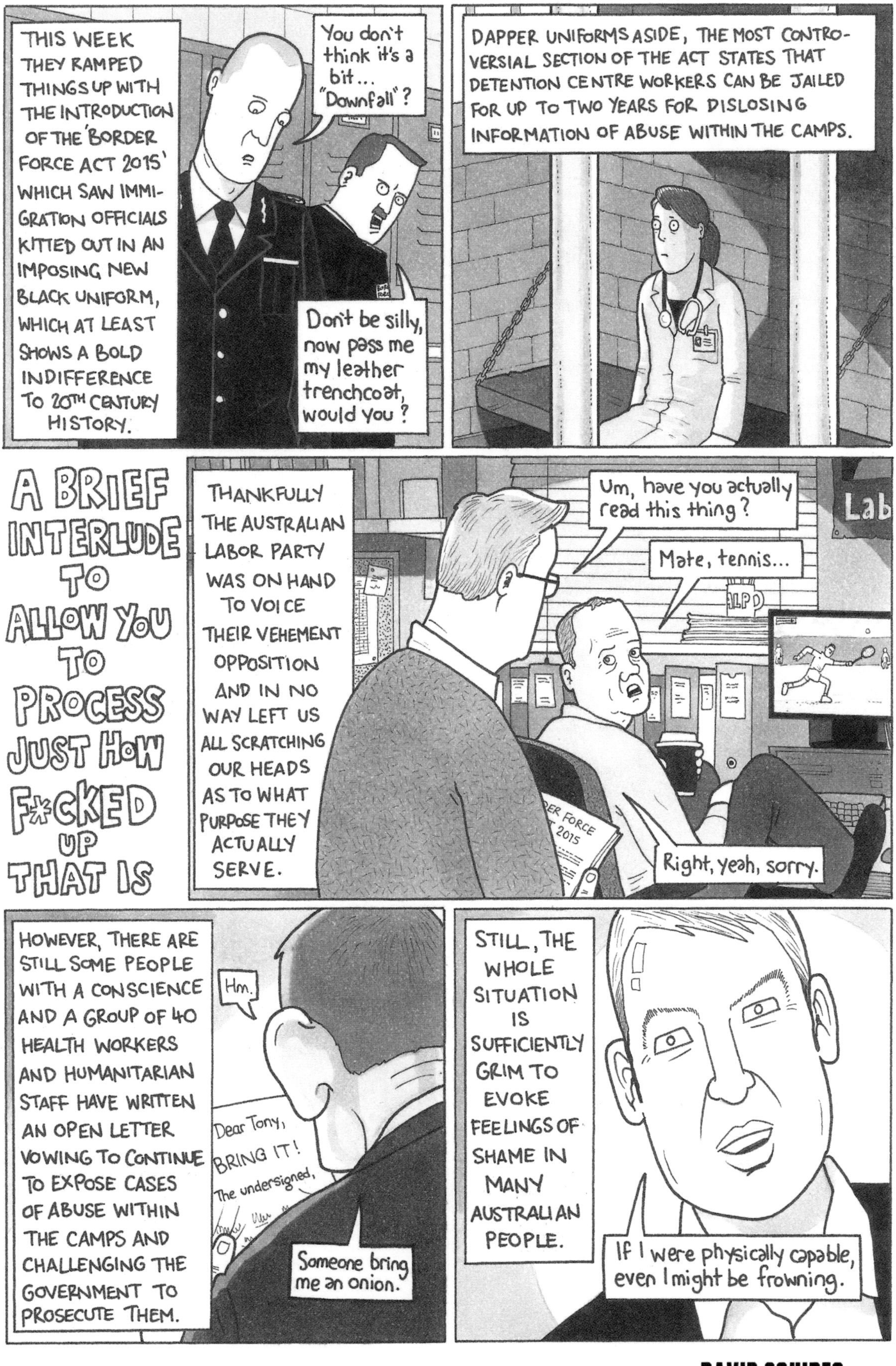
THIS WEEK THEY RAMPED THINGS UP WITH THE INTRODUCTION OF THE 'BORDER FORCE ACT 2015' WHICH SAW IMMIGRATION OFFICIALS KITTED OUT IN AN IMPOSING NEW BLACK UNIFORM, WHICH AT LEAST SHOWS A BOLD INDIFFERENCE TO 20TH CENTURY HISTORY.
You don't think it's a bit... "Downfall"?
Don't be silly, now pass me my leather trenchcoat, would you?
DAPPER UNIFORMS ASIDE, THE MOST CONTROVERSIAL SECTION OF THE ACT STATES THAT DETENTION CENTRE WORKERS CAN BE JAILED FOR UP TO TWO YEARS FOR DISLOSING INFORMATION OF ABUSE WITHIN THE CAMPS.
A BRIEF INTERLUDE TO ALLOW YOU TO PROCESS JUST HOW F*CKED UP THAT IS
THANKFULLY THE AUSTRALIAN LABOR PARTY WAS ON HAND TO VOICE THEIR VEHEMENT OPPOSITION AND IN NO WAY LEFT US ALL SCRATCHING OUR HEADS AS TO WHAT PURPOSE THEY ACTUALLY SERVE.
Um, have you actually read this thing?
Mate, tennis...
Right, yeah, sorry.
HOWEVER, THERE ARE STILL SOME PEOPLE WITH A CONSCIENCE AND A GROUP OF 40 HEALTH WORKERS AND HUMANITARIAN STAFF HAVE WRITTEN AN OPEN LETTER VOWING TO CONTINUE TO EXPOSE CASES OF ABUSE WITHIN THE CAMPS AND CHALLENGING THE GOVERNMENT TO PROSECUTE THEM.
Hm.
Dear Tony,
BRING IT!
The undersigned,
Someone bring me an onion.
STILL, THE WHOLE SITUATION IS SUFFICIENTLY GRIM TO EVOKE FEELINGS OF SHAME IN MANY AUSTRALIAN PEOPLE.
If I were physically capable, even I might be frowning.

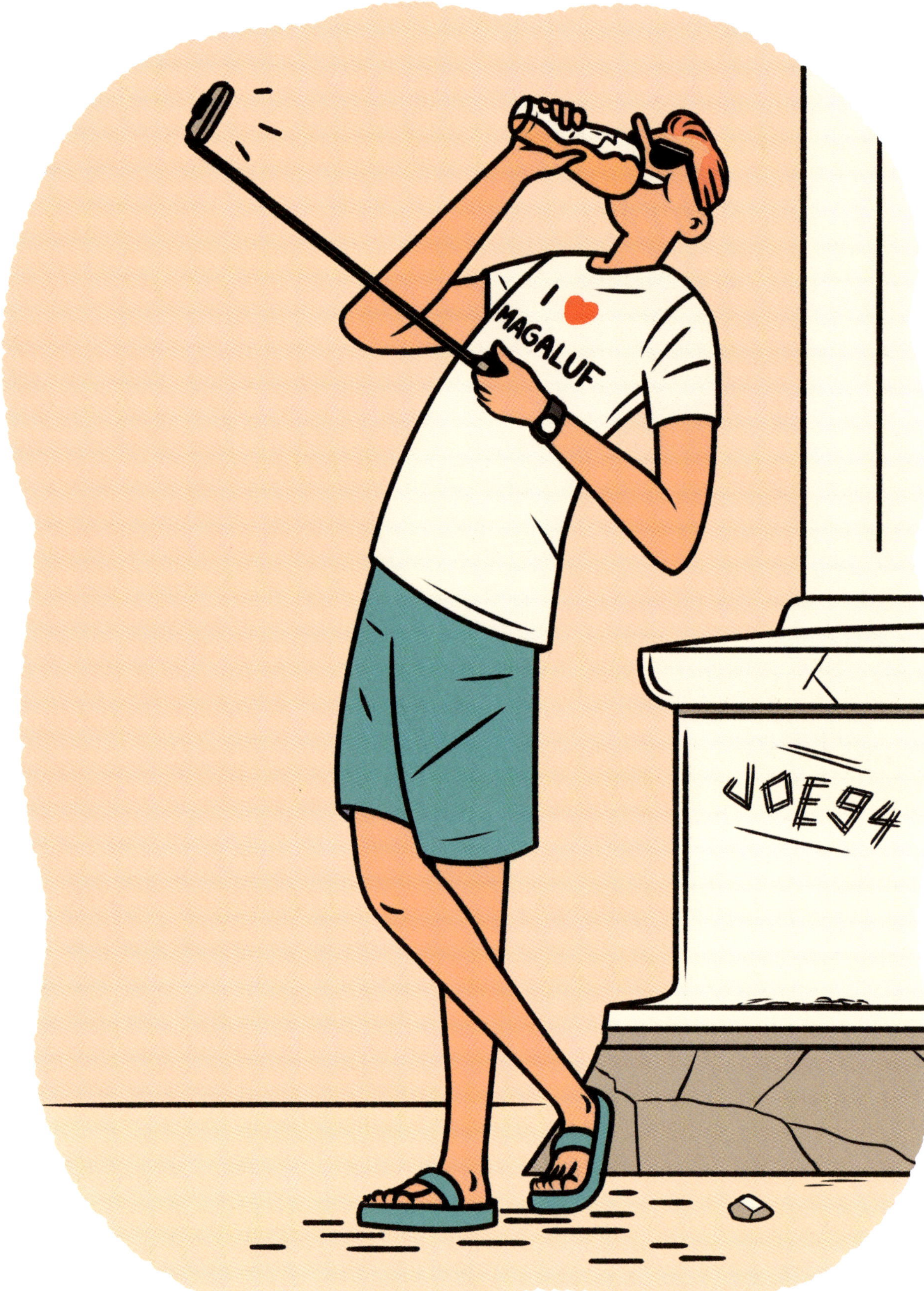
I ♥ MAGALUF
JOE94

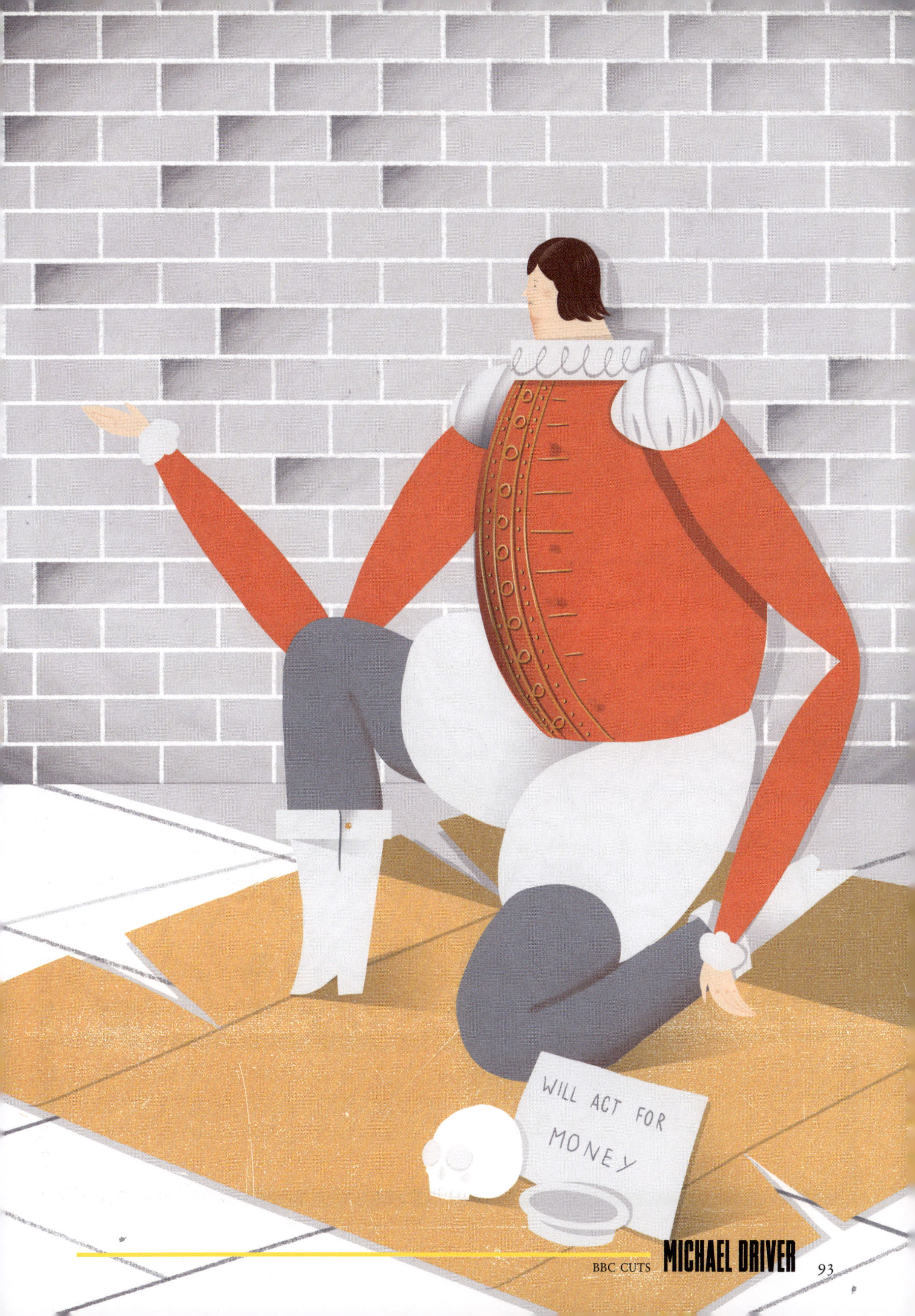
WILL ACT FOR
MONEY

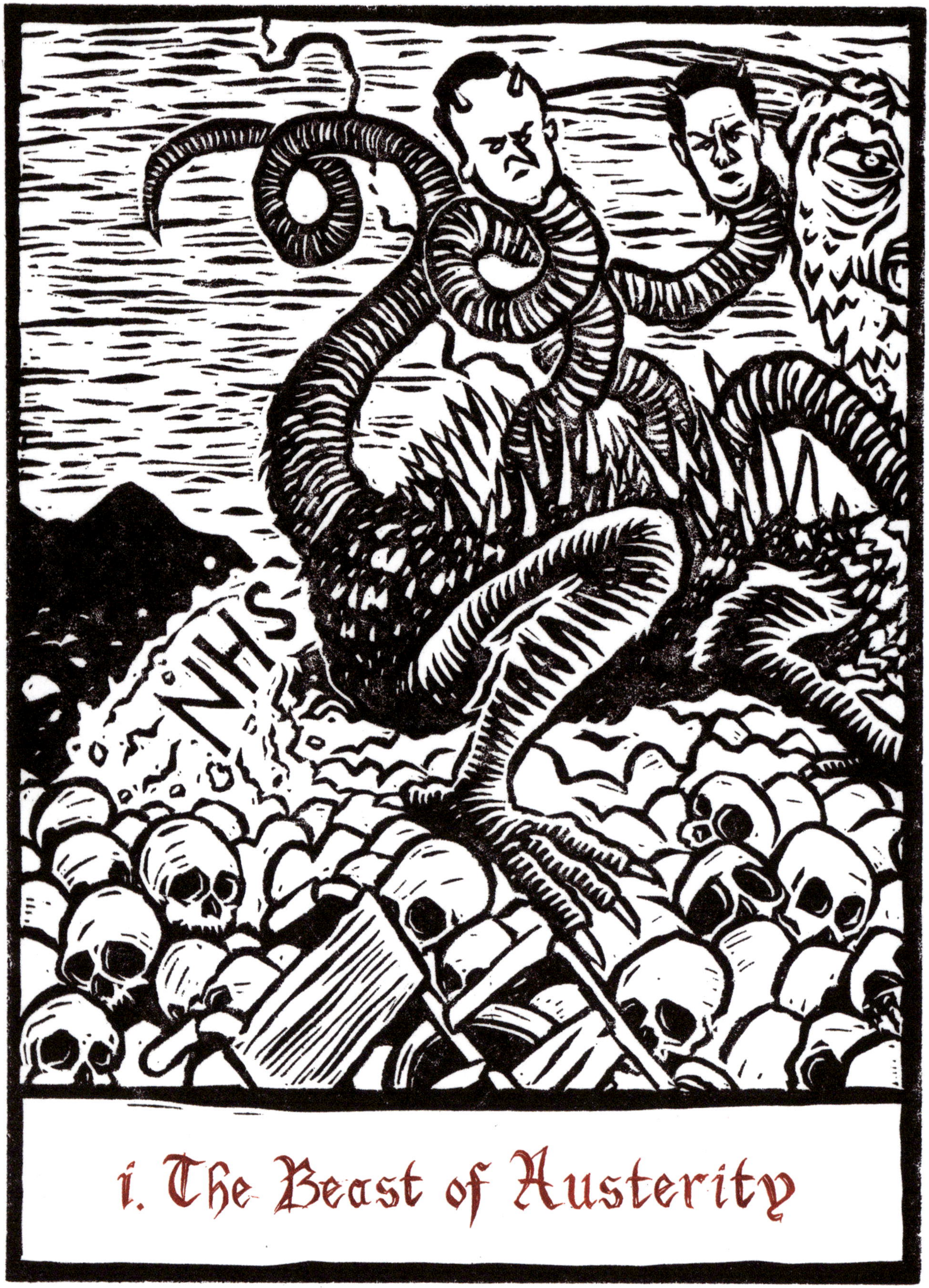

i. The Beast of Austerity

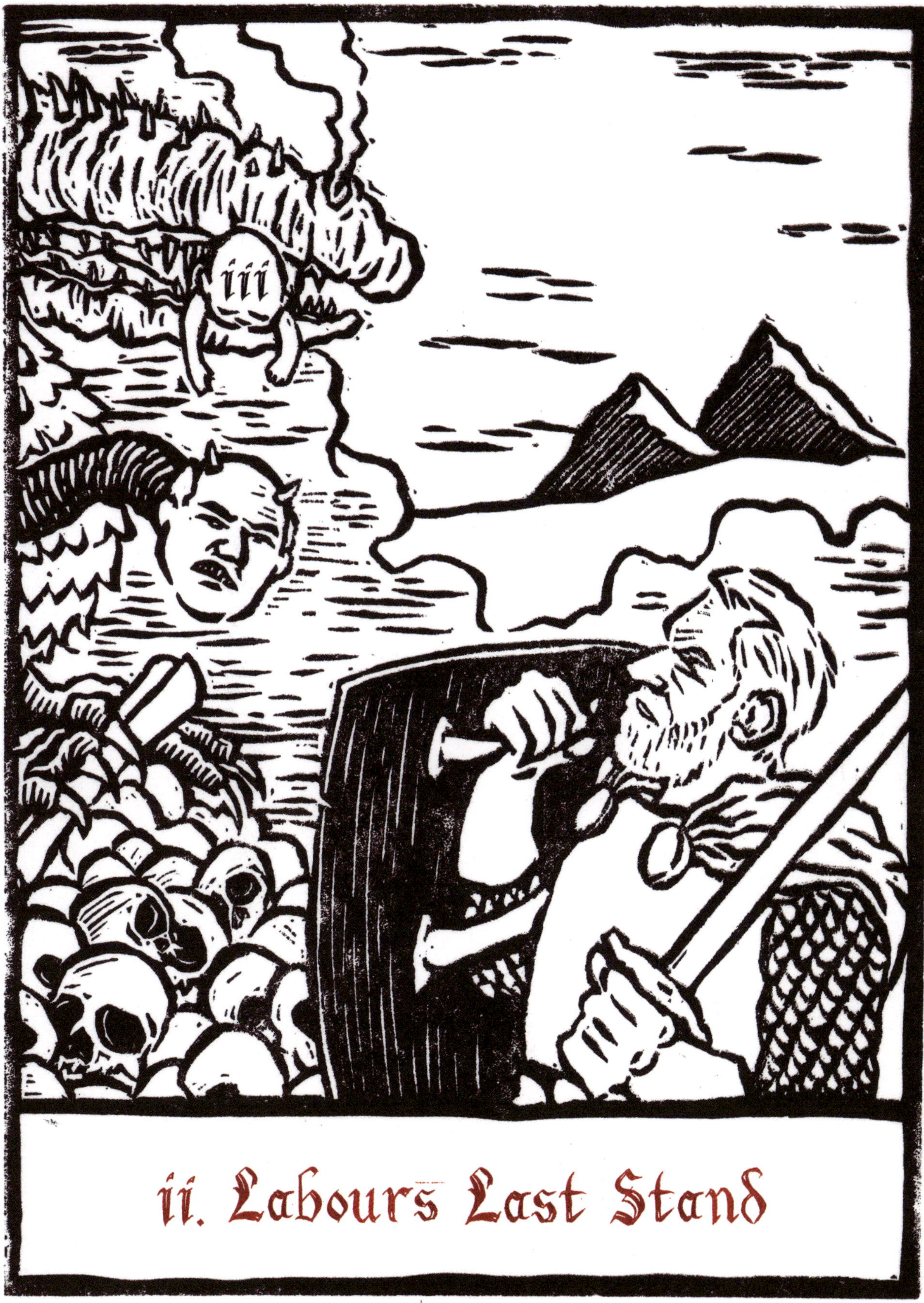

ii. Labours Last Stand

THE STATE OF IT

Dr. Palmer's one regret –
No Cecil head.
His thirty grand
Dirty in the hands
Of an African.
'My grant to the wilds'.

Migrant Child,
Limbless in the blaze.
Make room for the trucks –
They bring our tiffin,
Hampered by the crash of jets.
Wings drift.

Sun on the breast of a gull;
A boy falls. Grit sticks
Beneath the skin of his knee.
All hail Corbyn.

Dirt-faced, crotch-stink Helen
Plugs bulbs into decade-aged peat
And Pirate Pat from 73 knocks
To fuck her for a fiver.

Corned beef hash for tea
Again.
Heat it up in a foil bowl;
Watch the bulbs die

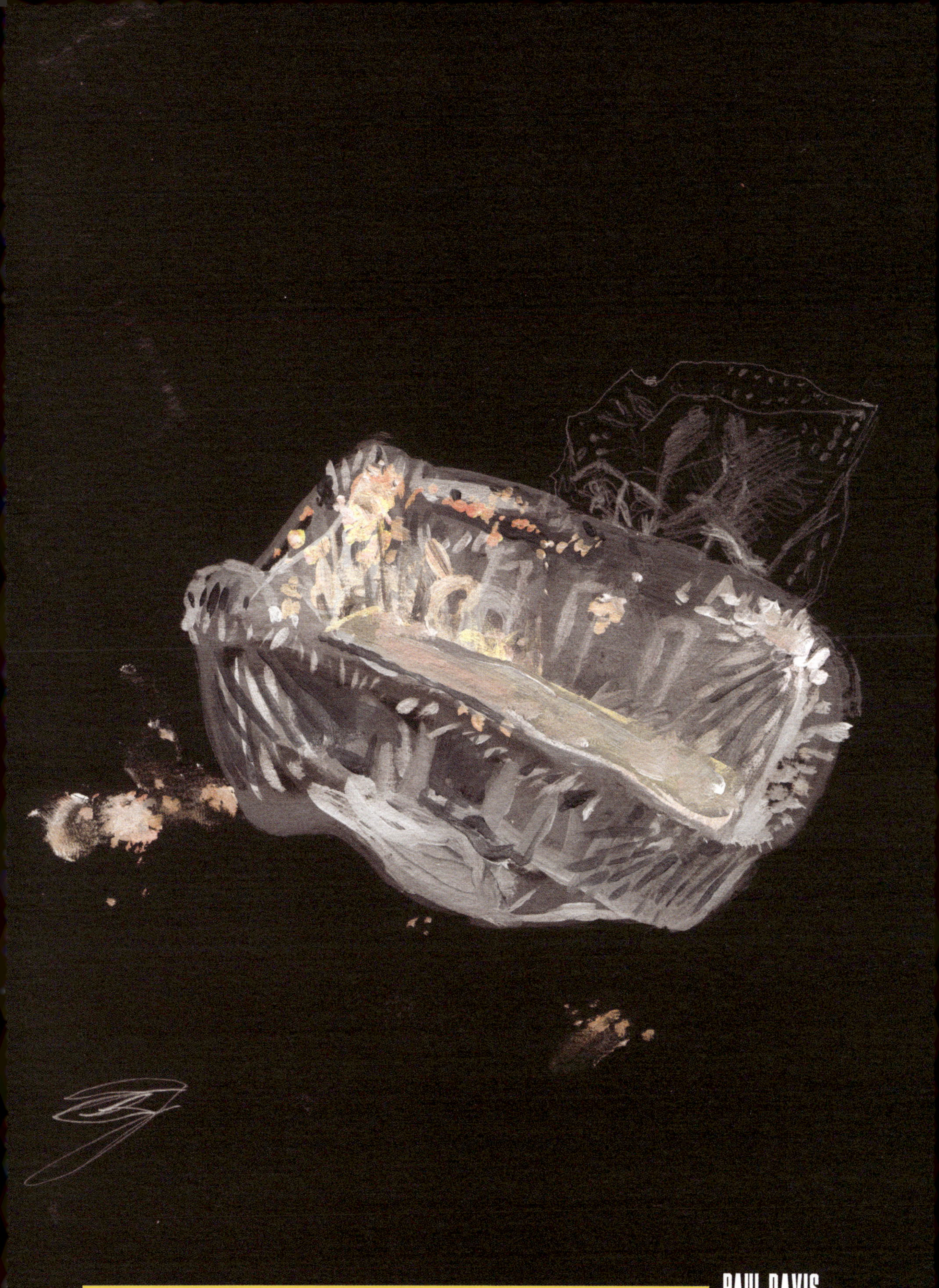

MARTINA PAUKOVA

HEATH'S MATES / 3–9 AUGUST

"I illustrated the child abuse allegations relating to Edward Heath. After reading about the defences from his former colleagues – playing upon Heath's unmarried and asexual nature – I imagined this man in his private setting, with this out-of-place lurking deviation. Thus this tacky candy dispenser in a posh flat."

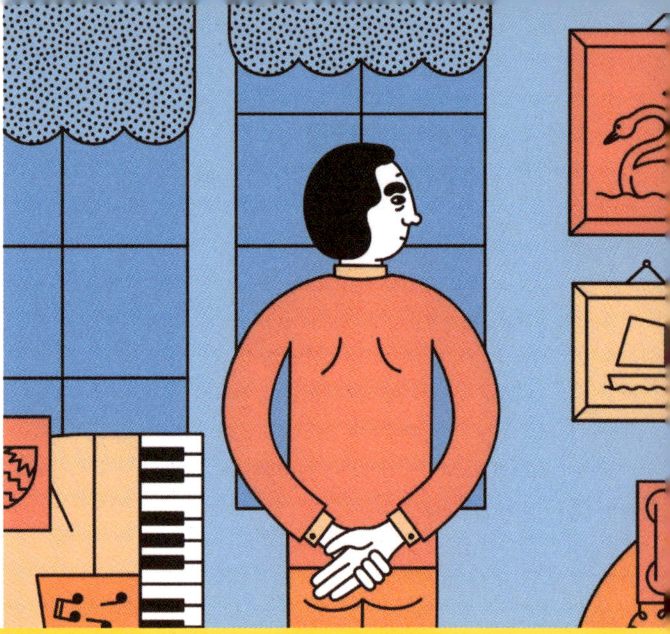

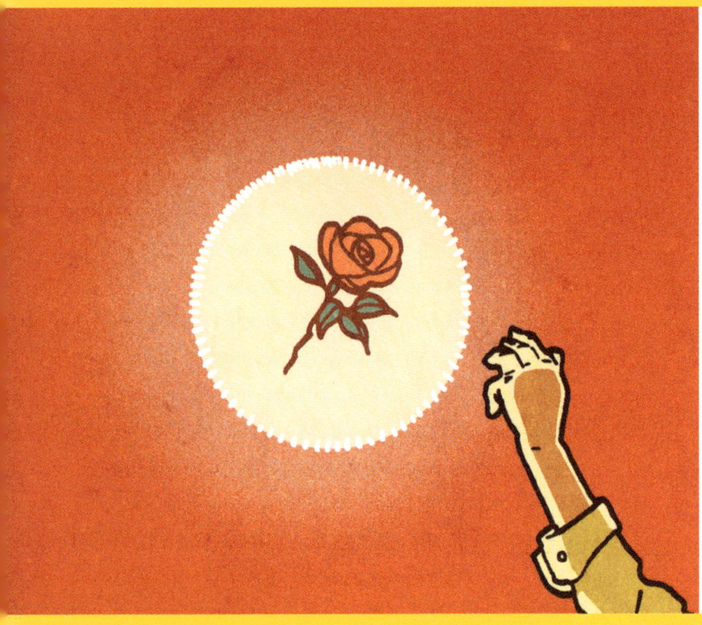

ROBERT G. FRESSON

LABOUR IN-FIGHTNG / 10–16 AUGUST

"I illustrated the struggle for leadership of the Labour Party. Jeremy Corbyn was topping the polls and, terrified for what this might mean, everybody else seems desperate to smear him. Conversely, Corbyn has been refraining from commenting on his rivals, giving his campaign a noble and ultimately more convincing edge."

EVA BEE

REFUGEE CRISIS / 17–23 AUGUST

"The refugee crisis made a resurgence during my week. My piece reflects on the fragility of the refugees' situation as they arrive in countries across Europe by boat. The power is in European hands to either help or dash their hopes, as we've seen with the violence faced by migrants trying to enter Macedonia."

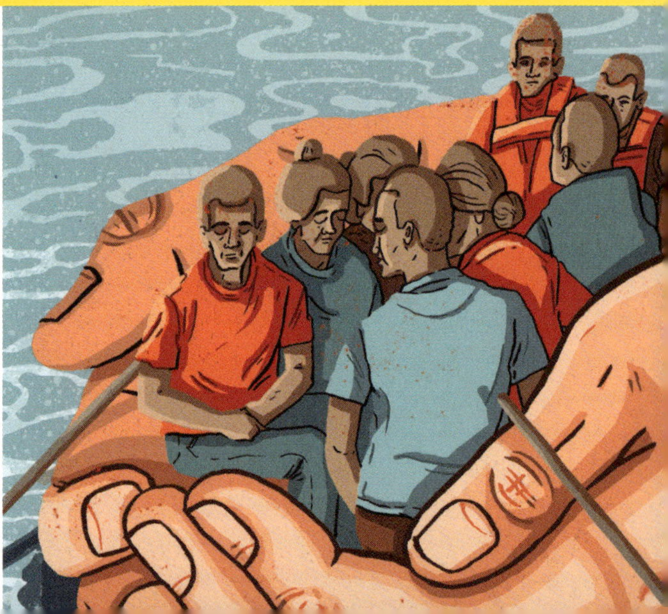

BEN JENNINGS

PUBLIC SPECTACLE / 24–30 AUGUST

"My piece is a response to the horrific shooting of two journalists on live television in Virginia, during which the perpetrator filmed and uploaded the killing to social media. This absurdity of genuine violence turning into some sort of online public spectacle is frightening."

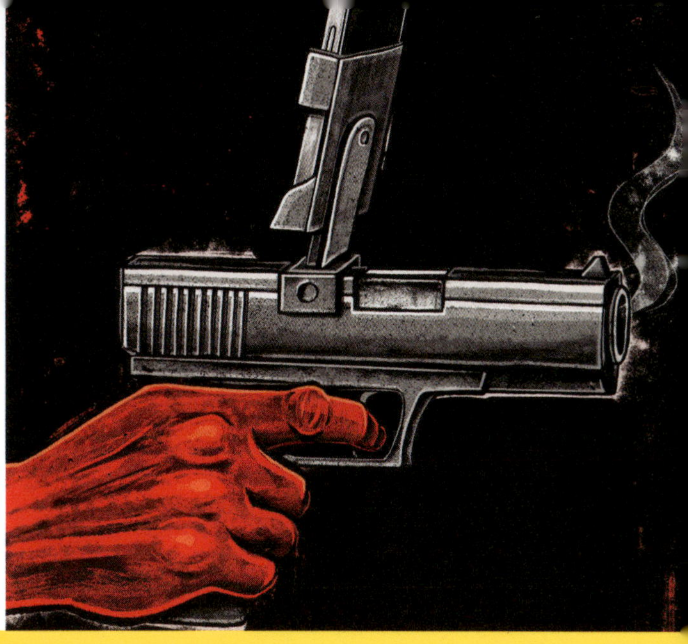

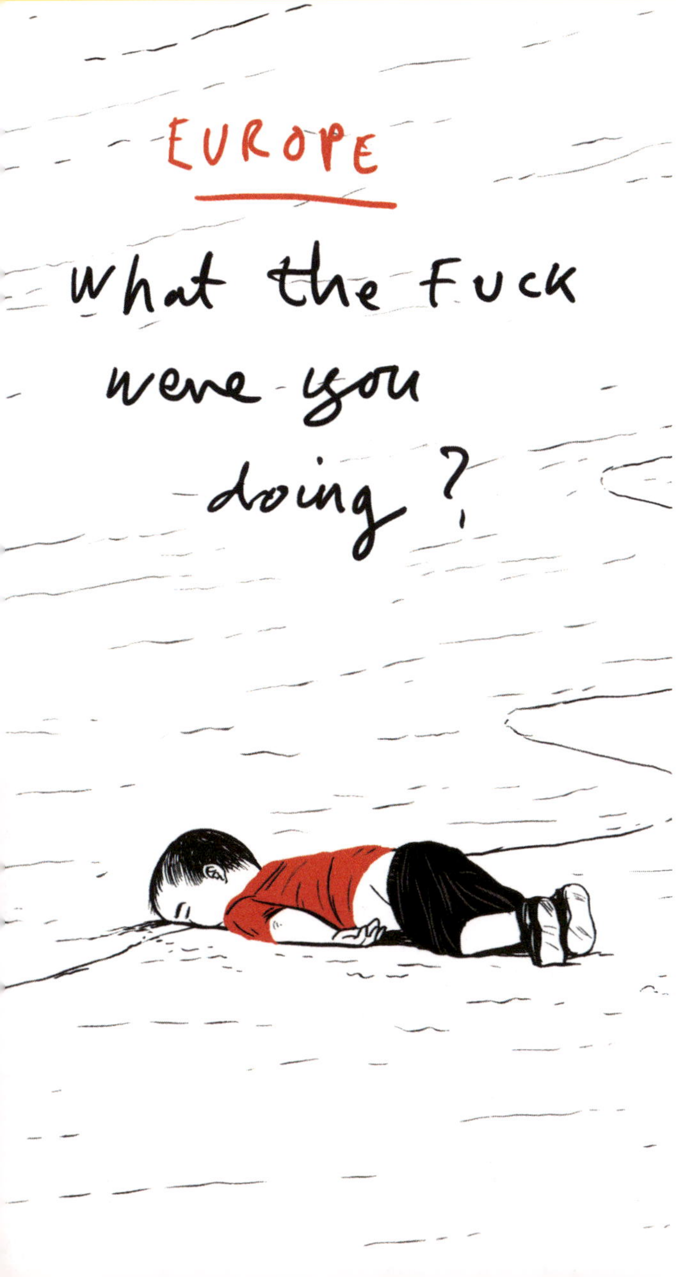

PAUL BLOW

WHAT THE FUCK WERE YOU DOING? / 31 AUGUST–6 SEPTEMBER

"Like so many, I saw the photograph of Aylan Kurdi during my week on *Yellow* and cried. As a father, the image of the poor wee boy was too much to bear, my pain and sorrow for the father and his suffering all too real. I could not escape the power of the image and neither could the world. The outpouring of charity and the compassion shown by people was overwhelming, especially against the backdrop of governments refusal to accept more migrants. So, it was this that prompted my illustration, an image using the power of the photograph, but recontextualising it and venting my own anger at Europe for letting this tragedy happen in the first place. In this image I've used text which I don't usually do, but felt it was appropriate. The image may offend – but my intention is to question the role of government, especially our own, when a humanitarian disaster has been unfolding over a long period. Where was the compassion and where was the help? Ultimately, I think it reflects on all of us. What the FUCK were you doing?"

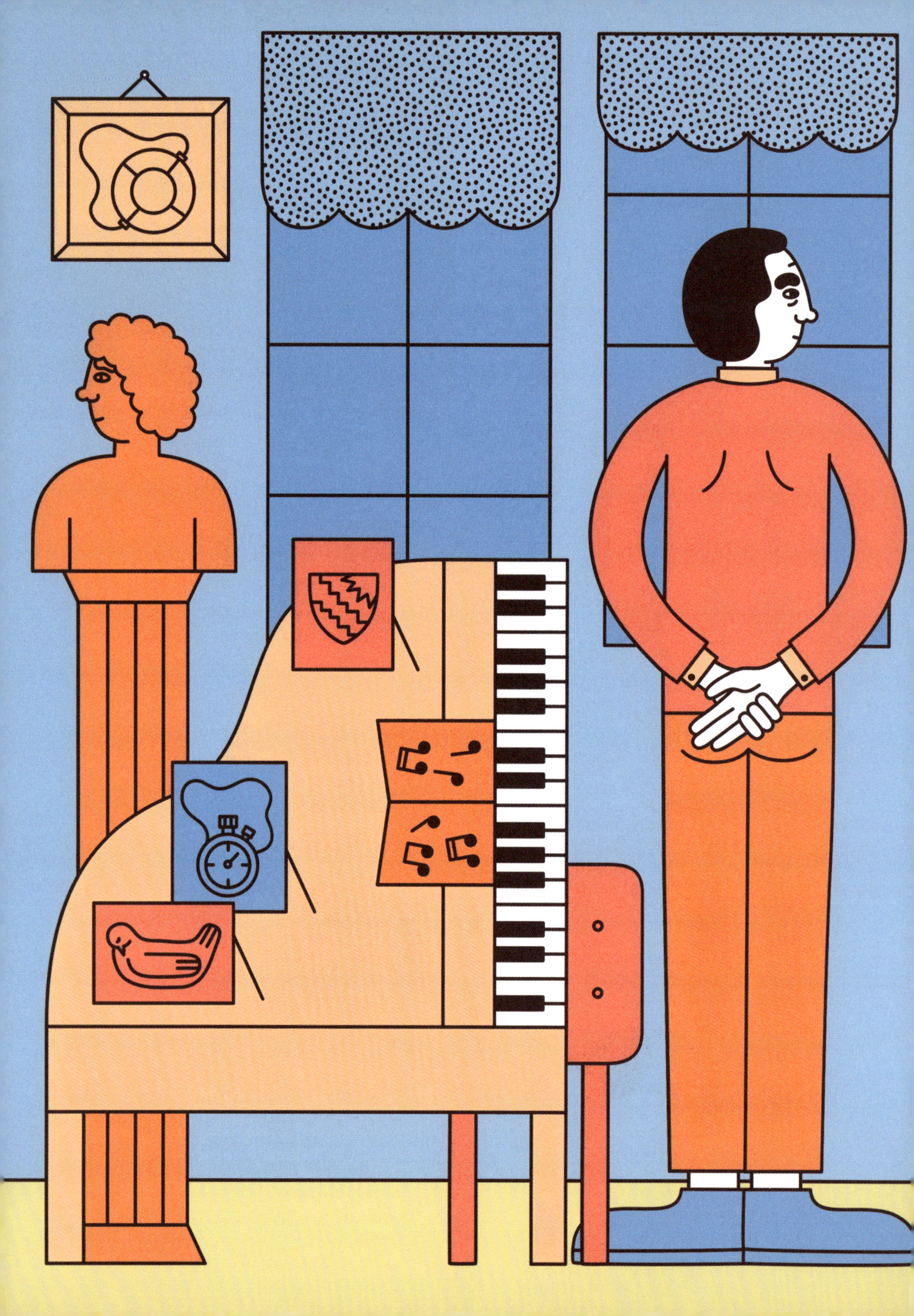

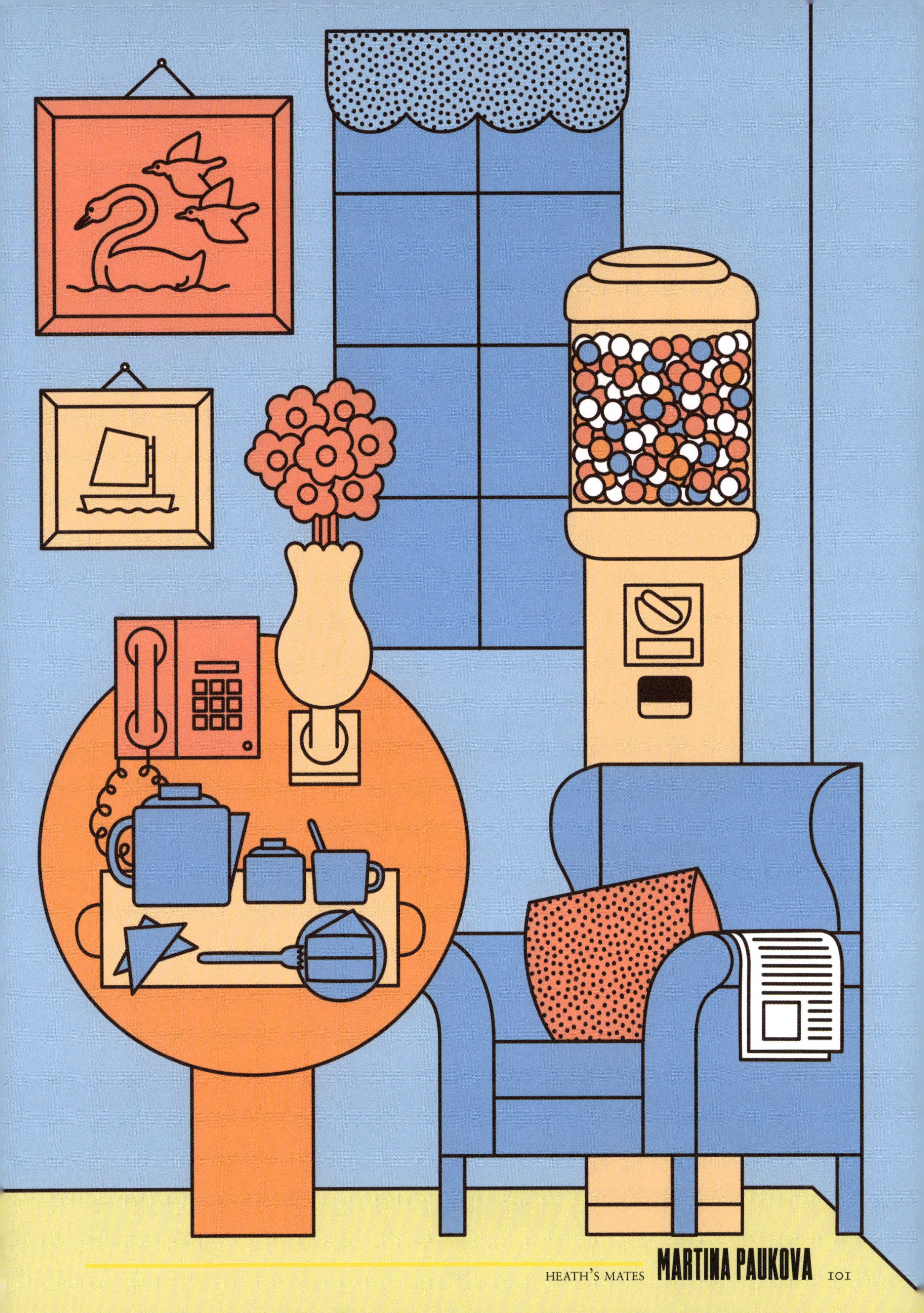

THE HEAVEN OF WESTMINSTER

Once upon a time there was a little god called Dave, who was the leader of the heaven known as Westminster. All the other gods hated little Dave because they wanted to be the leader, but no-one could do anything to get rid of him because Dave was a little prince with his tubby thumbs in every porky-pie. More people were led to believe in Dave, rather than his rival god Ed Face (because of pies) and so it came to pass that Ed Face was cast into the fiery pit of irrelevance in an epic battle that confused pretty much everybody.

Dave remained, telling barefaced lies, stealing the ideas of other gods and continuing to look very plump and shiny. This was a surprise as previous leader gods had a tendency to appear like they'd been punitively starved of sunlight and love after a few years in charge.

With Ed Face out of the way, a human called Promethejez Corbyn – who'd been hiding in the backbenches of heaven for many years prior – stood up and said the word "socialism", to which everyone gasped and got the uncomfortable feeling that something might be missing in their pockets. Then he said the words "refugees, not economic migrants" and everyone screamed "TERRORIST". Many humans liked the sound of Promethejez's words, but they made Dave pull frowny faces. So Dave called the Dismal Council, headed by Murdochistopheles himself – dark lord of Hyperbole, destroyer of nuance – and asked them to unleash the word-harpies to utterly trash Promethejez. Strangely though, none of the harpy attacks worked, because they were all based on utter nonsense, and so Promethejez grew in power.

Will Promethejez succeed in delivering the flame of social democracy to the people? Will we see him gutted by a massive fucking bird? Will Dave ever shake off the reputation as a pork molester? To find out, tune in next time to PROMETHEJEZ.

NEXT: Promethejez and the Limit to the Press' Credibility.

BY CHARLOTTE CHURCH

Singer and campaigner

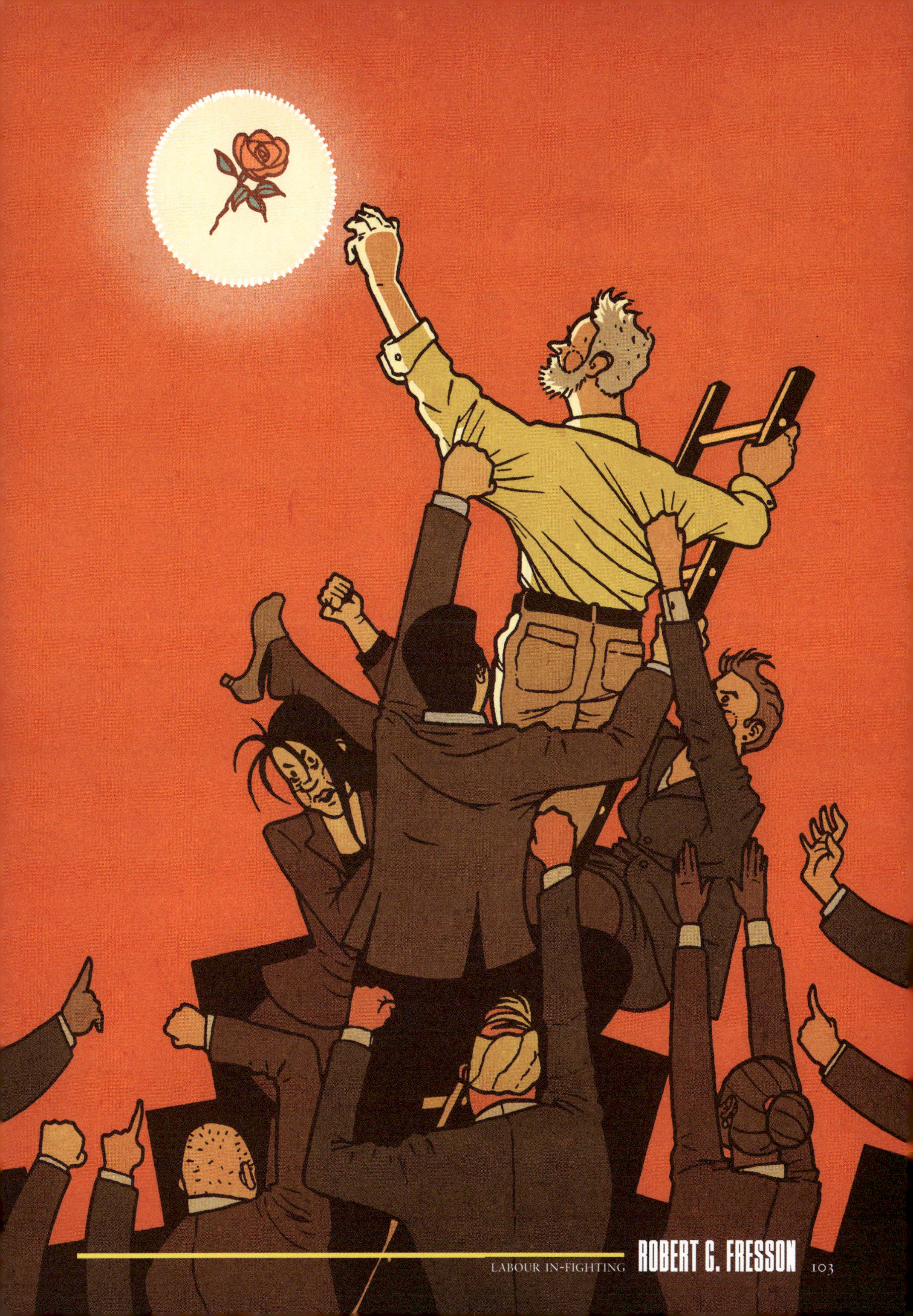

~~PEST~~

~~MIGRANT~~

~~REFUGEE~~

HUMAN

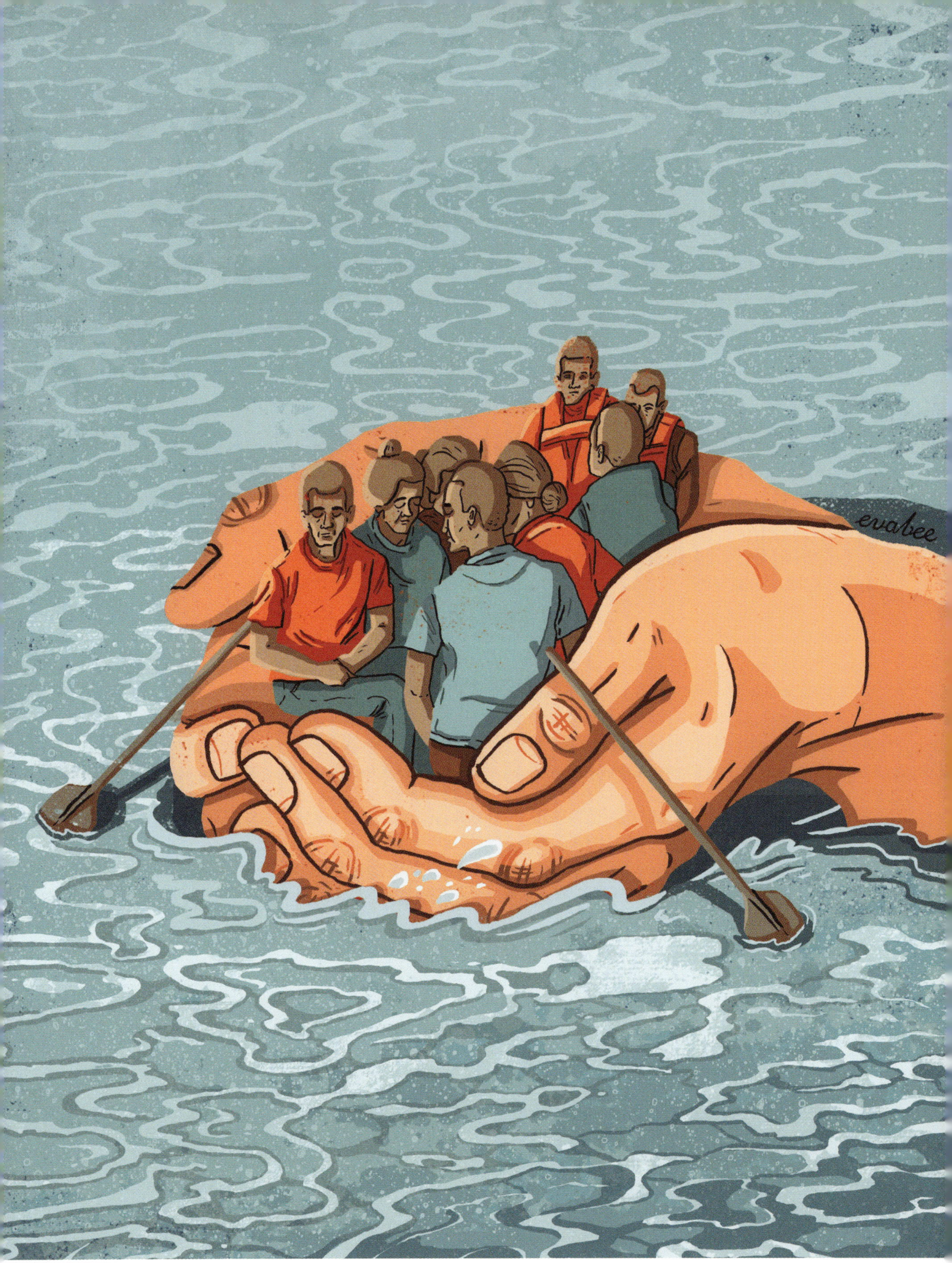
evabee

VIRAL WITCH HUNTS. LIVE TWEETED MURDER SPREES. USER-FILMED NEWS REPORTS. THE INTERNET HAS ALLOWED ALMOST ANYONE TO BECOME A BROADCASTER.

WE ASKED WARREN ELLIS – CREATOR OF CULT FUTURE-JOURNALISM COMIC *TRANSMETROPOLITAN* AND FORMER TECHNOLOGY COLUMNIST FOR *VICE* AND *ESQUIRE* – IF WE SHOULD WORRY.

IF THE INTERNET HAS 'DEMOCRATISED CONTENT', WHERE'S THE DIFFERENTIATION BETWEEN BROADCASTER AND VIEWER?

Citizen journalism doesn't exist in a vacuum. Mainstream, reported or curated news streams haven't gone away. There's no binary condition here. All that's new is that the viewer can also broadcast on a new scale of reach. The relationship is more fluid: the viewer can broadcast and sometimes the broadcasters are just viewers.

MAINSTREAM JOURNALISM IS INFLUENCED BY CORPORATE COMMITMENTS. CITIZEN JOURNALISM IS INFLUENCED BY PERSONAL BIAS. HOW CAN WE KNOW WHAT TO TRUST?

All journalism is subjective on some level. Hunter S. Thompson once said that if you want pure objective journalism, install and watch a CCTV camera. I think this is one reason why dashcam footage fascinates a lot of people. In the last century, those in television, over and over again, had to tell people 'television is not your parent'. You choose what enters your world through your media devices. If you grow up with the inability to make decisions about trust and truth for yourself, your problems are probably bigger than news provision.

IS THERE SUCH A THING AS TOO MUCH NEWS?

Twenty-four hour TV news cycles have shown that, in fact, there is less reportable news than the audience can take. Just look at the crap that CNN or BBC News 24 fill their schedules with. It's worth considering that news is only one part of our media diet – a thing we dip in and out of during the day. In this respect, there is probably never enough strong, wide reportage.

WHAT DOES IT SAY ABOUT SOCIETY THAT MILLIONS OF PEOPLE WATCH MURDER CLIPS ON YOUTUBE?

The same thing it said when it was about people attending public executions or touring asylums on Sundays. The internet doesn't change people, it's just a newer way to mediate the things that were already, always, in us.

IS THERE A CASE FOR CENSORING THE INTERNET, SO THAT PEOPLE CAN'T UPLOAD CONTENT SUCH AS SNUFF VIDEOS?

No. Who does the censoring? Who does the moderation? How can that ever be a pure and reasonable process? Yes, there is a case for a mechanism that decides what ISN'T news. I don't need newsflashes about Kanye breaking a nail being pushed to my phone. But once you get into that notion you're inducing amnesia upon the record, and that becomes very dangerous very quickly.

Yes, videos of people being beheaded are awful and the reasons why they're uploaded are awful. But those two separate acts should not be forgotten. They should not be treated as if they never happened. I'm not saying that we should all be forced to bear witness. But perhaps somebody should bear witness. And the record should show that it happened, and why.

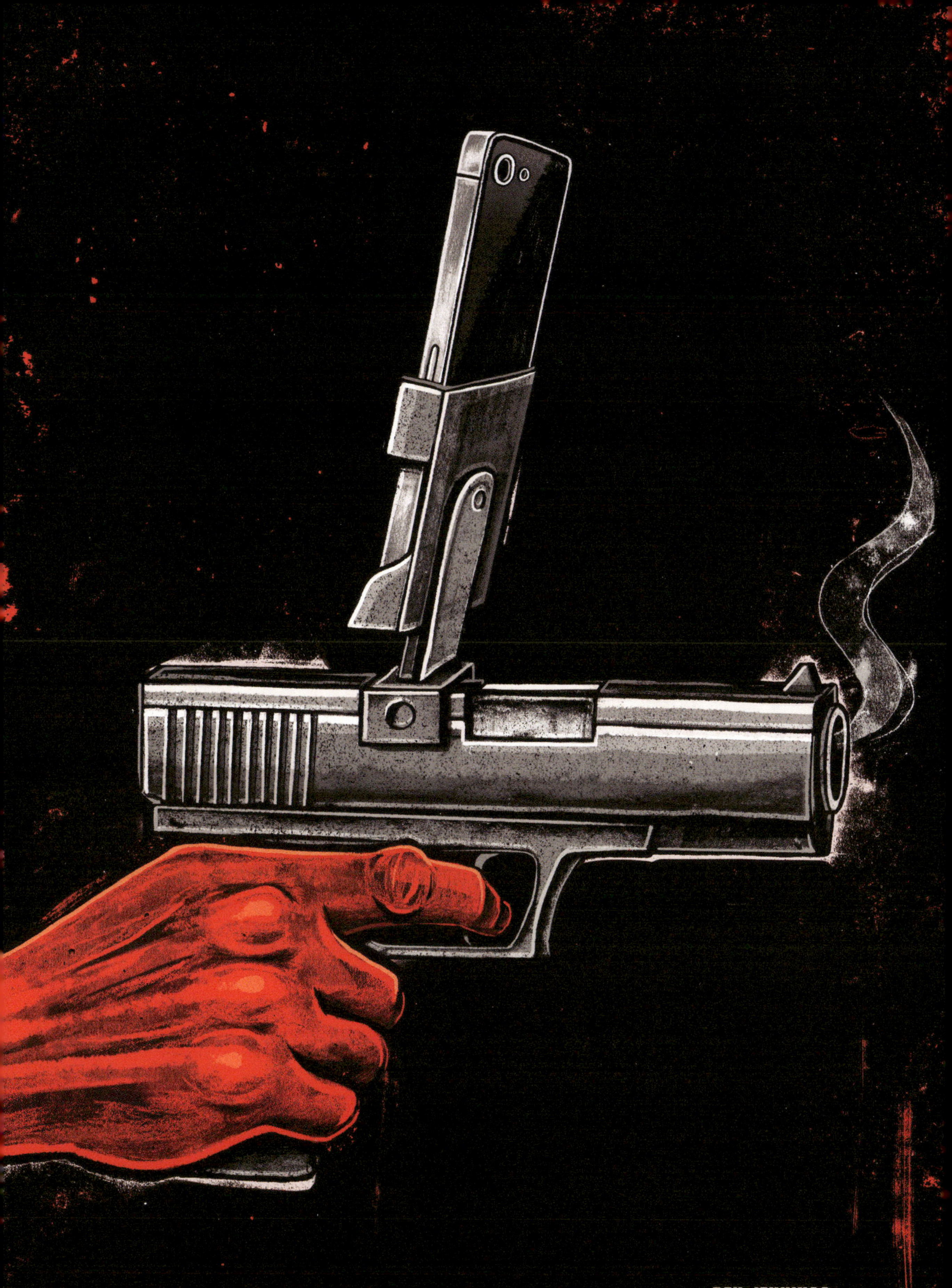

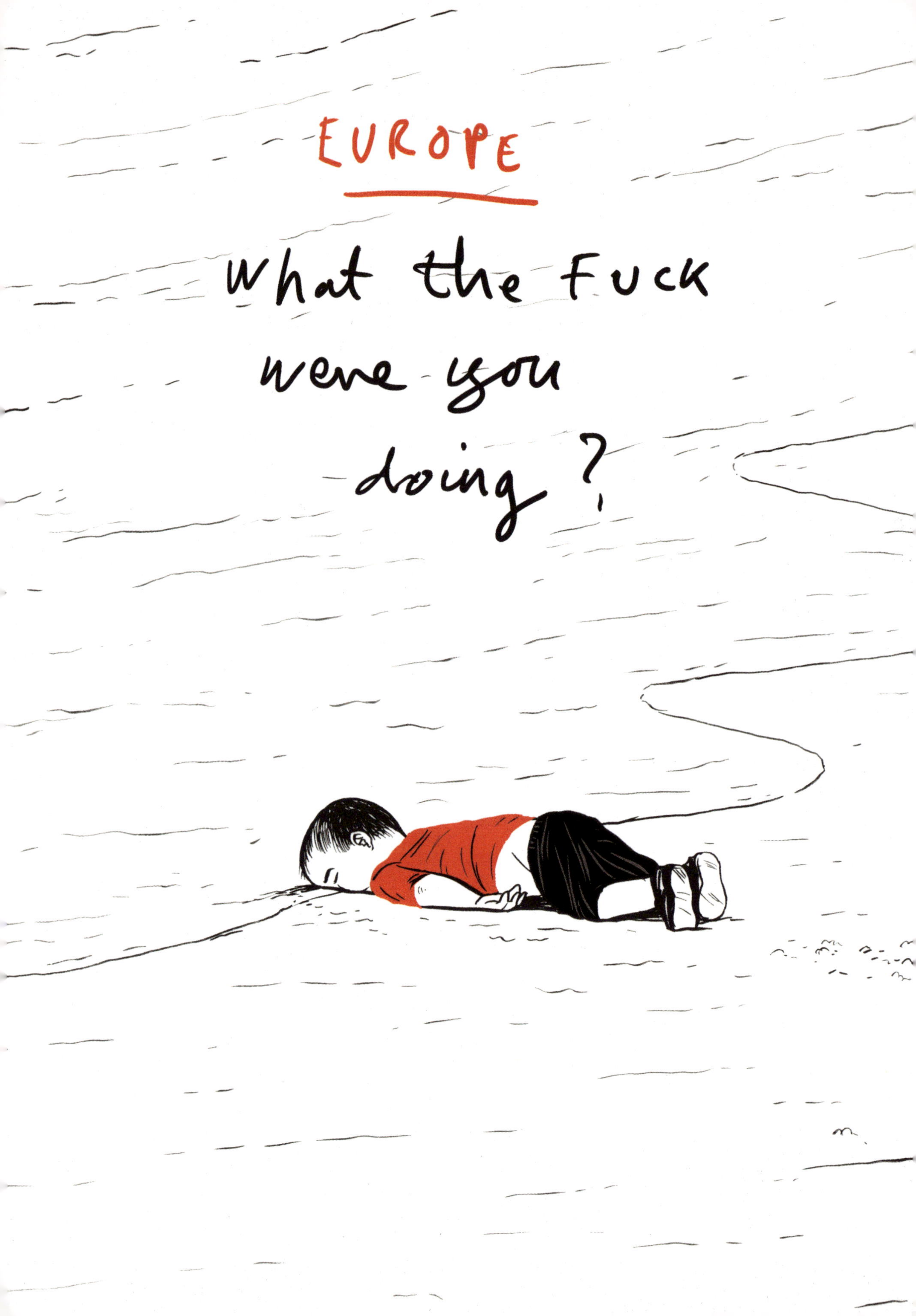
EUROPE
What the Fuck
were you
doing?

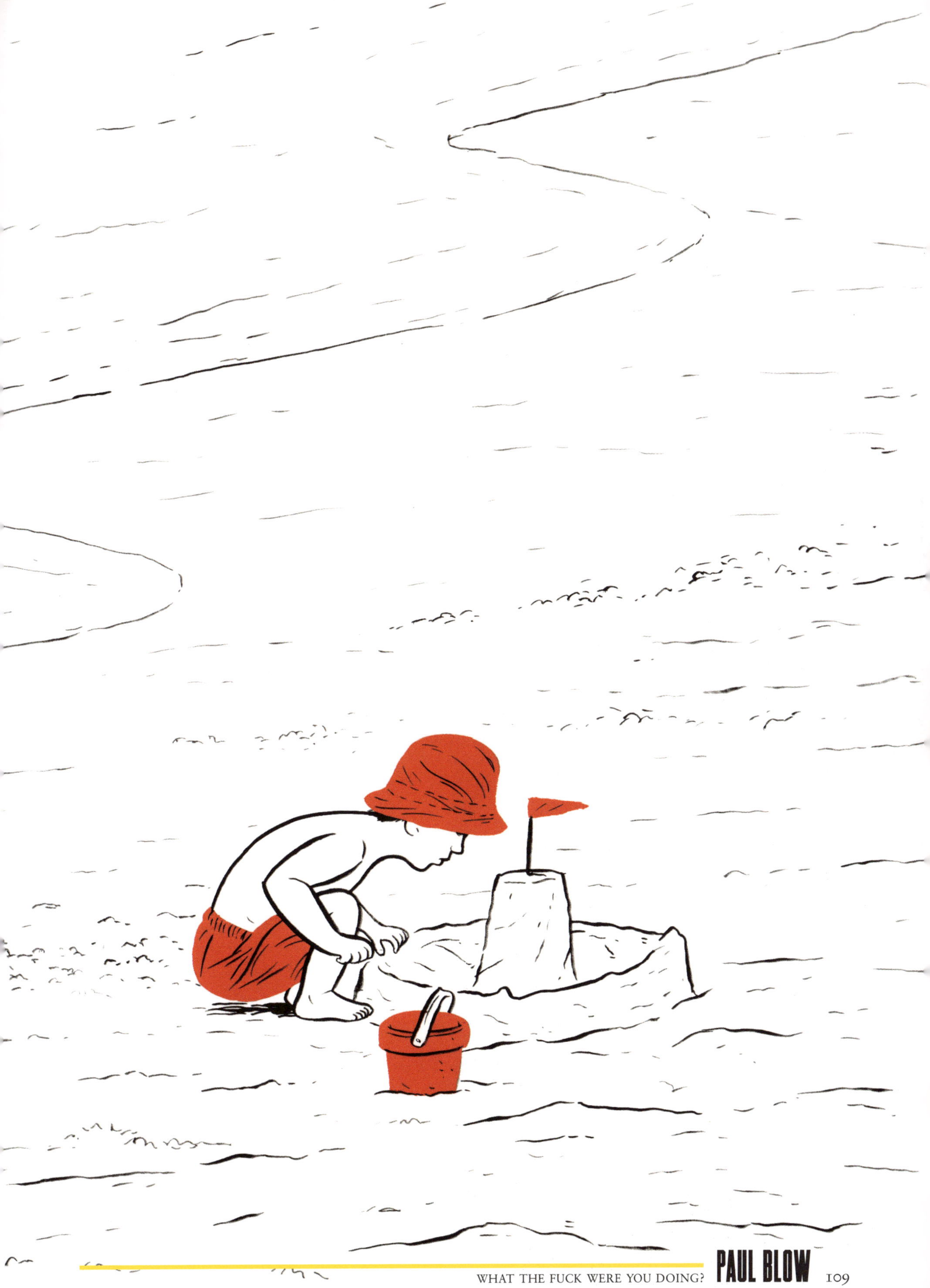

BEN THE ILLUSTRATOR

YAKUZA SPLIT / 7–13 SEPTEMBER

"The Yakuza break-up isn't just a story of in-fighting, but a human interest story. Tattoos are one of the most known elements of the Yakuza culture. In my piece, the tattoo breaks the tradition of not tattooing down the centre of the torso, much like how members of Yamaguchi-gumi broke the faithfulness within their syndicate and now find themselves forming a new gang."

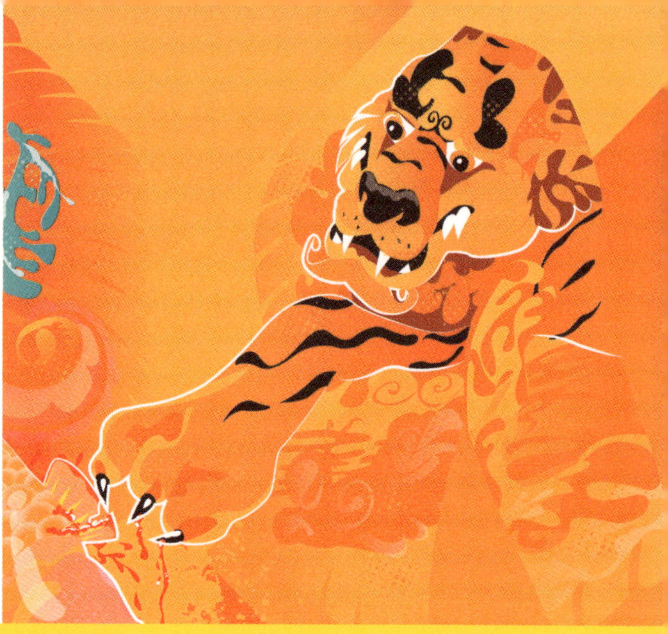

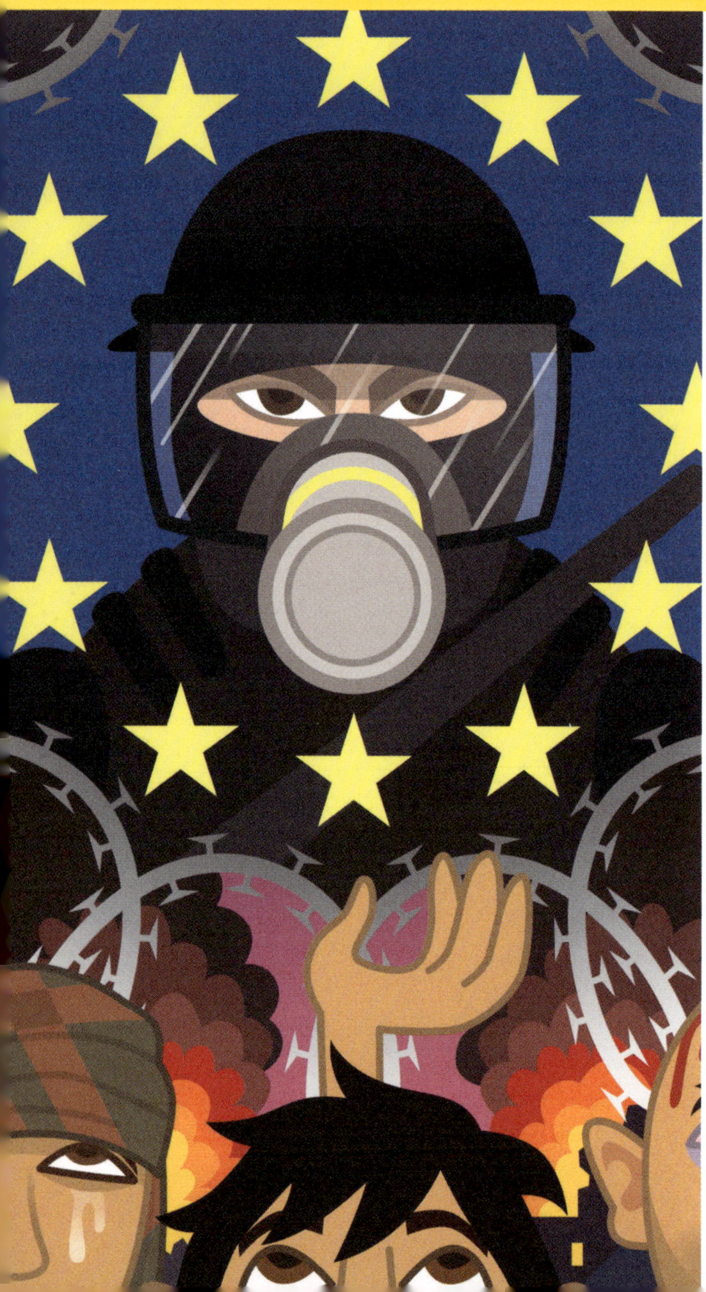

PETE FOWLER

THIS SHOULDN'T BE HAPPENING / 14–20 SEPTEMBER

"I decided to focus on the plight of refugees on the border to Hungary and the riot and chaos that followed the closing of the border, with the Hungarian police responding in, some would say, a heavy handed manner.

"My work rarely touches on real world events. Although I have a very keen interest in what's going on, I tend to draw mostly from my imagination. But recently I've been looking for some way to respond, as a human, to what's going on around us. You can't get away from the mess that's being made. With a purely emotional take on our fellow humans' struggles, I wanted to portray the situation, perhaps sitting to one side of the fence a little, I must admit.

"My initial thoughts when watching the story unfold via Twitter and news sites was 'this shouldn't be happening'. I don't think I can really say more than that to be honest."

MARK LONG

PIGGATE / 21–27 SEPTEMBER

"I was tempted to draw something explicit. The allegations are unsubstantiated, but that hasn't stopped everyone being amused by it. It doesn't matter if Cameron did it or not, it's just funny. Even if he didn't do it, we all think those Bullingdon boys are a bunch of wankers doing equally irritating things anyway."

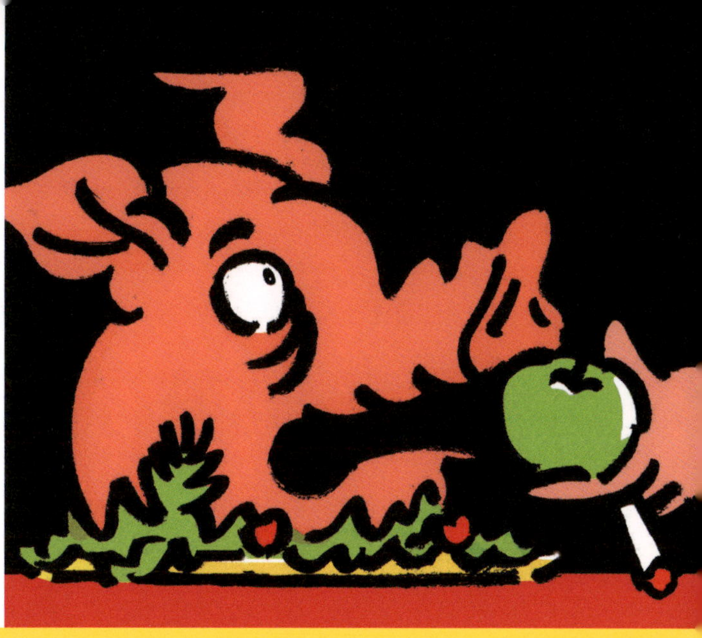

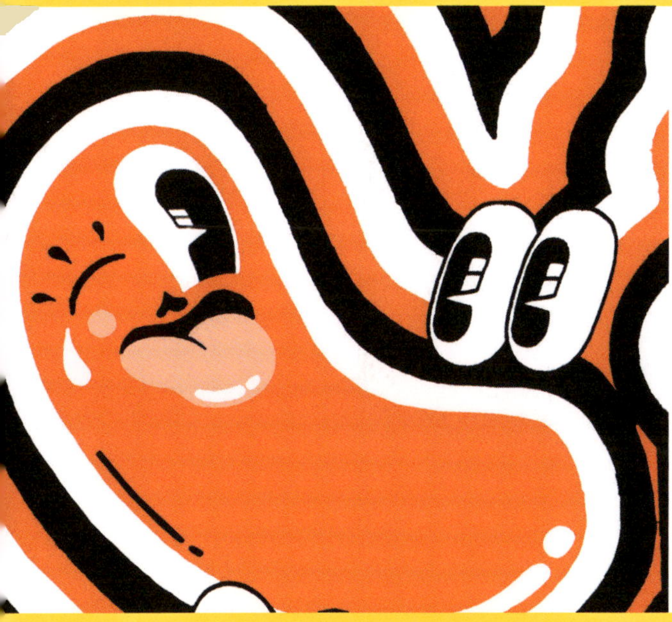

HATTIE STEWART

KIM KARDASHIAN EATS CHEETOS / 28 SEPTEMBER–4 OCTOBER

"After being inundated with articles about the Kardashians, I decided to create a satirical illustration based upon what I believe to be the most important article from the *Daily Mail – Kim Kardashian admits to eating Cheetos whilst pregnant with Kanye West's son.*"

SIMON SPILSBURY

ROLLING NEWS / 5–11 OCTOBER

"Daily news generally bores the crap out of me. I tend to be more interested in the newsreaders and weather forecasters, so I staged the illustration in the newsroom, so the news is delivered in words first and pictures second. I deliberately drew in a chaotic fashion as I imagine a newsreader's job is just that."

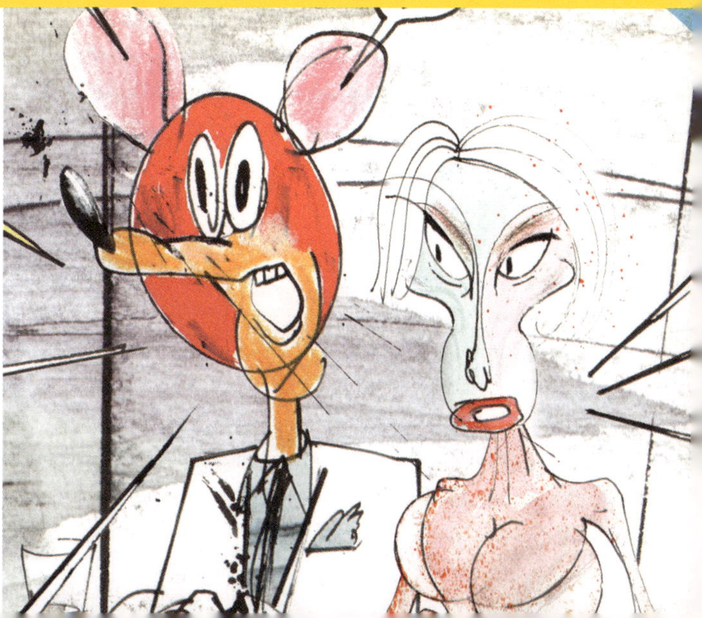

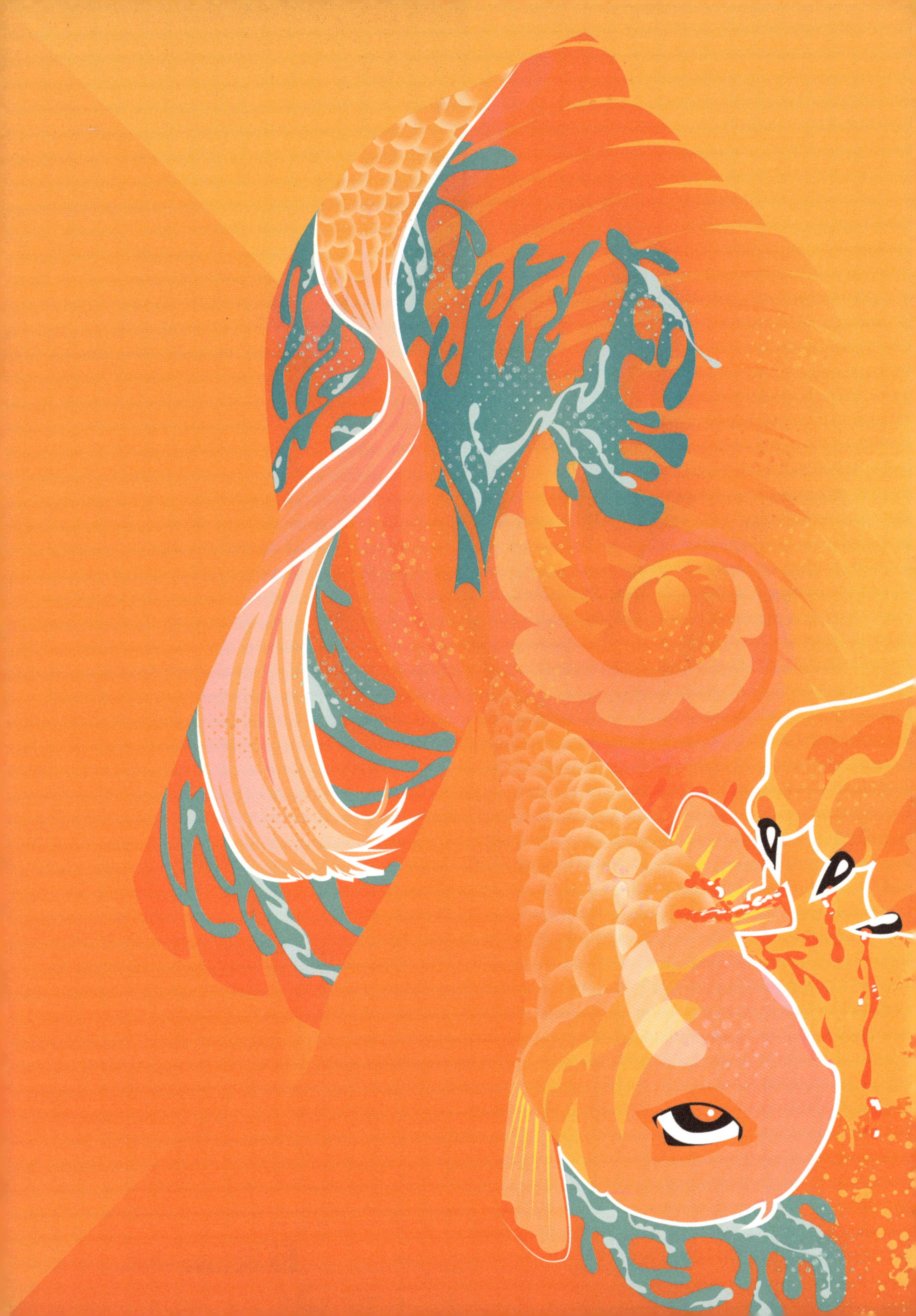

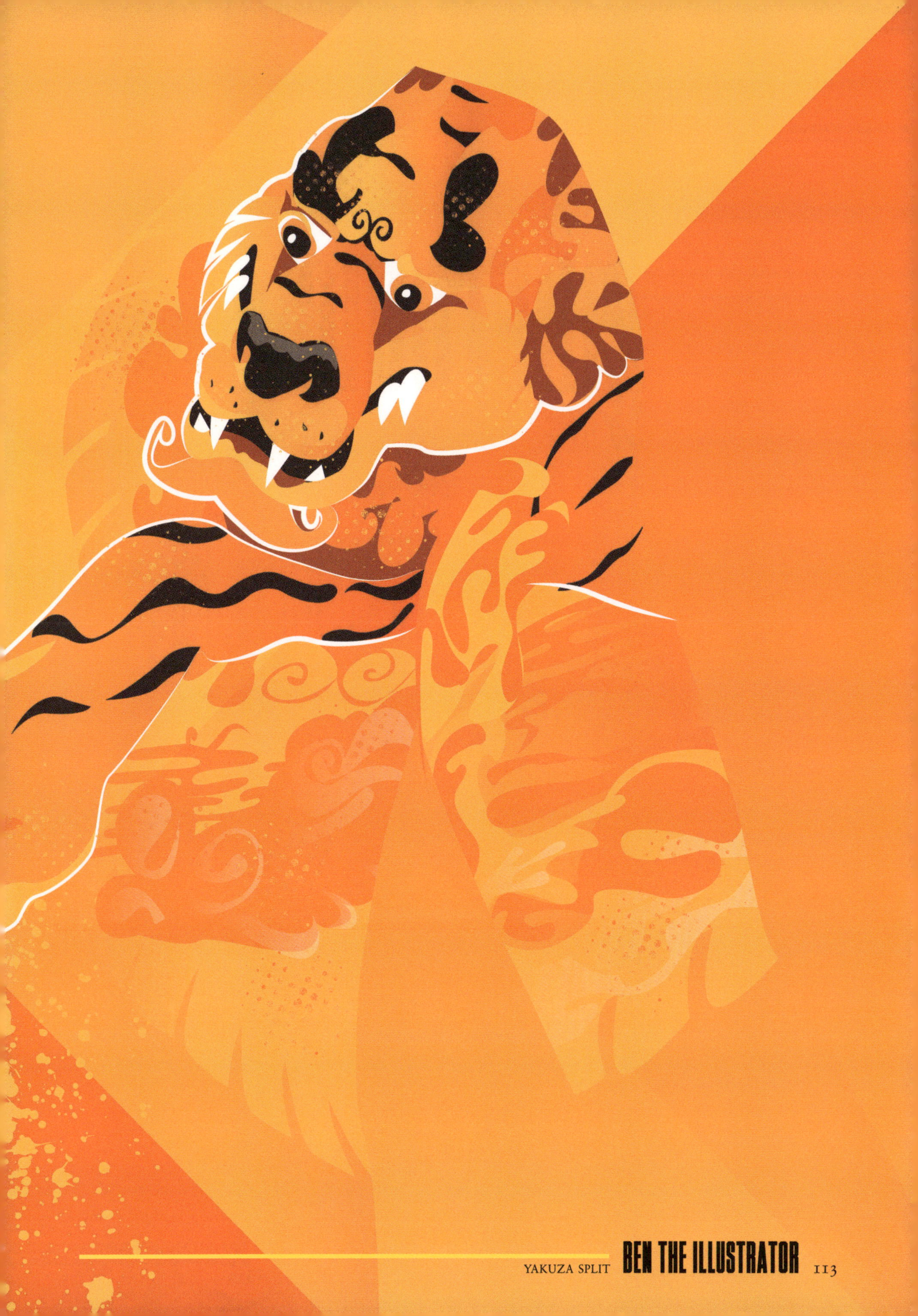

RHETORIC

Refugees are the inevitable losers of every invasion, occupation and war throughout history. This year, after a decade of Western misadventures in the Middle East, civilians from across Syria, Iraq and Afghanistan fled their homes in search of safer lands and European shores. The response from our politicians and media outlets was to call them 'swarms' and 'plagues'.

It's important we see the mainstream media as an extension of the political cartel; a conferred group of white men whose purpose is to uphold the policies of a staunch right-wing Government. The vitriol that surrounded desperate families seeking refuge culminated in the constant use of the word 'migrant'. Rather then being an accident, it was a deliberate attempt to sabotage their reputation – pushing the idea that these destitute refugees were travelling with self-serving economic interests at heart.

I'm still in two minds as to how beneficial the sharing of macabre images can be, such as Aylan Kurdi's infant body washed up on a Turkish beach. Are we simply trying to lessen our personal guilt by conveniently pinning images to social network feeds or if there is something to be lauded in trying to raise awareness?

One positive thing to come from that tragic photograph is that, as Kurdi's father stated, the world was offered a harrowing view into the reality of refugees, those ordinary men and women who are simply looking for somewhere safer to live.

Some artists feel they should be exempt from making political points in their work. I don't believe in direct obligation per se, nor do I think anyone has the right to dictate the nature of another's art. Yet we do have a collective responsibility, as the art that any society produces does not live in a vacuum. Every piece of artwork is somehow interconnected through its politics and intent, so if artists used their platform to steer the minds of people to think more critically, we could maybe become a catalyst for change. Historically, people have always yearned for alternatives and I feel art creates a more palatable platform to put forward progressive ideas, in ways that live outside the duplicity and spectacle of politics.

BY ANTHONY ANAXAGOROU

Poet, writer and founder of Out-Spoken

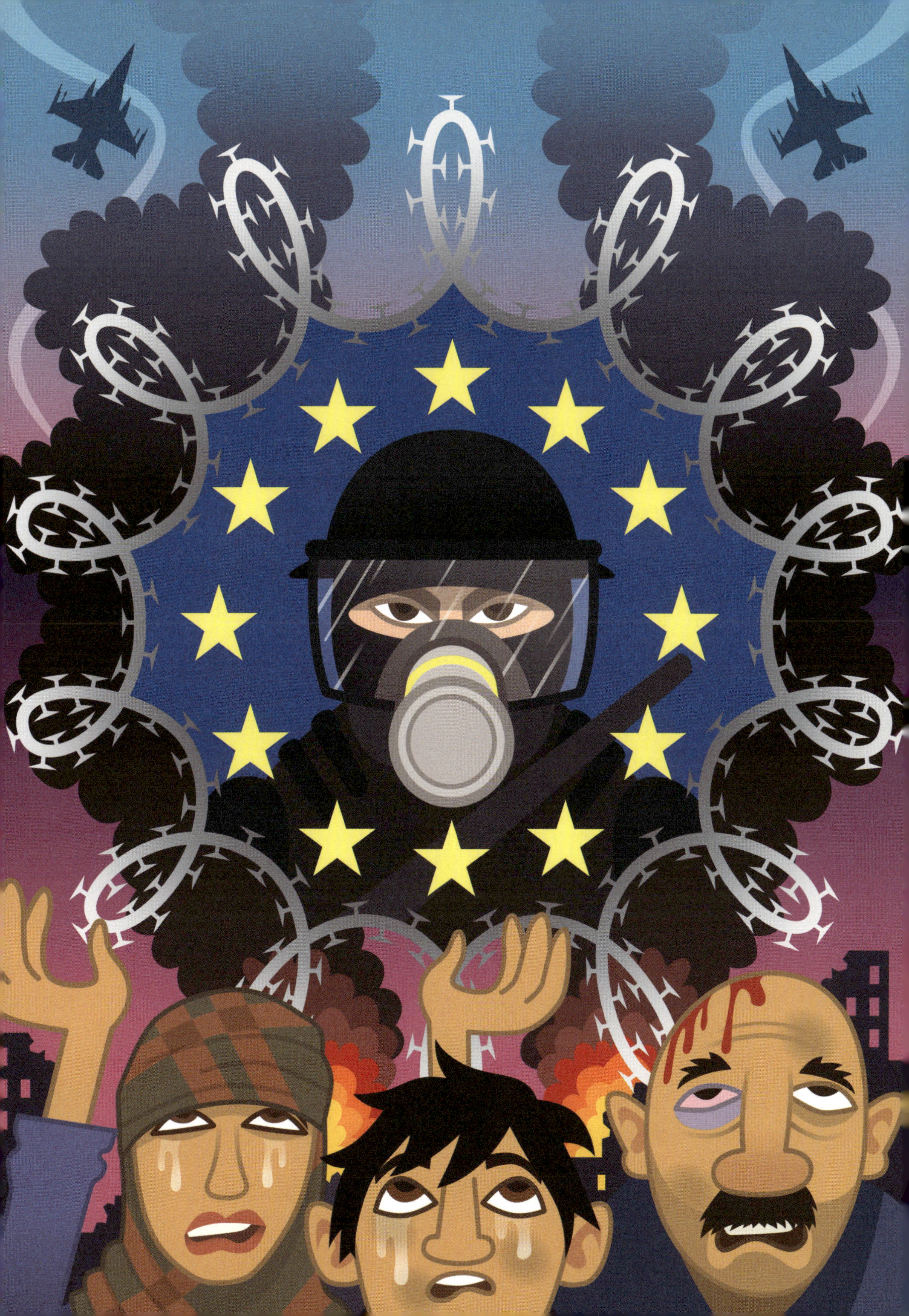

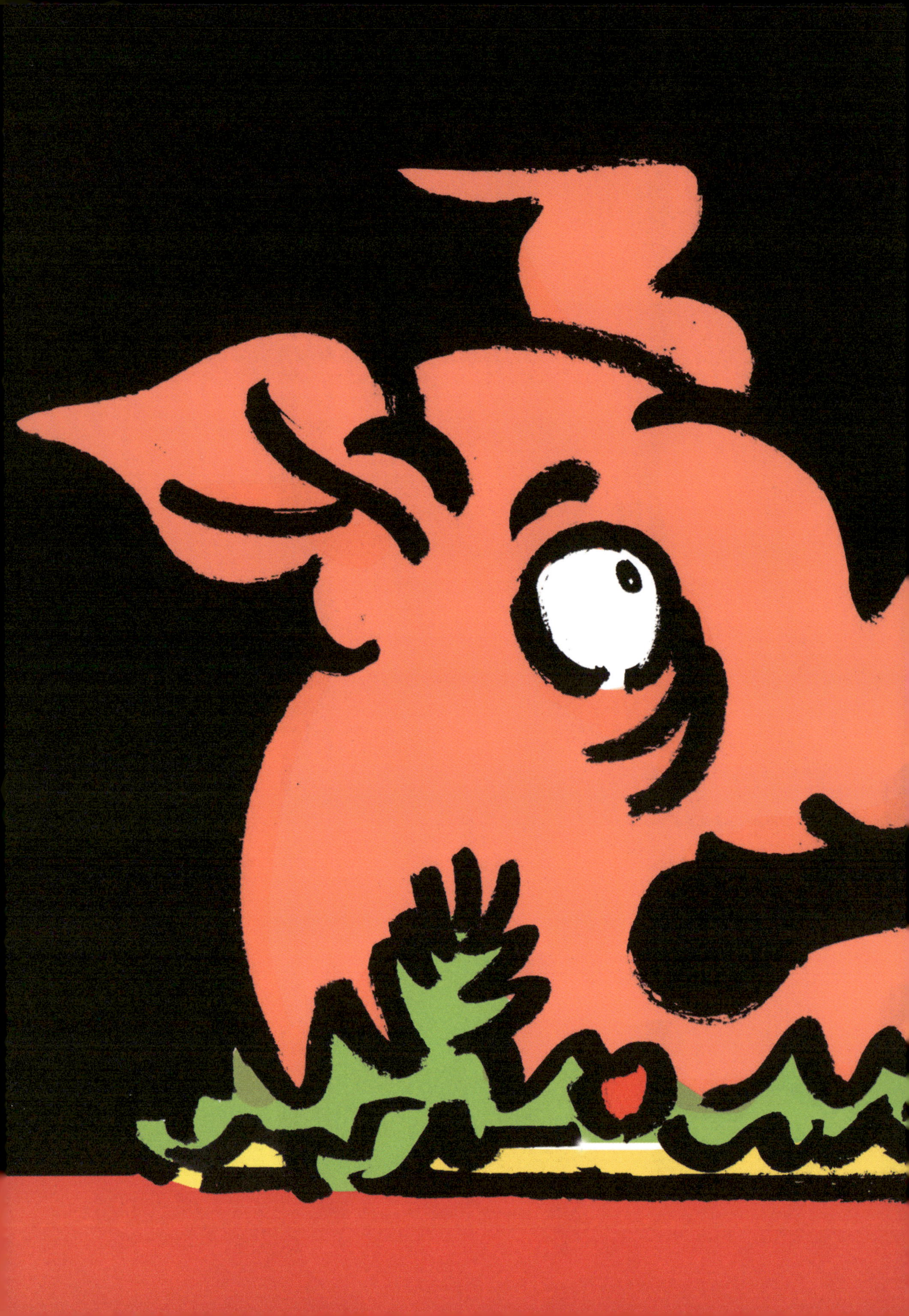

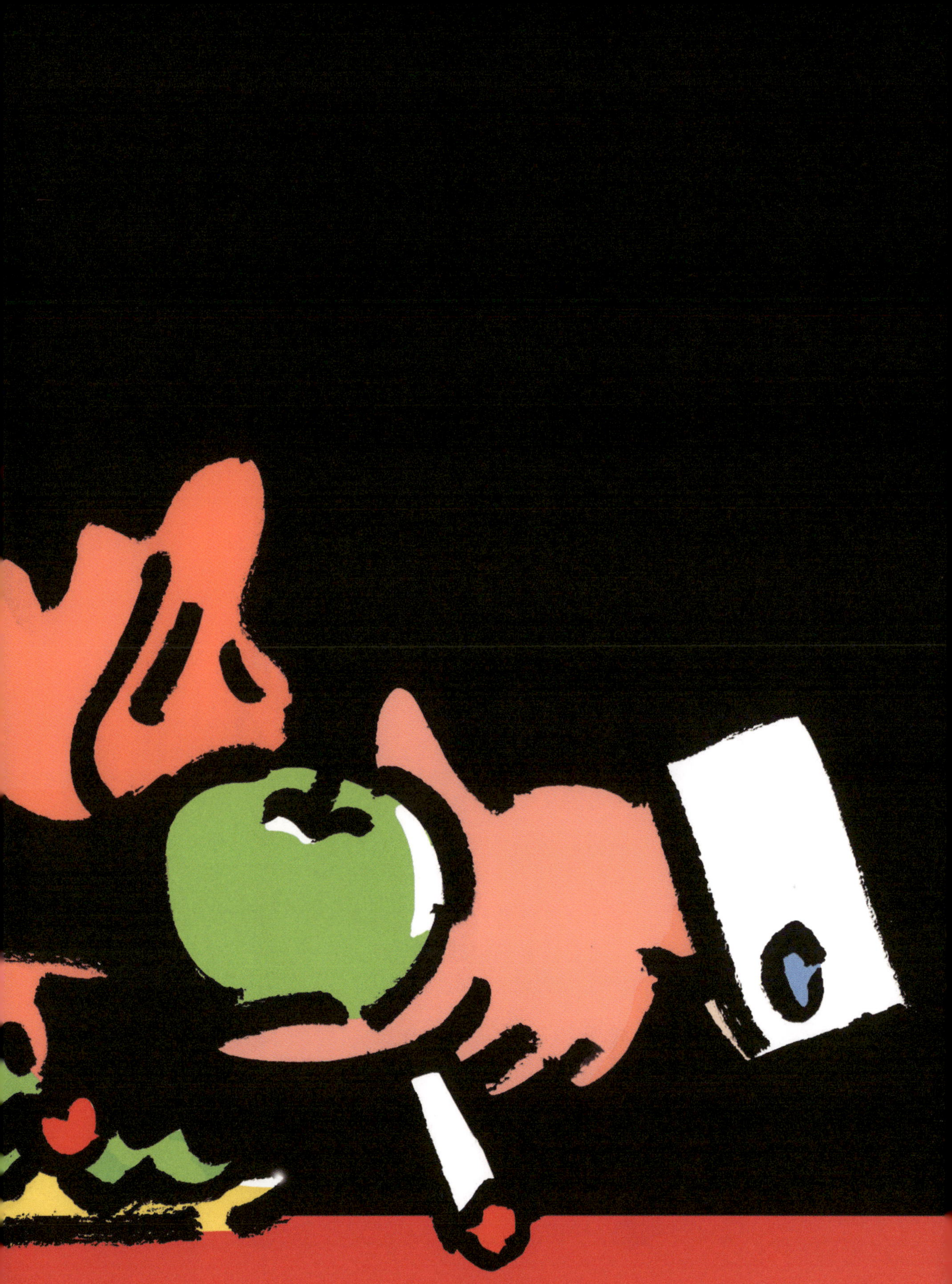

"THE NICE THING ABOUT BEING A CELEBRITY — IS THAT WHEN YOU B O R E PEOPLE, THEY THINK IT'S THEIR FAULT."

HENRY KISSINGER

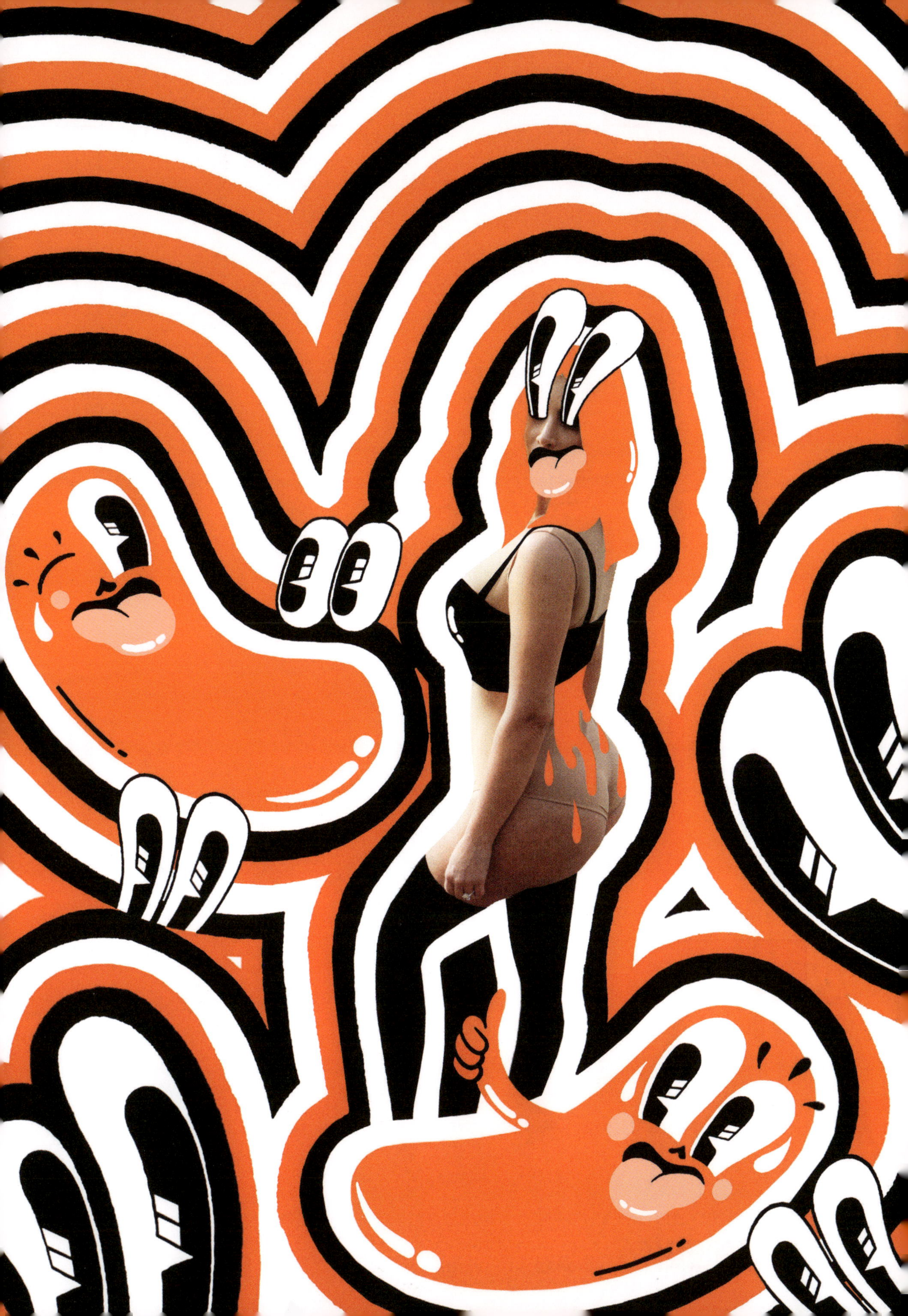

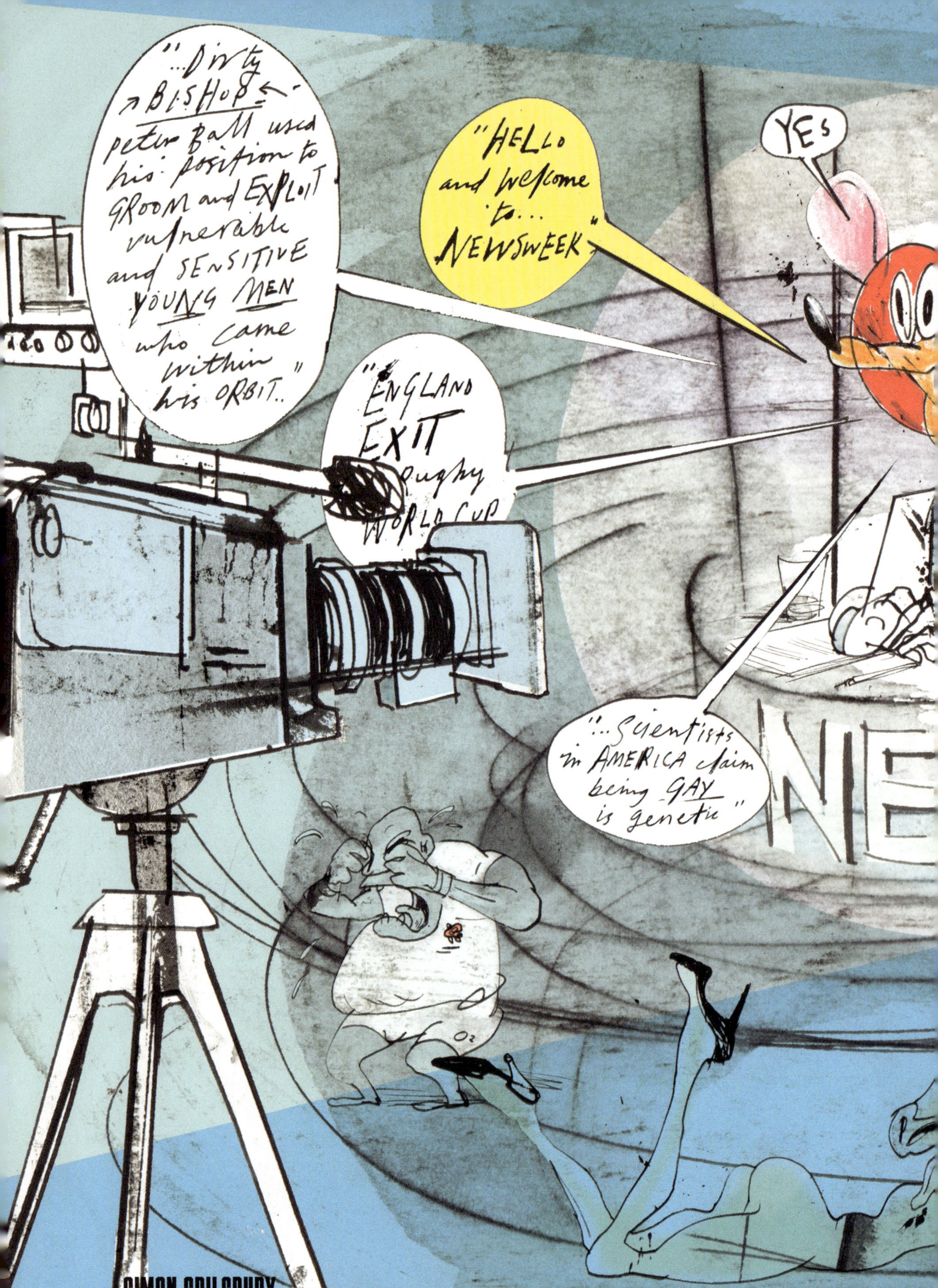
"...Dirty →BISHOP← peter Ball used his position to GROOM and EXPLOIT vulnerable and SENSITIVE YOUNG MEN who came within his ORBIT.."
"HELLO and welcome to... NEWSWEEK"
YES
"ENGLAND EXIT ughy WORLD CUP
"...Scientists in AMERICA claim being GAY is genetic"
NE

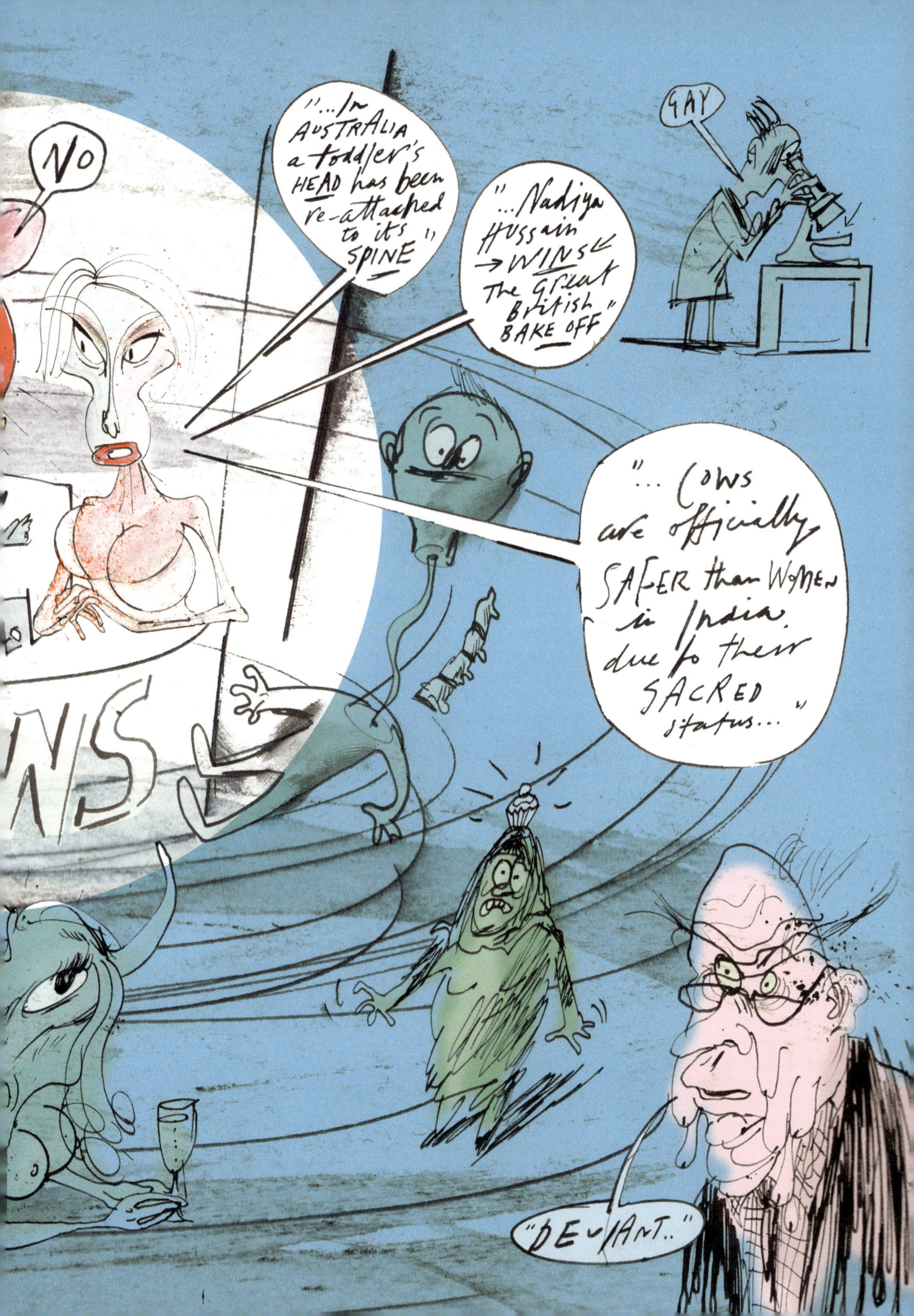
NO
"...In AUSTRALIA a toddler's HEAD has been re-attached to it's SPINE"
"...Nadiya Hussain WINS The Great British BAKE OFF"
GAY
"... COWS are officially SAFER than WOMEN in India due to their SACRED status..."
"DEVIANT.."

MALIKA FAVRE

PLAYBOY COVER-UP / 12–18 OCTOBER

"Reading the news is something that gets me down 95% of the time, so I knew I wanted to tackle something that would be positive. I read that *Playboy* was no longer going to expose nude pictures inside the magazine. I knew I had found my perfect news for *Yellow*.

"This decision comes at a time where porn is pretty much everywhere and doesn't exactly trigger the same reaction as when the magazine was founded in the fifties. After experimenting with initial ideas, I decided on a very minimalistic approach: zipping up the magazine cover itself to get the message across. Sometimes less is more, especially when it comes to sexiness and sensuality, so I wanted the approach to also reflect that."

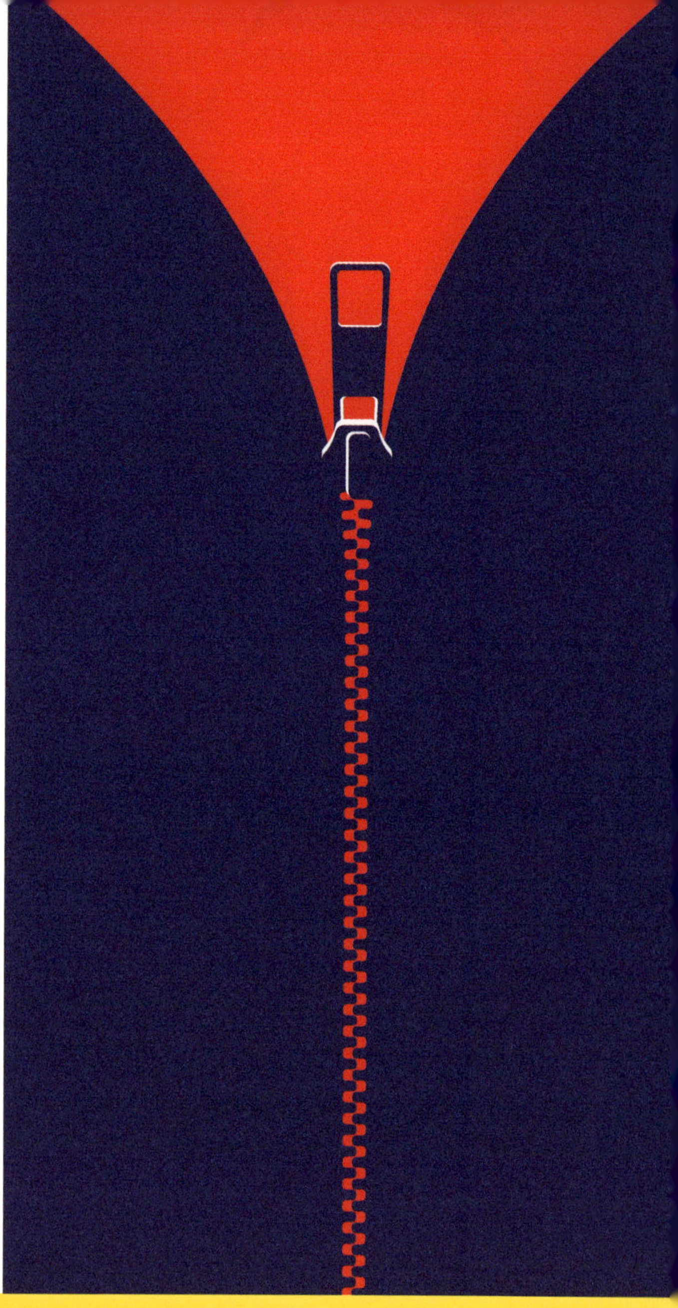

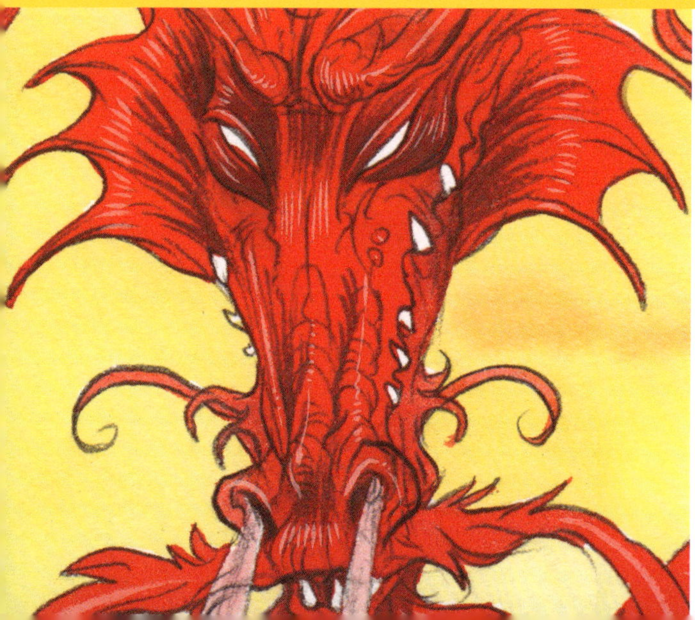

CHRIS RIDDELL

KOWTOW / 19–25 OCTOBER

"The first published cartoon I ever drew was of a Chinese Dragon clutching Hong Kong. That was in 1988. Some things don't change and I don't believe that human rights are ever a luxury that governments can choose to ignore. That pig's head is a gift that keeps on giving!"

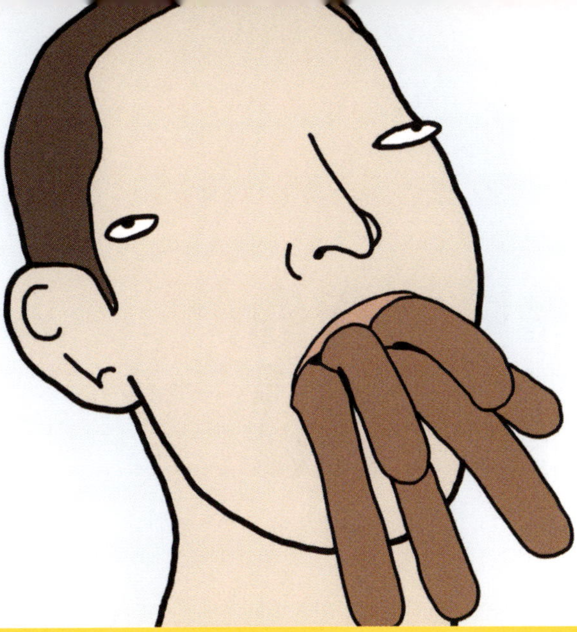

CHRIS SIMPSONSARTIST

CANCER SAUSAGES / 26 OCTOBER–1 NOVEMBER

"I did something about scientists finding out that sausages kill people now, and after all of these years of people thinking that sausages are a type of fruit, they've just found out that they actually contain a harmful poison in them that causes people to melt away."

MATTHEW THE HORSE

BRITISH CUCUMBERS / 2–8 NOVEMBER

"British cucumbers are dying out. It's a seemingly silly story, but as with most things, it's a signifier of a bigger issue: this time corporate greed. I wanted an image to decode and make sense of something that's immediate. When the profit-driven supermarkets have destroyed all our farms, I'll be sad."

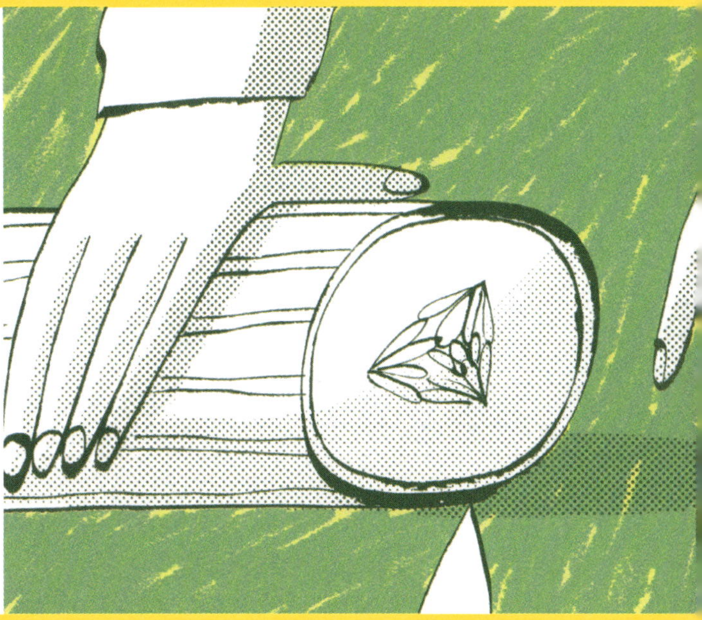

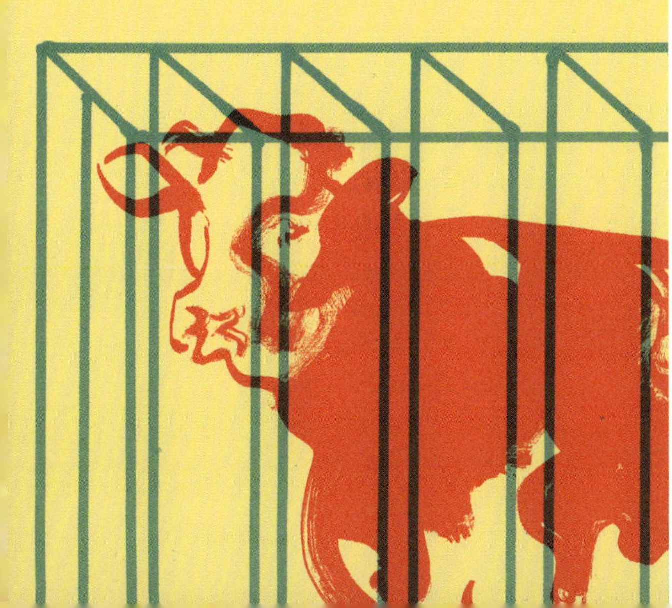

BRIAN GRIMWOOD

KILLER COWS / 9–15 NOVEMBER

"I was attracted by the 'killer cow' news story in *The Times* newspaper, where farmers are being told to protect walkers from their cattle. Apparently four walkers were trampled by cows in summer 2015, 74 in the past 15 years! Fortunately, I like drawing cows."

MEDIA TRUTHS

From music videos to TV adverts, billboards to magazine stands, the wallpaper of our daily lives reinforces a clear message: that women are decorative consumables. Whether it's a nameless model or a female celebrity, a headless torso or bottom, women's bodies are used anywhere and everywhere to sell just about anything. We are slim and airbrushed to perfection, we are overwhelmingly white, young, very slim, often with large breasts. We are posed and passive, and whilst we may be increasingly joined by a number of equally elite male counterparts, they are generally portrayed as more active and less vulnerable.

Despite the recent removal of Page 3, the topless image of a young woman that for 43 years graced the third page of the UK's best-selling newspaper, what we find is still far removed from the real lives of women in our society. Instead, both online and in print, our newspapers are packed with men in suits and sportswear, featured for their abilities and their talents. Women feature far less, and are likely to be posed rather than active, with the focus on their clothing or the lack of. The emphasis is on appearance rather than achievement, just look at male-dominated sports pages for evidence of that.

If our media portrayed the truth about women, it could have a profound effect on the aspirations of young girls. If we showed women as active rather than passive, talented and able rather than decorative, then women might be taken more seriously in the workplace. They might even receive equal pay. If our diversity was celebrated, rather than portraying a narrow 'perfection', girls might be less unhappy with their bodies and less likely to starve or abuse them. If women were treated by the media as full people rather than parts or things, we could begin to change the attitudes that allow women to be dehumanised and abused. History shows us that the sexual stereotyping of women is linked to violence against us. Sadly, without some much-needed changes, the media doesn't just lie about us, it contributes to our continued abuse and subordination.

BY LISA CLARKE

No More Page 3 Campaign

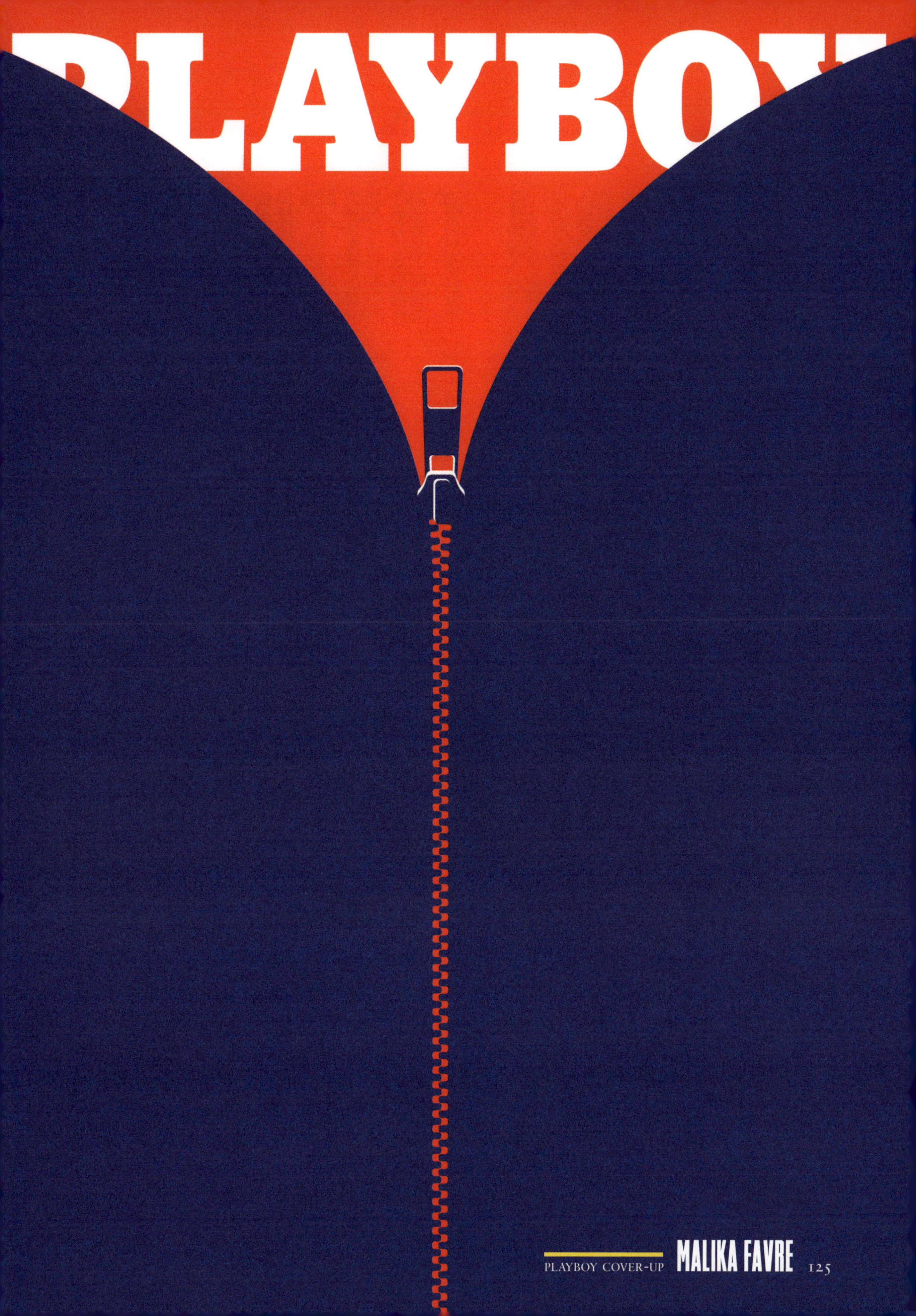

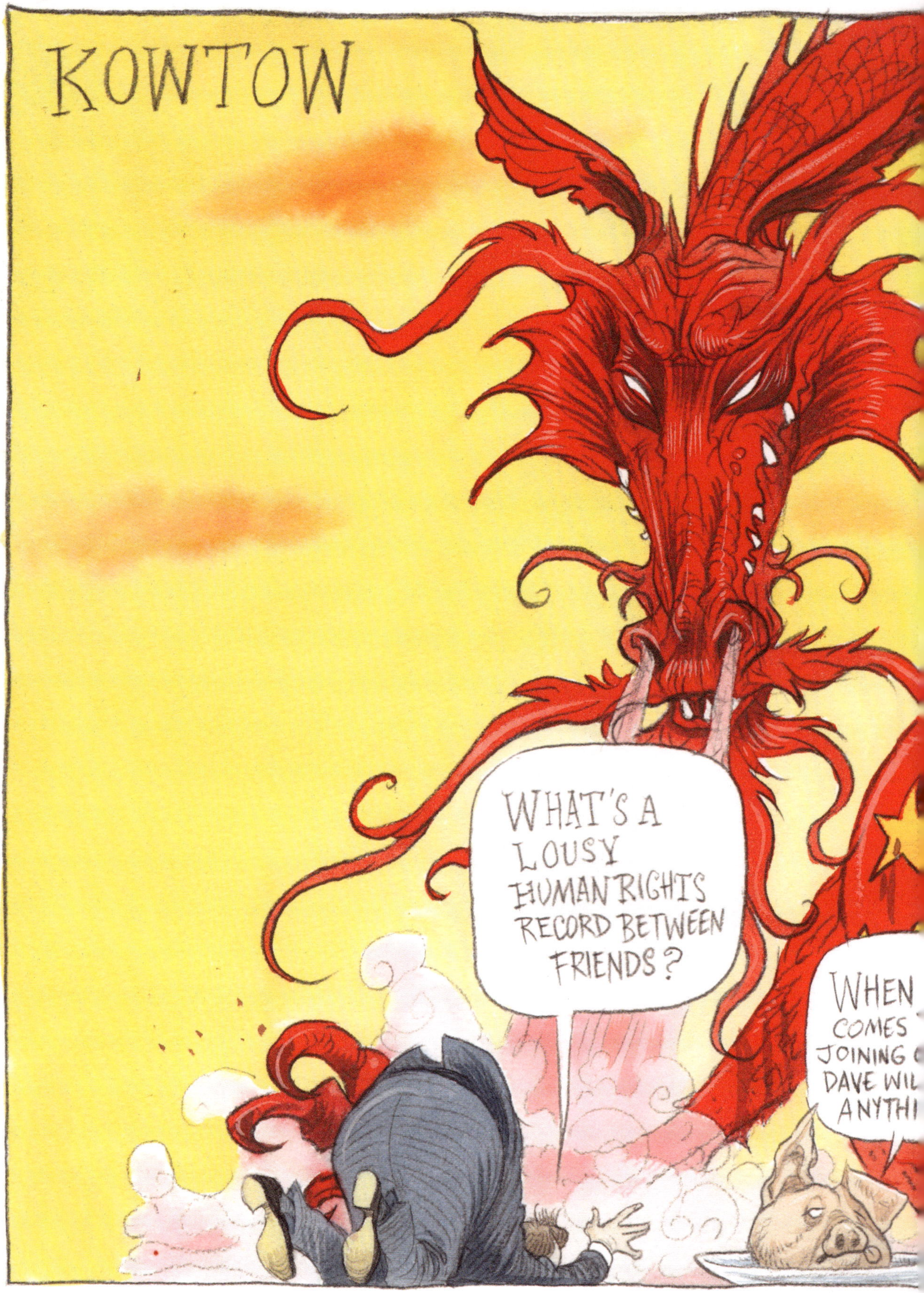
KOWTOW
WHAT'S A LOUSY HUMAN RIGHTS RECORD BETWEEN FRIENDS?
WHEN
COMES
JOINING
DAVE WIL
ANYTHI

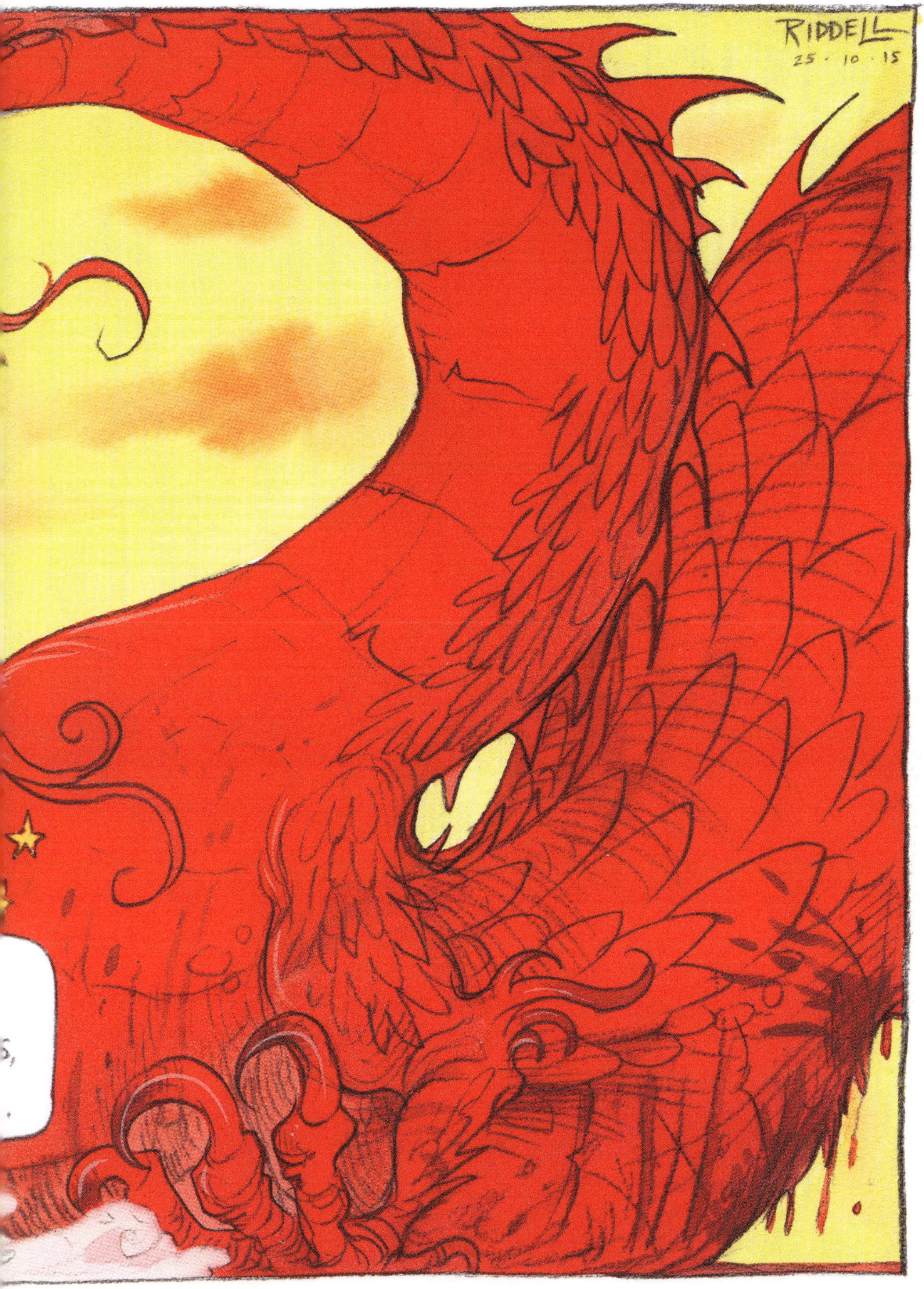
RIDDELL
25 · 10 · 15

do you want to die

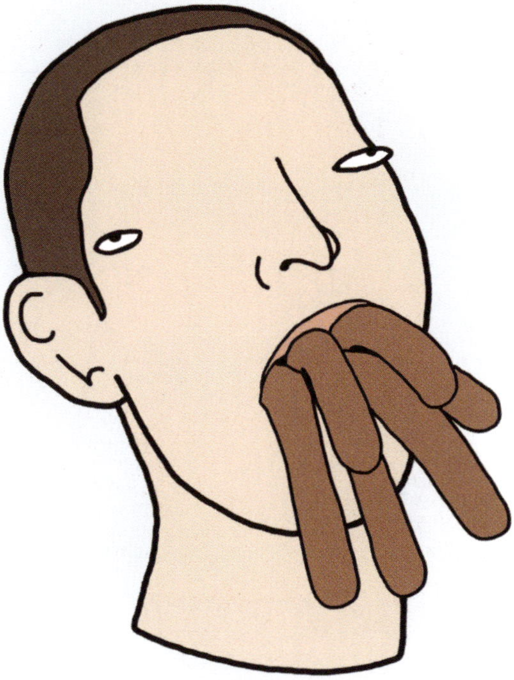

why papa why

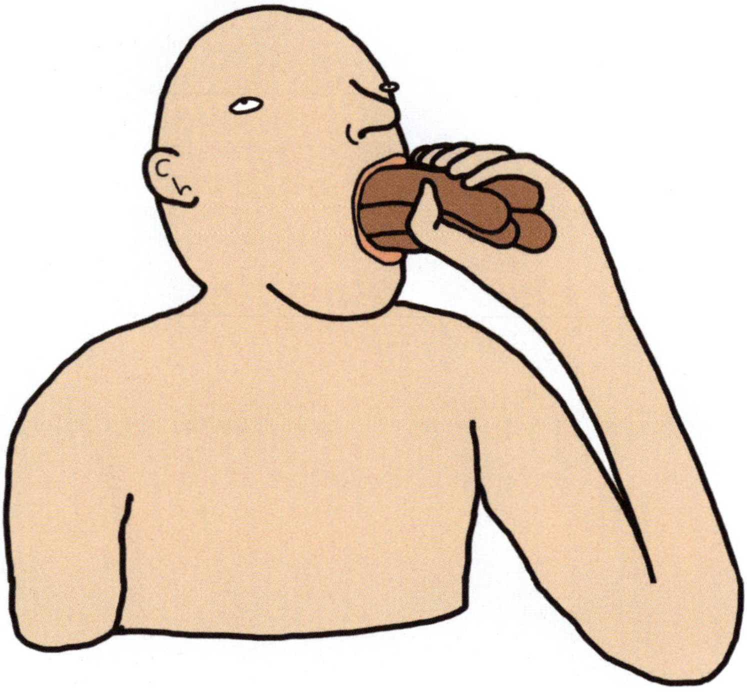

you are killing yourself

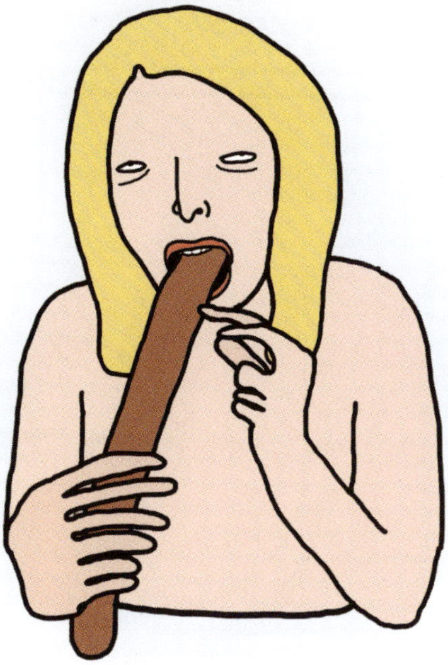

goodbye my sweet angel

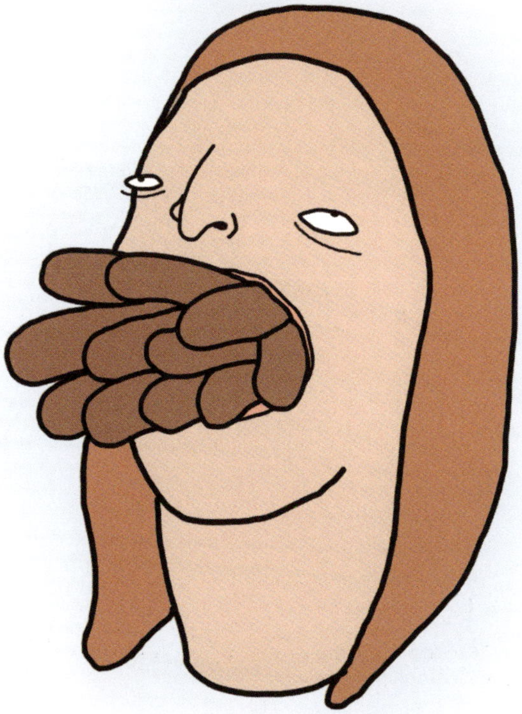

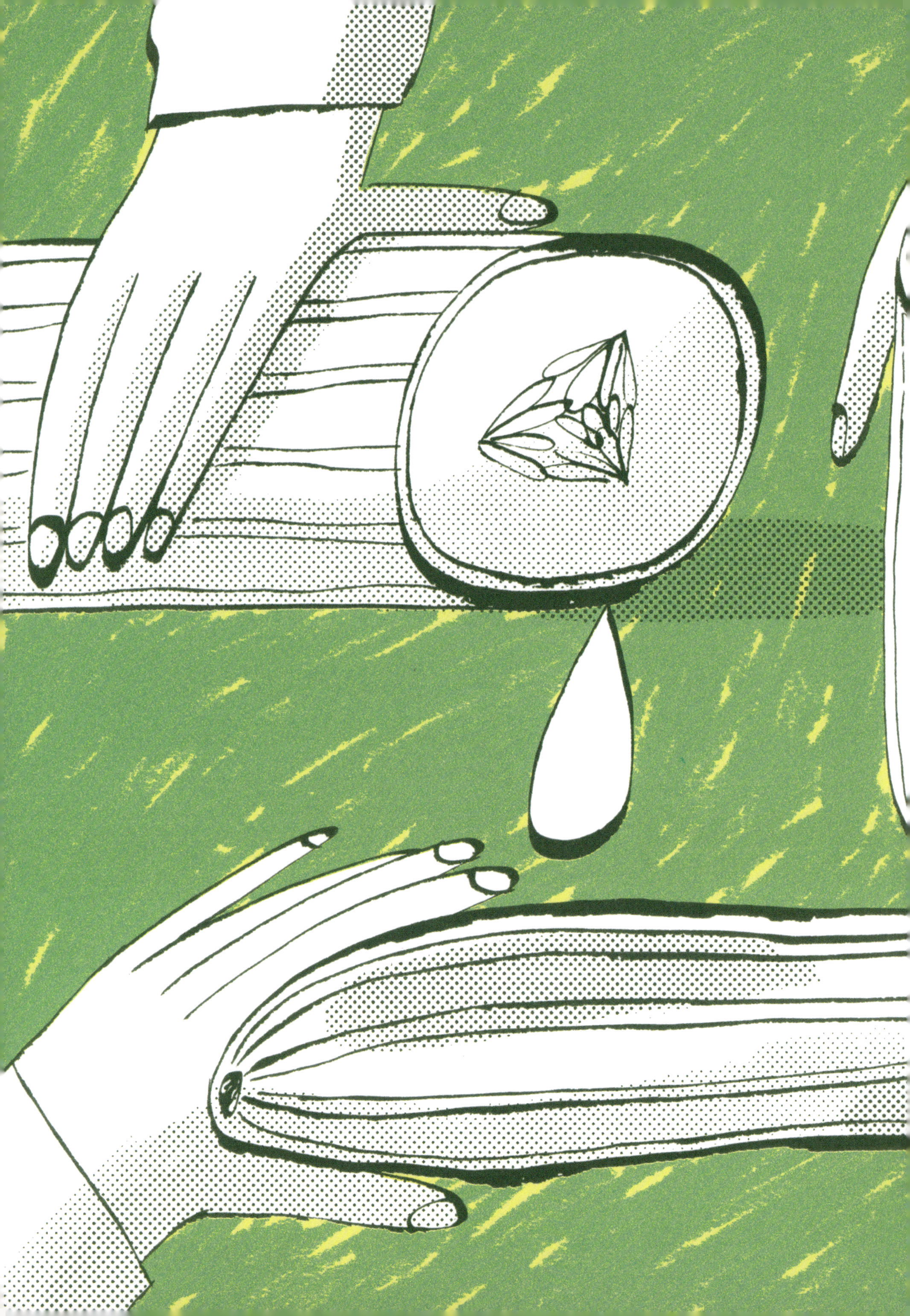

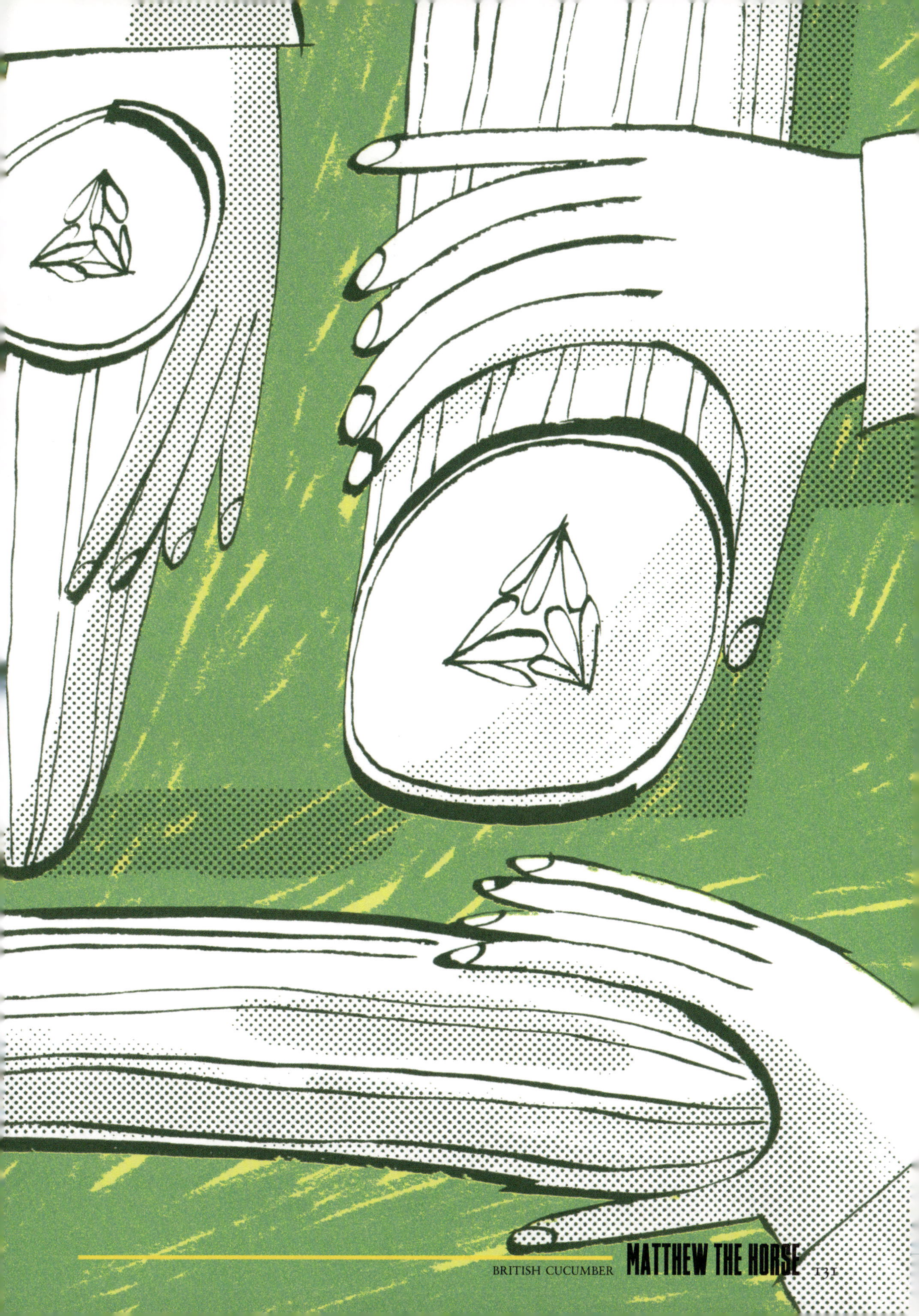

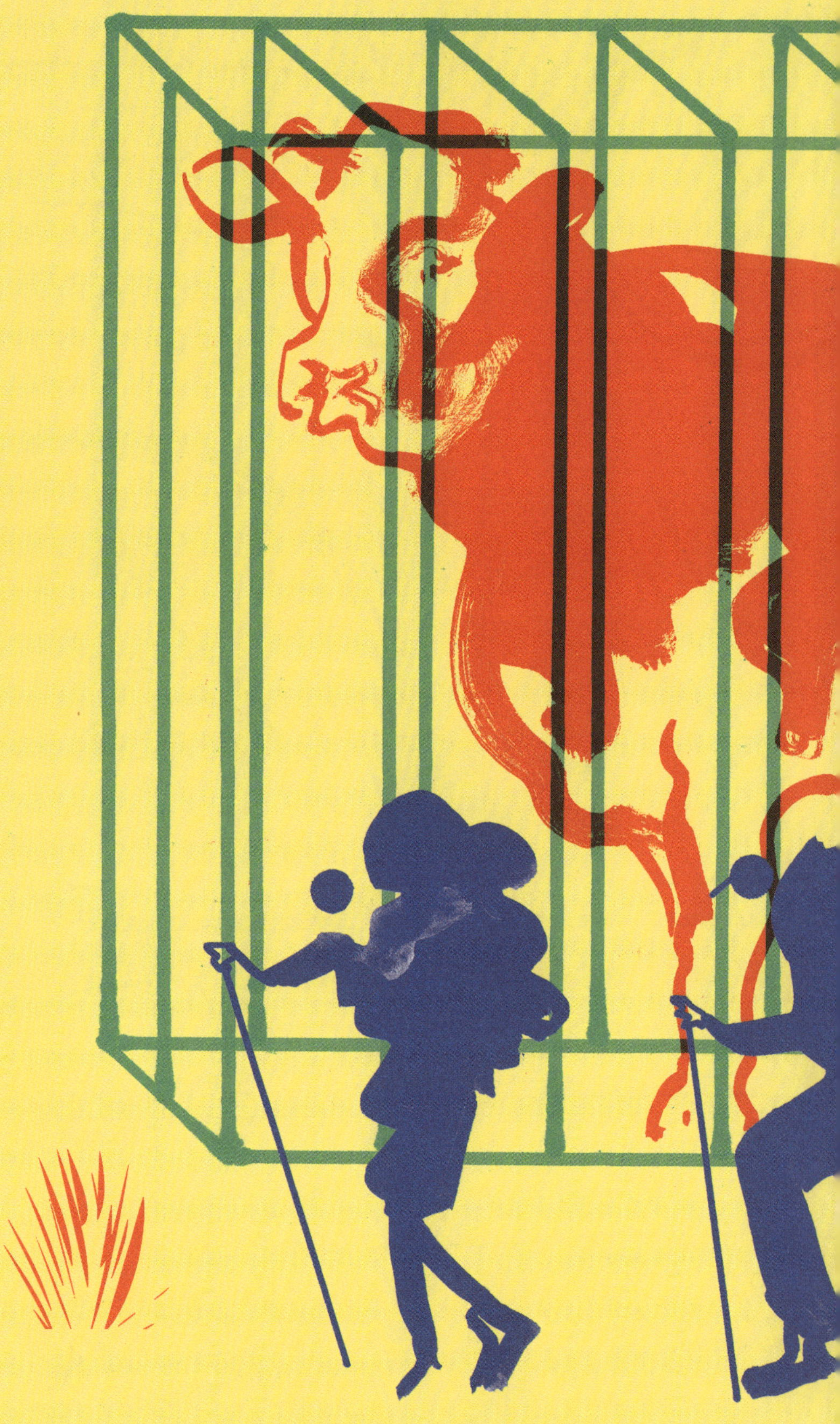

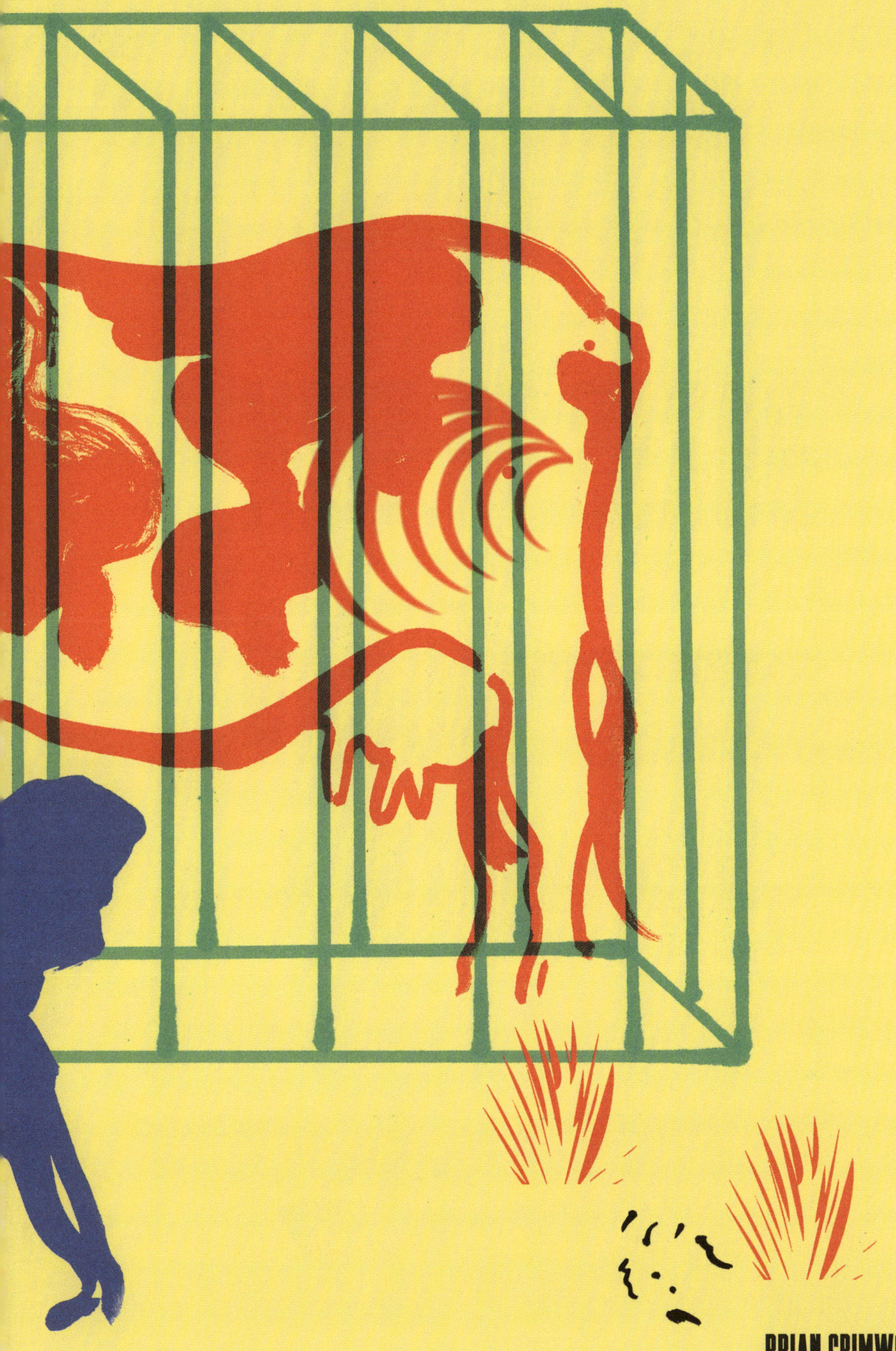

BOXES TO TICK

Illustrator

BRIAN GRIMWOOD

Founder of the Central Illustration Agency

The beauty of illustration is that it's a singular point of view. Every artwork is just one illustrator's vision, which is quite different to other artforms such as film, where you have numerous people working on one piece. I've always said illustration should excite the eyeballs, and probably the mind as well, as essentially its job is to make people question what they're looking at. Really, it's quite easy to create an acceptable illustration. There's a list of boxes to tick: you want the drawn elements to be interesting, you want the overall design to pull people in and you want the colour to be considered. Most importantly illustration needs a bit of lateral thinking and a good idea. But in order to tick all those boxes, you've got to have something to say.

There's a tension between 'fine' and 'commercial' art that's always been there, but personally I don't see any difference. Yes, an illustrator is given a brief, but that's also the case when you're creating personal work, it's just that you're giving yourself a brief and then creating within your own barriers. All my favourite fine artists were commercial anyway. People like Picasso used to do book covers and posters and all sorts of things. I don't think there should be any huge gap between commercial and fine art. The artwork in the Sistine Chapel was commercial, some Pope gave a brief and said, 'Oh I need my ceiling doing.'

Commercial work has its pros and cons, of course. Sometimes I'll create an illustration for a magazine, usually to brighten a dull article. Next thing you know, the editor will put a headline on the drawing, like the art has inspired the writing. In some cases it can make the drawing look naff, like I've just illustrated a headline. It's funny how that works and can be quite frustrating.

The way in which clients use your illustration can at times make it look like the artist is not imaginative, like we're given some words and copy them into art, but in fact it takes a lot of thought to illustrate for a magazine or newspaper article. You get this A4 page of often dull copy and then have to work some magic on it. But, all-in-all, drawing for a job is a privileged life. Illustration is quite a fashion industry, the commercial side of it comes in waves. An art director will generally use photography or illustration to fill a brief and every seven years the trend swings from one to the other. Not many people can pull it off, but if you can hold out then it's an amazing way to earn a living.

ACKNOWLEDGEMENTS

Taroh Kogure (Enjoy The Holy Grail!), The Mill, PERSORA Gallery, Dee Screen, Rebecca Mahoney, Jack Humphry, Georgia, Lewis & Jonah, Sarah & Andrew Jordan, Gill and Derek Hamilton, Nan Jean, Ned Read, John-Marc Comperat & Clare Williams, Dirty French de Wreede, Charlie Penrose, Nathan Hull, Zoe Menday, Ceri Jones, Jamie Smart, Chris Cahill, Jeremy Leslie, Sam Calvert, Liam Thomson, PRAH Foundation, Laura Hounsom, Joe Stubbs, Henri Yoki, Alison Watson, Helene Harris, Cristiano Loschi, Sky Molyneux, Will Riga, Marge Walsh, Elliott Zierolf, Kholoud Al Zaabi, Alexander Rea, Clayton Adams, Wei-Lin Allen, George Gendle, Johnna D. Wesley, Jonathan Anders, Toby Matthew Snowdon, Rick Jones, Farihah Zaman, Nick Tidey, Chris Myers, John Jakubowski, Matt Bray, Christian Rommens, Lloyd, Suzy Fischer, David J, James Stefan Dann, Sixpenny Publishing, Olivia Cline, Olwen Moseley, Anna Newman, Nancy O'Neill, McDavid Henderson, Cheryl G. Banks, Cynthia Worby Nero, Tu Family, Anthony Montaigne, Martin Schoonheim, Samantha Wilco, Geir Terje Ruud, Megan Hutchinson, Caroline Panico, Matt Burke, Rob Stothard, Andy Gott, Chad Yochens, Susannah Huntington, Deirdre Teo, Adrienne S, Daniel Chiha, G & S Henderson, Dr. Carl Butler, Leo Loveday, Mitch Crystal, Samuel Sjöström, James Yale, Zoe Bowcott, Matthew Young, Tim Garbos, Rick Jones, Micha Wertheim, Kristina Hermes, Nicholas Rapp, Rory Walsh, Marta Baraibar, Helen Ireland, Thomas Wielemaker, Jen & Marcel, Bruce Kean, Francisco Sebastian Chavez, Gabriel Jower, Nayantara Krishnamurthy, Immanuel Anosike, Ruth A. Nyman, Jen Gray, Wayne Jones, Kenneth Knowles, Moaraj Hasan, Marc Cook, Anne Uphoff, Paul Lewis, Vishal Desai, Alexander Lyons, Curly & Rachel, Sean Chou, Janet Keller, Sebastian Mawassii, Alex Burton-Keeble, Margot Diaz Learned, Evan Bare, Danny Jak Midwinter, Matthew Savage, Lauren McNab, Tony Hadyar Cardier, Michelle Girard, Kayla Dickensen, Jae Roh, RODRIGO A. CALDERON, Stephanie Pereira, Kate Bryant, Robert Cordwell, Wayne Schneck, Karen M. Buckley, Simon Dormer, Raul Valenzuela, Theodore Rhys Moorefield, Sydney F Shea, Kim Taylor, Lily Owens, Shayna Pilnick, Camila Arantes Dias, Ramon Hurtado, Martin Humpolec, Chris Bowden, Rohan Maharaj, creechnasty, Emmet Smith, Marcy Kirtack, Olena Sokolova, Ignacio Barba, Simon Busborg, Alexis Charnee & Mary Clark, Vanessa Lee, Kantak, João Bastos, Mahamed Momin, Mark Vlasic, Lua Monteiro, Lillie Jean Sharam, Geert G., Stephen O'Callaghan, Ellen Robinson, Paul Vooght, Maria Pia Mazza, Mike Caruso, Reinhard Fischer-Fuerwentsches, Rachel Ang, Sławek Wzorek, Alessandro Ciancio, Cali Piper Livingstone, Katrina Hopewell, John Power Jr., Muffin, Dom & Pipa, Sean Mulholland, Ric Bixter, Matthew Wood, Kimberly Gosewisch, Jean Kemp, Susan McConville, Raphael Odini, Aziz Karim, Thomas Nugent, baldyzuzu, Edgar Rouwenhorst, Bob Runk, Joan Hazard, Conrad Green, Gioacchino Repetto, William E. Boswell, Jack Galilee, Patricia Raynor, Mark Monteiro, MaryJo Fisher, Jerry Nurzinski, Yen Quach, Lisa, John Paulo Cardoso, Andy Mallalieu, Michiel Peters, Caitlin Biggerstaff, Kayla Halleur, John Buchholz, Dominique Herrera, Charles Satterfield, Jan Lüönd, Christophe Gévaudan, Grace S, Ash Kayser, Samuel Sharp, Melissa Polkey, Andrew & Rebecca Gallup, Yoo Kyung, Gretchen Roy, Kenneth Godfrey, Candy Systra, Nicholas, Jacqueline Hefley, Massimo Schneider, Sebastian Arrese, Baluppe, Marina Blake, Candice Warnock, Nicole Yeo, Riccardo Coppa, Pernille Sys Hansen, David Ruiz, Emanuele Iacono, Roger Marsh, Alexandre Lopez Stamm, Charlie Evans, Michael Hart & Yvette Tardiff, Rebecca Roden, Minoru Uchida, Gregory Brassil, Mr Dunne, Foose Moose, Freddie Hilton, Valentino Borghesi, Jeemie J, Bo Lee, Stephen Langdon, Oliver J Smail, Joel Estopà Nussbaum, Dorothée Pomme Redon, jstefka, Dennis Alexander Carey, Roos Taillieu, Sahil Shah, Heba Malaeb, Lani Hollander, Tom Calver, Calvin Garza, Kate Walling, April Bell, Christine Luc, Christiaan E Heerema, Bella Hughan, Monika Jasmine Sharma, Jess Stone-Weaver, Val Woodhouse, Debbie Trencher, Heather Henbest, Sarah Watson, Jacob Venables, Philippe Martin, Chris Longshaw, Sam Navin, Kwame Henderson, Mike & Jessica Kammann, Matthew Garcia, Denise Stovell, Jaleesa Titus, Natasha R. Chisdes, Augie Ilag, Asa & Danru Sum, Elizabeth T Sanders, Sophie, Stefan Kappeler, Jan Arnow, Eiko Bron, Senthil Ananthan, SAS, Cameron Farrior, Logan Celeste Jackson, Gemma Milne, Apathetic-ASympathy, Yaseen A Hussain, Bruce Bean, Steven Scaglione, Brett Boyles, Rosita Elias, Bethany Thompson, Patricia Repullés de L'Hotellerie-F, Tim Handley, Stefan N, Judi Tinnell, Aron T, Marian Blythe, Aurélien Berthelot, Jami, Sinister Purpose, Roman Trystram, Claire Wallis, Fred Boak, Hanne, David Court, Jean-Philippe Stanway, Martin Dumbrell, Shaunda L Bowman, Josh Morton, Nick Hoobin, Jen Carr, James Beaumont, Kurly, Humberto Godinez, Svend Holstein Ipsen, Xin Tan, Jeff Faulkner, Maria Miller, David Perta, Reuben Randall-Milne, Megan Jolliff & Vincenzo Savastano, Matthew J Wilson, Clement Lapeyre, Carianne Lance, Diane Detelich, Zerv, The Gent Family, G.M.J. MARVIS, Catherine Dock, Diego Farbo, Omri Mamon, J Matusiak, Henny Portman, Tim Cooper, Molly Culver, Lewis Garvey, Mojo, Jenn Robison, Susan Gilbert, 13th Monkey, Lauren McGuire, Jack Winston Harwood, Tom Ferguson, James Poulette III, Annatina Luethi, Catherine Nasserbakht, Yvonne Budden, Human Rights, Nate Kemp, Beth Connors, JazzyDan, Brittany Gardner, Jasper Kok, Bob Turner, William Banfield, Hanna Ahlström, Brendon Marczan, Harry Kaczka, Meredith A Stafford, Denise Prickett, Matt Mendenhall, Elen Haf Moore, Ronan Eales, Chris Pennington, Max & Zach Tohill, Nicolas Caridi, Alan Henderson, Alison F. Guerin, Kat Gottfried, Joshua Walker, Jota Erre Coto, Chris Rosa, Jackie Burhans, Eva Cox, Matthew Riva, Annie Dayton, Simon Tripcony, Tommy Watchorn, Nigel Downer, Daniel T Smith, Michele Mercaldo, Lumi, Elise H Welch, Justin Bonneau, Erik Rosner, Holly Spooner, Emily Yao, Michael McCranie, Jamie Smith, Lily Bass, YCSWYD, Robert E. Schnare Jr, Margot Martens, Scott Homann, Neil Britt, Charlie Rettig, Donna Murphy, Fern Culhane, William M. Strom & Sarah Weiss, Laura Simpson, Robert Bakelaar, J.S. Leonard, Derek Anderson, Alexa Rohn, Joe Mani, Robin O'Canna, Nuria, Bekky Harrison, Eric Mattson, Liah Moss, Taylor Colona, House of DB, Max Cable, Bernard Gijbels, Jacqui Jones, Romeo T. Villaseñor, Rochelle A. Ferrara, Sutton Lasater, Fannie Ko, Laurence Kaplan, Adrian Cull, Mike Gibson, Richard Stephens, Douglas Candano, Austin Russell & Thomas Beal, Randi Paris-Salb, Kaleb Fergin, Jacqueline Mandy Lowther, Laura Lynne Wright, Lauren Dowding, Yao Yue, cynumber9, Tom Brearley, Karosu, Clyde Saunders, Michael S Wang, Philip Hampton, Adam Lee, Chris Edrington, Valerie A. Wasserman, Kristin Ackerson, Rhiann H.G. Stewart, Finbarr Farragher, Nico Siewert, Lara Stoll, Tracy Zimmerman, Don Heider, Stephen Carratt, Nicole Clark, Delaney Gibbons, R. Sharon Wilson, Dawn R. Paine, Amy Elder, Vinh Nguyen, Sebastian Garn, Deborah Petite, Maria Iztaccihuatl Arana, Sue Damment, Trine Daely, Jill & Richard Sheinberg, Joshua Milwer, CJ Busenkell, Kären Anne, Ulrike Webering, Robyn Downing, Pete Schlax, Shane Campbell, Jean Dotson, Stephanie Walton, Andrew Dwersteg, Hazel Symons, Rui Ventura & Rita Carvalho, Carsten Semmler ,Bethanie Ariana Emmons, James Boyle, David Schulz, Babs Mondschein, Sarah Vines & Robert Allen, Fru Kenworthy-Browne, Robin & Margaret Dean, Yasmine S Mehmet, Ardys Otterbacher, Daniel Herbert, Andrew Graeme Beggs, Andy Thomas, Kevin Sharp, Candace & Mike Wilkinson, Jennifer Anthony, Diletta Giuntini, Penny Lindon Suttle, Oli Seymour, Lindsay Rollins, Rebecca Leach, Michael Masleczko, Alyssa Argento, Wilder Atlas Chua, Matthew Parsons, Sheila M. Johnston Wannan, Tracy Bowie, Scott Moore, Mary Brisson, Ryan Kirk, Maryann Beaver & Joe Kovach, Roy and Macy Melley, Ross Early, Thomas W Davis III, Ashley Doty, Fulvio Ariani, Cat Noonan, Jessica Abel, Nevena Christi, Randi Haugland, Karol, Chase Pashkowich, Ryan Stanich, Nate Richardson, Alex Fitch, Priscilla Ng, Laurie Nelson, Anna Heym, Gianluca Punzi, Marie Yuan, adc, Daniel R. Leonard, Galen Q, Patrick Danaher, Michael Dolloff, John Vincent Green, Claire Brown & Kevin Stach, Katherine J. Santos, Tina M. Gonsalves, Matt & Lindsay Manco, Lori Hymowitz, Nick Burton, Fede Schwalb, Rayvon Fouché, Rowan Eland, Jean Kemp, Grace

Arsenault, Tim Chapman, Schanoird, Wayne Fletcher, chuck dorris, Sam Myers, James C. Nielsen, Michael Duxbury, Eleanor Wood, Joseph, George Koza, Kristin M. Tamayo, Jason & Shelia, Karissa Cook, David Lars Chamberlain, Olexandra Pruchnicky, Lyman Ng Quan Li, Ryan Adams, Robin Ball, Sabrina Killian, Debbie Fong, Ellen Steevensz, Antero Paavola, Daryna Kratenko, Jacob Z George, Benjamin Sterling Lunday, Martin Jantzen, ATS, Daniel M. Salzman, Cody Chretien, Colleen Wu, AwesomeEMO, Matthew Sirrine, Natasha Mujawar, Billy Young, Dr Thomas Moers, Bence Büdi, Ahmed Elsirir, Subha Wijesiriwardena, Jean-Philippe Poirier, Ross McIntosh, UpstartThunder, James M. Meyers, Beatriz Gonzalez, Melchior Schöller, Amy T. White, Lisa Frankis, Nick Johnston, Sarah Lloyd, Susan M. Miller, Florian Betria, Elizabeth Gilbert, Lisa Marie Marks, Kieran Ross, Chris Bowen, Ollie Pattinson, Emeric Thérond, Yellow T, Sue Yee, Samantha & Charles Hannon, matt manco, Jonny Gordon-Farleigh, Lewis Moran, Talya Steiner, Felix Liu, Elliott Glick, Shannon Stolting, Ben Nasrallah, Dahbia B.L., The Lake Family, The Lupton Family, Paul Sampson, Nick Taylor, Tristan Vena, Lucy Ward, Bob Counts, C Campo, Marjorie Murray-Ure, Alice Ralph, Professor Lawrence Zeegen, Central Saint Martins Library, Casey Bozkewycz, Gabi from Hamburg, Petur HK, Annabelle Lozzi, Huib J., Joshua Glantz, Jason Guidry, James Robertroy, Jae Long, Michael Borkowski, Christopher 'Kaine' Romero, Maria-Elisa & Chris, Jordan Walsh, T Frankland, S'angie, Harmonie et Chris, Dochoppel, Alan Drummond, Facu, Kurt Ofer, Claire Pulford, Jenny & Joe Costne, Mark Movic, Yawming wong, Kirtis Clarke, Danielle Roberge, David Hughes, Leslie S., Nicolai Maverick, Stefanie, Harbano, Simon Overell, Clint Weaver, David Brimble, Lamon Bethel, The Butler kids, Charis Charalambous, Stephen Holt Davis, Dr. Ihab Algadi, Niklas Hartmann Have, Hayday, Victoria L. Bicunas, Anne Conn, Mr Mike Ryan, Aaron Schutte, Peresso Design Studio, Monika Neall, Sandra L. Planisek, Robert C Shelton, Anna Ballinger, Derek Luciani, Ruby Angelica Muller, Marc Champagne, Vanessa Kotiadis, Filip Zywica, Holly Catford, Pinda Chohan, Ronnie M. Weger, Daniel Ham, Amy L. Reams, Vaughan Greene, Deborah Franze, Riley L, Paul Arpais, Paul Parker, J. A. Schmehl, Milesa DeLoose, Ermy Ju, Sarah Melone, Stewart Wagner, Alexander S Palmer, Nikola Vuletic, Stivl, David Greene, David Ormondroyd, Caleb Whitaker, Martin Pellegrine, Ralph Cosentino, Rebecca Hart, Gustaf Olsson, Chris Mack-Riddel, Malcolm Robertson, Rajesh Warrier, Nicholos A. Bouck, Bek Trembirth, Tom Madigan, France-Leigh, Andrew Nicholas, Jeremy North, Mary Clark, Kat Irannejad, Tobias Jensen, Natasha Kapodistria, Ron Hamilton, Stephanie Crocker, Dagmar Eisenbach, Pedro M. Bonnin, Justin Bell, Patrick W Sonnenberg, Gruffyn Millward, David Coston, Duncan Rieger, Katy Minns, Geoff G, Bernadett Istvan, Susan & Stoorie, Kasper Randorff, Irreverent Ink, Wijtze Valkema, Cynthia Flores Guevara, John Waring, Gavin West, Hansesgaard Jeppesen, Diane W, Laura Caldwell, Kevin Matthew Smith, Louie Jenkins, Rob Allport, Matt Whelan, Giulia Galbarini, Solipsis, Florent Moyer, Yong-Namm Lee, Florian Horsch, Yuki Nakagawa, Jake Barlow, Trenton Kenagy, Barbara A. Leasure, Rory McCawl, Catherine Bell, Idea Starter Company, Steckline- Fuentes Family, Kate Ahmat, Daniel Smyth, Claudio Vögtli, Stephen Holland, John R Hofker, Päivi, Archie Lyons, Matt Forrest, Ruth Tedman Hartstein, Andy Rudkin, Rosie Cooke, Pavel Luzhetskiy, Georgie Surrey, Marin Devine, Jeff Hilnbrand, Boaz Halachmi, Charles Gabouleaud, HM, Emma Palmer Brown, Cassandra Sheekey, Marcelo Gaio, Grandson Design Studio, Michael Schroeder, Ryan Hanna, Martin Beisswenger, Will Brabant, Jerome A. Dennis, Rick "Poppy" Claypole, Pella Stenberg-Lundgren, Scott Howard Bennett, Anna-Lucia Stone, Brian Segedin, Alex Mankiewicz, Ben Smith, Katherine Paul, Nilly von Baibus, György Péchy, Jazmine R. Hudson, Hash Milhan, Mindaugas Dudenas, Michael L. Weed, Muhammad Fahmei Hassan, Jordi pujol, Simon Morton, Tom Payne, Kevin & Leah, Vinciane Piérart, Jeeves Williams, Bogdan Grigore, Chloë Grenier, Phil Wareham, Mel Scaffold, Ruth Wood, Henry Comyn, Mitch Ross, Benny Bean, Nick W. Castone, Angela Steatham, Malou Osendarp, Cristian Pandele, Neil Frankland, Karen M. Henton, Linda Avriani, Anthony Istrico, Grace Helmer, Miguel Santos Herrán, Benoit Maso, Ade Mills, Liam Daly, ML Erskine, Helge, Johanna Klefbeck, Pamela Williams, Patrick Hogan, Alice McCarthy, Serge M, Julieann O'Malley, Tom Hoffman, Tor Wirsén, Mick Watson, Jeremy Michael D'Lima, Noel Savory, Jemima Yong, Sona Harrison, Chris Plowman, Felix Wong, Jaime Solís Riera, Rodrigo Okuyama, James Fishlock, Rachel Perez Rumpf, Lana Simanenkova, Alexander Würthwein, Shannon S, Michal Dino, Roddy Marsland, Romain Gaullier, Chris Bradley, Kathleen Ragusa, Jonathon Mclean, Charlotte Allsop, Emily R. Brooks, Scott Cosby, Mal Padgett, J W Ziehler, Colin Hutton, Michael Burns, Rosanna Hawkins, Tammy Wright, Paul McNally Design, Adam Mark Taylor, Edward Manson, Joe Lawrenson, Max McBride, Caroline Bärwald, Gary Clap, Jerry Peace, Peter G.T.M. van der Ham, Christine Ince, Jeff Treadwell, Emilija&Vedran, Marlowe K Earl, Chloe Batchelor, Lynne Speight, atomicimagery.com, Michael Schaefer, Kirsty Martin, Sow Ay, James Unwin, Yumi Tamashiro, Laura Pera, Lloyd Kinsley, Antonio Trifirò, David Benedetti, Umberto Trevisani & Annalisa Brunazzo, Joanne Ng, Alex Lewis, Andy Miles, Hillel Koren, Wei Guo, Jesse Hagger, Pedro C. González, Ariëlla F. Reinders, David Nicolaou, Juliette Keyte, Maria Lo Bello, Arda Aksaray, Jeanne Axelrod, Patrick Turbet, Jancis, Ben McGeachie, Adam Dahlstedt, Fredrik Hedin, Fauquette's Family, Craig Davis, Cezar Chan, Dean Jackson, Cathy Haworth, Daniel Kan, Tom Hinton, Danny Jenkins, Thirteen, Hamzah Gamil, Christopher Masterman, Charlie Morgan Evans, Thibault Clack, Jack Storey, Maja Rundqvist, Richard Turner, Michelle Speck, Thomas Köller, Jake Bullman, Chris Madden, Hasim Karaman, Henning M. Lederer, Alex Mcgrath, Pete Prior, Jakub Kyncl, Emma Tucker, Nikki Simpson, Josh Phillips, Daisy Wilde, Justine Gastault, Ashima Bawa, James Barrick, Andrew Canham, Alphonso N. Dandridge, Alexander Sel, Ryan Yewell, Richard Evans, Francisco Brain, James Gerlis, Pauline Hay, Mauro farina, Anand Nagrick, Robin De Groote, Torstein Raabye Haugen, Linh Truong, Matt Breckons, Marco Buscaglia, Tom Cocks, Andrew Corrigan, James HG Pope, Peter Allen, Stephanie Hartman, Jessica Bader, Andy Bell, Antoine Verdet, karn mazzei, chelsea starna, Amanda Koster, Marigail Sexton, Ben White, Nicole Chorney, Georgina Staines, Sorab Del Rio, Craig Farras, Stephen Attong, Keller, Nate, Brittany poole, Ryuji Kawamoto, Erynn McConnell, Geo Dench, Jen Sutherland, Rajiv Mandalia, Stephen, Kim Brown, Mia Quagliarello, Michelle, Jill Ellen Burwell, Alexi Wheeler, soufflet, Susan Joy-Sobota, Joseph Kuk, Aaron Dunn, Jackie Fox, Kaal Dewar, chris mcclary, Emma Raby, Luís Castro, Delaine, Arjun Mahadevan, Tyler Micheli, Steven Hanson, Alex Drozdovsky, Nick Cross, Olivier Mallue, Simon Perez Wilson, Stephen Howe, Muhammad Yasin Ali, Erika Flak, Rachel Holden, Peter Kongstad Schmidt, Sus Kongstad Schmidt, Christopher Slatner, Marsal Llenas, Mike Eckel, Jeanne Eckel, John Bennett, Kathrin, Fei Alexeli, Alex Holstein, Mapology Guides, Jim Jourdane, Kt Gelston, James McMurray-Cole, Max Ford, Felix Kirk, Diane Frandsen, Ben O'Hara-Byrne, Damon Troth, Steven Druker, Lovejit Sarkaria, Shukri Habib Ali, Brett Cloke, Evonne Okafor, Joe Stone, Calab Crow, Jon Dalladay, Nabil Nadifi, Dave, Call of the Brave, Luc Benyon, Alex Demetriades, Karen Dalziel, Jade Moore, Charles Samuel, Trumpet B. Cat, Jukesie, Phil Woodsford, Dwayne Blee, Richard Wilcock, Sarah George, Tariq Thobani-Hacker, Jon Hodson, Brendan Jordan, Dan Edwards, Jim Thornton, Adrian Clabburn, Rachel A, Allie Buxton, David Luton, Neel Rastogi, Jane Mason, Darryl Bresland, S Foot, Sam White, Julie Murray (Drynan), Matt & Cole, Our Name is Mud, Anthony Lagomarsino, Mike Turner, Gavin Simpson, The Inventors Club, Jim Greayer, Sarah Weiner, Mizotion, Paul Cook, Mark & Alice Fresson, Simon Platt, Amber Hunter-Love, Maureen Bowes, Indra Adnan, Karen Preston, Howard Teece, William Russell Bethune, 陈武洋.

DANIEL HUMPHRY

EDITOR

Daniel Humphry is an award-winning editor and creative director who has worked in creative agencies, publishing houses and freelanced from his sofa for the last decade. He has helped develop books and magazines for clients around the world, including *One Thing I Know* for Creative England and *B+V* for German shipyard Blohm+Voss. Daniel is the founding editor of street press comic *OFF LIFE* and also harbours elicit dreams of screenwriting cartoons.

You can find more of his work at: danielhumphry.squarespace.com

STEVE LEARD

ART DIRECTOR

Steve Leard is a graphic designer and art director, specialising in branding, illustration, book and editorial design. He has worked for design agencies, large publishing houses and for freelance clients. He's the founding art director of street press comic *OFF LIFE*.

You can find more of his work at: leard.co.uk

NOTE ON TYPE

TIMMONS NY / SABON

Yellow uses Timmons NY. It was designed by Matt Willey with assistance from Henrik Kubel. Matt donated the font to the BuyFontsSaveLives campaign, which sells typefaces to raise money to support Cancer Research UK and Macmillan Cancer Support.

The body copy is set in Sabon, a serif typeface designed by the German-born typographer and designer Jan Tschichold (1902–1974) in the period 1964–1967.

You can help by purchasing fonts at: buyfontssavelives.com

NOTE ON PRINT

L.E.G.O.

Yellow is a hardbound book and was printed by Legatoria Editoriale Giovanni Olivotto (L.E.G.O.) in Italy. L.E.G.O. was originally founded as a bookbinding workshop in 1900 and today, more than 100 years later, its history is still linked with that of the Olivotto family.

You can find more of their story at: legogroup.com

Published by Studio OL

www.StudioOL.uk

978-0-9934799-0-8

A CIP catalogue of this book is available from the British Library.

Editor: Daniel Humphry
Art Director: Steve Leard
Production Manager: Sarah Hamilton
Sub Editor: Anna Hamilton
Copy Editor: Lucy Rice
Hero: Aron Jones

Printed and bound by L.E.G.O. Italy